Ontology and Metaontology

ALSO AVAILABLE FROM BLOOMSBURY

Heidegger, Ethics and the Practice of Ontology, David Webb
Metaphysics: An Introduction, Jonathan Tallant
Pragmatist Metaphysics, Sami Pihlström
Quine: A Guide for the Perplexed, Gary Kemp
Quine's Naturalism, Paul A. Gregory
The Bloomsbury Companion to Metaphysics,
edited by Neil A. Manson and Robert W. Barnard
The Bloomsbury Companion to Philosophical Logic,
edited by Leon Horsten and Richard Pettigrew
The Science, Politics, and Ontology of Life-Philosophy,
edited by Scott Campbell and Paul W. Bruno
Transcendental Ontology, Markus Gabriel

Ontology and Metaontology

A Contemporary Guide

Francesco Berto and Matteo Plebani

Bloomsbury Academic
An imprint of Bloomsbury Publishing Plc

BLOOMSBURY
LONDON • NEW DELHI • NEW YORK • SYDNEY

Bloomsbury Academic
An imprint of Bloomsbury Publishing Plc

50 Bedford Square
London
WC1B 3DP
UK

1385 Broadway
New York
NY 10018
USA

www.bloomsbury.com

First published 2015

British Library Cataloguing-in-Publication Data
A catalogue record for this book is available from the British Library.

ISBN: HB: 978-1-4411-9195-3
PB: 978-1-4411-8289-0
ePDF: 978-1-4725-7329-2
ePub: 978-1-4725-7330-8

Library of Congress Cataloging-in-Publication Data
Berto, Francesco.
Ontology and metaontology: a contemporary guide/Francesco Berto and Matteo Plebani.
pages cm
Includes bibliographical references and index.
ISBN 978-1-4411-9195-3 (hardback)–ISBN 978-1-4411-8289-0 (pbk.)–ISBN 978-1-4725-7330-8 (epub)
–ISBN 978-1-4725-7329-2 (epdf) 1. Ontology. I. Plebani, Matteo. II. Title.
BD311.B47 2015
111–dc23
2014021253

Typeset by Deanta Global Publishing Services, Chennai, India
Printed and bound in India

To our parents, who made us part of what there is.

Table of Contents

Acknowledgements

We are most grateful to Doug Edwards, David Liggins, Tuomas Tahko, Stephan Torre, Achille Varzi and Alberto Voltolini for their helpful comments and remarks on various parts of this book. The division of labour for it has been as follows: we wrote the Introduction together. Chapters 1, 3, 7, 8, 11, 12 and 13 were written by Francesco Berto. Chapters 2, 4, 5, 6, 9, 10 and 14 were written by Matteo Plebani. We reviewed each other's chapters.

Parts of Chapters 1, 3, and 7 draw on Chapters 2 and 4–6 of Francesco Berto's Synthèse Library book *Existence as a Real Property*. Thanks to Springer for allowing us to use that material.

Parts of Chapter 9 draw on Matteo Plebani's survey of nominalistic strategies in the philosophy of mathematics ('Nominalismo in filosofia della matematica') for the online journal *Aphex*. Thanks to the editors for allowing us to use that material.

Parts of Chapter 11 come from Francesco Berto's entry 'Impossible Worlds' for the *Stanford Encyclopedia of Philosophy*. Thanks to the editors, and particularly to Ed Zalta, for allowing us to reuse that material.

Introduction: What Is Ontology? What Is Metaontology?

Chapter Outline

1 Ontology ...

Biology studies living things. Psychology studies mental functions. Astronomy deals with celestial phenomena and mathematics deals with numbers. They all study *something*, of course, but none of them studies *everything*. They do not address the whole of reality, or all that there is. Ontology does.

This characterization of ontology can be traced back to Aristotle, who in Book Four of his *Metaphysics* introduced the idea of a 'science of being *qua* being', or of being as such. Yet Aristotle did not use (a Greek counterpart of) the word 'ontology' to name such a science, although the term comes from *ón,* the present participle of *eînai*, the Greek verb for 'to be'. The word is a more recent seventeenth-century coinage (nor did Aristotle use a Greek counterpart of the word 'metaphysics' – we will get back to this). After having been dismissed by much early analytic and neo-positivistic philosophy, ontology made an impressive comeback in the second half of the twentieth century. One initiator of the renaissance was Willard van Orman Quine, who made mainstream the idea that the task of ontology is to write down something like a complete catalogue of the furniture of the world. What we want from ontology is a list of *all* there is, and ontology gets the list right insofar as it misses nothing that is there, and includes nothing that isn't there.

However, many still think that there is something perplexing about the study of *what there is*, which sets it apart from the other above-mentioned disciplines. Laymen have a rough understanding of what biology, psychology or mathematics are about, and few doubt that living creatures, or the functioning of the mind or the realm of numbers, are legitimate areas of rational investigation. But, first, what does it *mean* to study being *qua* being, or what is? And, secondly, via which *methods* or procedures of inquiry should such a study be carried out? While there are many excellent introductions to ontology on the market, few deal extensively with these two issues – questions to which professional philosophers give conflicting answers. This provided our motivation for writing the book.

2 ... And metaontology

As its title makes explicit, this book is an introduction to ontology as well as an introduction to *meta*ontology. And the term 'metaontology' is a very recent coinage: as far as we know, it officially entered the philosophical landscape as the title of a 1998 essay by Peter van Inwagen, one of the greatest contemporary ontologists. Now, van Inwagen understood metaontology as dealing precisely with the two issues just mentioned: if the key question for ontology, as Quine told us, is 'What is there?', then the (twofold) key question for metaontology is 'What do we mean when we ask "What is there?"', and 'What is the correct methodology of ontology?'. By using the prefix 'meta-', van Inwagen meant to suggest a kind of higher level reflection: 'meta-X' as the inquiry on the central concepts and procedures of discipline X.

It is only natural that the reflection on the proper methodology of a discipline historically comes after the discipline itself has flourished and developed its own conceptual tools. Perhaps the main element of novelty in early twenty-first-century ontological research is that many of its practitioners pay more and more attention to metaontological issues. 'Metaontology', as Ross Cameron 2008: 1 said, 'is the new black'. This book aims to give a textbook presentation of the discipline in line with such recent developments.

Now the metaontological turn has brought a rediscovery of some traditional and pre-Quinean approaches to ontology. As for the first of those two meta-questions, 'What do we mean when we ask "What is there?"': the catalogue metaphor embedded in the Quinean view has it that the goal of ontology is to write a list of everything that falls under the notion *being*. But the original Aristotelian idea of a 'science of being *qua* being' was concerned, first of all, with the very concept of being, that is, with the meaning of the notion itself. Quine did have something important to say on the meaning of being, as we will see in the first part of the book. Other recently developed metaontological stances differ from the Quinean approach in their conceptualization of being as such, and from this they derive different views of ontology's tasks. Some say that the primary goal of ontology is not to write a list of all there is, but (as also Aristotle set out to do in the *Metaphysics*) to identify the most fundamental or basic entities: those which ground all the rest, and on which everything (else) depends.

Some claim, as Aristotle himself did, that *being* can mean different things – that there are different ways of being – and that the primary goal of ontology is to identify these meanings, or ways of being. Some even introduce a distinction between *being* and *what is there*, and claim that some things should be included in the universal catalogue because they are there, although they lack being.

As for the second meta-question, namely 'What is the correct methodology of ontology?', the new methodological consciousness of twenty-first-century ontology has revitalized deflationist perspectives on the goals and ambitions of ontology itself. Quine's methodology for ontology was naturalistic: he believed that we should include in the universal catalogue the kinds of entities our best natural science commits us to (he also had views on how such 'ontological commitment' ought to be understood, as we will see). He thus denied that ontology has a special philosophical autonomy, allowing it to float freely from the findings of natural sciences. Contrary to the beliefs of his master Rudolf Carnap, Quine believed ontological questions to generally make perfect sense and to allow substantive replies. Nonetheless, other philosophers nowadays are much more Carnapian: they think that ontological questions make sense only when appropriately restricted or qualified. Some have a more strongly dismissive approach, and believe that most of these questions are just shallow: they reduce – as some founding fathers of analytic philosophy also thought – to confusions concerning the meanings of some expressions of our everyday language.

3 ... And metaphysics

Ontology entertains a complicated relationship with metaphysics, which is itself one of the most traditional parts of philosophy. The border between ontology and metaphysics in the works of contemporary philosophers is fuzzy. Some just use the two terms interchangeably. Sometimes the relationship between metaphysics and ontology is understood as of one between a discipline and one of its sub-disciplines.

As a first approximation, metaphysics is the branch of philosophy which asks what reality is like – as opposed to such other branches as epistemology, which asks what we can know about reality and how; or ethics, which asks how reality ought to be. Textbook presentations often say that metaphysics is an investigation into the most *fundamental* and *general* structures and features of reality (Crane and Farkas 2004; Garrett 2006).

Just as the word 'ontology', so the word 'metaphysics' comes onstage later than the Greek philosophers who can be considered the founding fathers of the discipline. It has a tangled history too. When Aristotle's works were ordered after his death, some of them were put after his writings on physics. They belonged to a discipline Aristotle called 'first philosophy', and which dealt with such fundamental topics as being, causation, God and other issues. Such writings then got the label of 'what comes after the books on physics', in Greek: *tà metà tà physikà* – hence, 'metaphysics'. Physics was taken as the study of the material world, subject to change, movement, generation and corruption. 'First philosophy', as the discipline that studies the most general and fundamental aspects of reality, was believed by Aristotle to transcend physics in some sense. In order to fully understand the foundations of reality, for him and for many others after him, one has to resort to incorporeal, nonphysical entities, such as God. So the name 'metaphysics' also came to mean a study that goes 'beyond physics' in this sense: it deals with a realm that surpasses, or is anyway not reducible to, the physical world.

Now when ontology is understood the Quinean way, that is as the quest for a catalogue of all there is, it may then be seen as in some sense a preliminary to metaphysics. One first writes down the complete inventory of reality – one says what is there. Then one wonders about the nature, structure and fundamental features of the kinds of things listed in the inventory.

Even if one agrees with the view of ontology as preliminary to metaphysics, the border between the two remains fuzzy: as we will experience throughout this book, ontological issues (so understood) naturally tend to shade into metaphysical ones (so understood). Thinking about the relationship between ontology and metaphysics in the aforementioned terms can help to understand the following pattern, often recurring in contemporary philosophy: authors A and B can seriously disagree on the metaphysical status of entities of kind *F*, which they nevertheless agree to include in the ontological catalogue. Here's one example that we will delve into in the third part of the book. The notion of *possible world* is extremely useful in most branches of contemporary philosophy. One starts by taking 'possible world' to stand for a way reality as a whole could be or could have been. This quickly leads to the natural twofold question: are there really possible worlds distinct from the actual one – that is should we include them in the ontological catalogue? And if so, then what kind of entities are they? Now philosophers A and B can agree on including possible worlds in their ontologies: they both reply 'yes' to the first ontological question. However A thinks that these things (possible worlds) are just like our actual world, but causally and spatiotemporally isolated from it. In particular they are, as we may say, (mostly) *concrete material objects*: things endowed with a mass, which occupy some space and are subject to the flow of time. On the contrary, B thinks of them as *abstract objects* – things more similar to numbers, functions and, perhaps, concepts, than to these physical surroundings of ours. So A and B have diverging metaphysical views on possible worlds.

It is fair to say that such characterization of the relation between ontology and metaphysics, despite being widespread, is not uncontroversial. To begin with, it is possible to accept the ontology-as-catalogue metaphor without taking ontology to be preliminary to metaphysics. If one thinks of metaphysics as an attempt at 'writing the book of the world' (Sider 2011), then the ontological job will look like writing the index of contents to the book of the world. And the index of contents is often written when the book is close to completion. Some authors, for example, Bergmann 1967 and Grossmann 1992, believe that we just cannot decide whether some putative kind of entities should be included in the ontological catalogue without first giving some characterization of *what* the kind is like. These philosophers will tend to understand 'ontology' itself as meaning the study of the fundamental and most general structures of reality. They will then tend to use 'ontology' just as a synonym of 'metaphysics', or to blur any distinction between the two (for a comparison between this way of understanding ontology and the one followed by us above, see the introduction to van Inwagen 2001). Besides, the development of non-Quinean metaontologies, as we will see, has brought even more pressure on the mainstream way of drawing the line: for it presupposes the 'Quinean catalogue' view of ontology, which is questioned in some alternative metaontological approaches. This quick overview should make clear that this book, dealing with ontology and its methods, is perforce also, to some extent, a metaphysical book.

4 ... And science, and common sense

Let us stick again with the 'catalogue' or 'index of contents' metaphor for ontology. Another natural preliminary question about writing the catalogue or index of contents to the book of the world is: what is specifically *philosophical* – as opposed to scientific, on the one hand, and plainly commonsensical, on the other – about this task?

Sciences such as physics, chemistry, astronomy, biology, etc., already teach us a lot about the makeup of reality. We can learn, for instance, that the surface area of Saturn, measured in square kilometres, is $1.08 \cdot 10^{12}$ (Liggins 2008a), that some biological species are cross fertile, that spiders share some important anatomical features with insects (van Inwagen 2004), that the event of a solar flare can release several billions of joules of energy. Also, we share commonsensical knowledge on lots of things constituting the furniture of the world. We know that fragility is a feature of crystal glasses, that bananas are yellow when ripe, that a bikini is composed of a bra and a slip, that Emmental cheese has holes in it and that the Clinton-Lewinsky affair was a scandalous incident. Suppose we look at examples such as these and start writing down the following list:

1 Planets, like Saturn
2 Insects
3 Bananas

4. Spiders
5. Bikinis
6. Holes, for example, in pieces of cheese
7. Numbers, like $1.08 \cdot 10^{12}$
8. Properties, such as fragility, ripeness, and genetic features
9. Biological species
10. Events, like solar flares and the Clinton-Lewinsky affair
11. ...

Would a list of this kind tell us an ontologically satisfying story? One problem is that it seems randomly constructed. It resembles the classification of animals in Borges' *The Analytical Language of John Wilkins*:

Those that belong to the Emperor
Embalmed ones
Those that are trained
Suckling pigs
Mermaids
Fabulous ones
Stray dogs
Those included in the present classification
Those that tremble as if they were mad
Innumerable ones
Those drawn with a very fine camelhair brush
Others
Those that have just broken a flower-vase
Those that from a long way off look like flies

One would like to impose more order and structure to our inventory of the furniture of the world: we want our list to be *systematic*, in some sense.

A related issue may be one of insufficient generality – though pinning down the exact level of generality is no easy task. Ontological catalogues don't typically stick with such entries as *bikini, insect* or *banana*, but comprise much more general categories. For instance, we may group planets like Saturn as well as insects, bananas, bikinis and human beings like Clinton and Lewinsky into a single very broad category. All things belonging to these kinds are, to retrieve a label we used above, *concrete material objects*: they all have mass, they occupy a place in the physical world.

But what about the sixth item in the list? Should we include holes in our catalogue of all there is? Holes being devoid of mass, they look quite unlike things belonging to the first five items. Is a hole something like an absence of matter, or a kind of nothingness? If so, how can holes exist? A parsimonious ontologist may deny that holes should be included in our ontological catalogue: out there in the world, there really are no holes. But then we have a problem: 'There are holes in pieces of Emmental cheese' is a truth of common sense, and for this truth to be true there must be holes in pieces of Emmental cheese – thus, there must be holes.

How about our seventh item – numbers, like $1.08 \cdot 10^{12}$? These also look very different from concrete material objects. Saturn has a very large mass – so large that it generates a gravitational field, which would attract you, should you get close enough. In fact, the number $1.08 \cdot 10^{12}$ is, so to speak, too light and thin to have any attractive force on you. It doesn't even make much sense to wonder about the thinness of a number, as well as about its spatiotemporal location. Indeed, $1.08 \cdot 10^{12}$ *does* nothing physical to you: it is causally inert, as we may say.

But how can we know anything about things we cannot entertain causal relationships with? Can we even be sure that they are there? Even if we were freed from our contingent spatiotemporal limitations, we could never cross paths with $1.08 \cdot 10^{12}$, for it's nowhere to be found in the physical world. Some may find $1.08 \cdot 10^{12}$ and its peers to be too obnoxious to be admitted in our ontological list of the components of the world. Numbers, sets and other mathematical entities must simply not be included in our ontology, these parsimonious folks may claim. On the other hand, refusing to include numbers in our ontological catalogue may also bring problems. If there are no numbers, how could it be true that, as mathematics teaches us, seven is a prime number? This can only be the case, as it seems, if there is a number (seven), which has the feature of being prime – thus, if there are numbers.

How about *properties*, such as fragility or ripeness, and biological *species*, such as spiders and insects – our candidate items no. 8 and no. 9? Considerations of ontological parsimony may lead some not to include them in the catalogue either. Of course there are material objects, some of which are ripe or fragile, some of which are human beings. Yet, why should we admit *fragility*, *ripeness* or the species *homo sapiens*, above and beyond the things which are fragile, ripe or human? Parsimonious ontologists might have arguments similar to the ones against numbers (properties and species are often grouped with mathematical objects under the broad label of *abstract objects*, which we also used above, and opposed to concrete material beings). We see, touch and interact causally with human beings, fragile glasses and ripe bananas, but nobody has ever seen or touched fragility, ripeness or humanity. One may object. We also directly speak of species: we claim that some of them are cross-fertile; and this can only be true if there are cross-fertile species, thus, if there are species. We also seem to know things about properties – for instance, we know that fragility is a property of crystal glasses; and this demands that there be properties.

How about item 10 in the list? *Events* – things that happen – make for another popular ontological category. Events seem ubiquitous in our daily life: Clinton's affair with Lewinsky was scandalous, but Kennedy's killing by Oswald was tragic; the French revolution was a momentous event, while Francesco's watering his flowers yesterday just passed unnoticed. And unlike abstract objects, we cannot easily dismiss events on the ground of their being devoid of causal powers. On the contrary, they seem to be the main actors of causal processes: we say that the throwing of a stone caused the breaking of the window, that the Clinton-Lewinsky affair caused the impeachment of the President, and that the latest solar flare caused the emission of billions of joules of energy in the Solar System. Events also present problems of their own, for instance, concerning the fine-grainedness of their individuation. Francesco walks to the same office every working day; but is the event of Francesco's walking to his office one single general event, which recurs many times across the year? Or are we talking of similar but distinct particular events, each with its own unique spatiotemporal setting? We may also have issues with the identity of the particular events themselves: is Oswald's shooting the same as Kennedy's killing?

Now notice that all of these concerns are not typical of disciplines like physics, mathematics or biology. Mathematicians talk about prime numbers; biologists talk about cross-fertile biological species; astrophysicists deal with solar flares. But, *qua* scientists, they will not typically wonder whether there really are prime numbers, species, properties or events – whether these things ought to be included in the ontological catalogue. Nor will they wonder what it means to ask whether the world really includes these entities or not. Nor will they typically wonder what they themselves are ontologically involved with when they claim that there are infinitely many prime numbers, or that genetic features are shared between spiders and insects.

Nor is common sense unqualifiedly helpful in all of these issues – even though, as we will see throughout this book, some ontologists take the deliverances of common sense, for example, as they show up in our ordinary talk, very seriously. Common sense often delivers vague, imprecise, ungrounded or occasionally inconsistent verdicts on the existence of various kinds of things. Here's one example. It is commonsensical to maintain that everyday objects have parts that constitute them. Bananas have a peel and a pulp, normally endowed human beings have arms, legs and a head. Also, according to common sense, scattered material objects may constitute further objects. A slip and a bra for instance, can compose a further thing: a bikini. Yet it is not commonsensical to think that this can always happen: intuitively, there's no object made up of Brad Pitt's face and George Clooney's body. So according to common sense, two objects sometimes compose a further one and sometimes do not. And there seems to be no commonsensical criterion to draw a principled line between the case in which bunches of material objects compose a further object as its parts, and the case in which they don't. But we need such a criterion to build a well-motivated ontological catalogue.

Here philosophy steps in again. As we will see in the third part of our book, specifically in Chapter 12, philosophical considerations may lead ontology to sharply depart from common sense on the question: 'When does the inclusion of two material objects in our inventory force us to include also one further object, composed exactly of them?'. A parsimonious ontologist may plainly deny the existence of bikinis by claiming that what actually exists are just slips and bras. A bikini is nothing but a slip plus a bra: once we have counted the slip and a bra, there is no reason to countenance a further object, the bikini. But then, an even more parsimonious ontologist may claim, slips and bras are nothing but bunches of atoms and molecules arranged in a certain way. Once we have countenanced the (properly arranged) atoms and molecules, there is no reason to further countenance slips and bras. Worse: countenancing them may bring lots of troubles concerning their persistence across time and change and their spatial boundaries. It's better to say that there really are no such things (we now see that, although ontologists look for the most general kinds of being, this does not prevent them from expressing their disagreements more concretely: 'Unlike van Inwagen, I include bananas in my ontology' – not just subatomic particles arranged banana-wise: van Inwagen 2001: 3).

There seems to be room for philosophical work, then – at least, if we are sensitive to issues like the ones just explored, for which physics and the special sciences, but also commonsensical shared beliefs, often deliver no clear verdicts. We may want to know whether apparently problematic entities like numbers, holes and properties can be admitted in our catalogue of the furniture of the world. If we don't include them, we need to make sense of facts, truths and bits of knowledge apparently involving them. If we do include them, we need to answer objections of various kinds to their ontological respectability.

5 The rest of the book

The book is neatly divided into two halves. Parts 1 and 2, making for the first half, focus on metaontology. There is a mainstream metaontological view among analytic philosophers: this is dealt with in Part 1. Its origins are traced back to Russell's *On Denoting* (Chapter 1), which provided the methodological paradigm of philosophical analysis for much of twentieth-century philosophy.

The mainstream view, though, is usually labelled as 'Quinean', for it is most clearly stated in such famous Quinean papers as *On What There Is*. Chapter 2 explains the pivotal theses of Quine's metaontology: that ontology's key question is: 'What is there?'; that in some sense the question can be answered in one word, 'Everything', for it is trivially true that everything exists, but in another sense it is not trivial at all; that it is inconsistent to make certain claims while holding that things of a certain kind do not exist (what is known as Quine's 'criterion of ontological commitment'); that there is a principled way to settle debates about the existence of things like numbers, propositions, properties, etc.

Chapter 3 delves into the details of the standard metaontological view, as developed, for example, in Peter van Inwagen's essays: being is not a (non-trivial) feature of things; being just is existence; being or existence is univocal – it means only one thing; the single sense of being is completely captured by the existential quantifier of elementary logic. It also deals with 'paraphrase strategies' to get rid of ontological commitments apparently brought about by our everyday quantification over unwelcome kinds of things, and with the ontological import of so-called identity criteria, recaptured by Quine's motto 'No entity without identity.'

The consensus about these matters is not universal. On the contrary, much top-level contemporary work in metaontology starts by calling into question the standard view. Part 2 of the book explores reasons of dissatisfaction with it, and a range of alternative options. Here, Chapter 4 discusses two ways to depart from Quine's framework. The first, that of *ontological pluralists*, agrees with Quine and van Inwagen that existence or being is captured by the quantifier, but holds that there is more than one mode or way of being, thus there is more than one (primitive) quantifier. Chairs and numbers, according to this view, both exist, but in two very different ways, and a correct description of the world should take this into account. *Neo-Fregeans*, on the other hand, think that linguistic categories, like that of singular term, are in some sense conceptually prior to ontological ones like that of object. This leads to a view of the relationships between language and reality (broadly linked to the so-called 'linguistic turn' of twentieth-century philosophy) with surprising results for the issue of the existence of abstract objects like numbers and directions.

Chapter 5 focuses on the view of ontology held by Quine's master, Rudolf Carnap, and on its legacy for contemporary ontology. Carnap believed that it makes sense to ask about what there is only on the background of some conceptual and linguistic framework. Assuming the framework of material things, for instance, it makes sense to ask whether there is a skyscraper higher than the Empire State Building, as people ordinarily do. But to ask, as philosophers have traditionally done, whether there are material things in some 'absolute' sense is to ask a very different question. Carnap called questions of the first kind *internal* and questions of the second kind *external*. This distinction, together with a certain deflationary attitude towards ontology associated with it, has been a source of inspiration for an amount of recent work in metaontology, ranging from the so-called 'quantifier variance' view to proposals to the effect that we must distinguish an internal and an external reading of quantificational expressions.

Chapter 6 introduces the burgeoning *fictionalist* strategies, according to which when we make claims that seem to commit us to the existence of controversial entities like numbers, possible worlds, properties, etc., we should not be taken at face value. The fictionalist motto has it that such claims can be 'good without being true', and much work in this area consists in making this motto plausible. However, we speak of fictionalist strategies, in the plural, for we will see in this chapter that fictionalism has been developed in quite different ways by its supporters.

Chapter 7 speaks of (neo-)Meinongian theories taking seriously the view that some things just do not exist (the name comes from Alexius Meinong, an Austrian philosopher who held this view). (Neo-)Meinongians are unified by their disentangling the quantifiers from (automatic) existential commitment, but their views are otherwise diversified, too. In particular, they have different non-quantificational conceptions of the meaning of being as well as different proposals on which non-existent objects there are, and on which properties and features they can display.

Chapter 8 explores recent work on the notion of *grounding* and its impact on the methodology of ontology. Advocates of the grounding approach tend to see reality as an ontologically hierarchical structure. They hold that the most important question about things of a given kind is not whether they exist, taken in the Quinean sense as a quantificational question. Rather, the most important explanatory task for ontology has to do with which position such things occupy in the structure. Are they fundamental entities, or do they depend for their existence on entities of another kind, and if so, which kind?

Having investigated the issues of the meaning(s) of being and of the methodology of ontological inquiry, in Part 3 of the book, which occupies its second half in length, we give a closer look at how ontological investigations are actually carried out. Here, Chapters 9 and 10 are dedicated to abstract objects of different kinds. Do objects like the number eighteen or Pythagoras' theorem really exist? And what about moral obligations: is there really something like a duty to keep your promise? On the one hand, abstract objects look peculiar: we cannot see, touch or smell them. They are apparently nowhere to be found in the material world surrounding us. On the other hand, is it really possible to renounce abstract objects like numbers and sets without renouncing mathematics? We will extensively review, in particular, the pros and cons of both *nominalist* positions, which try to make sense of mathematics without admitting abstract objects, and of *platonist* positions, which admit such objects and try to explain how knowledge of them is possible at all.

Is the actual world we are living in the only one there is? Talk of alternative ways the world could be or have been, also known as *possible worlds*, is ubiquitous in analytical philosophy, for the notion is extremely helpful to analyse a number of key philosophical concepts. Since David Lewis called our attention to the ontological and metaphysical status of these entities, the debate on them has been lively. Lewis proposed to take possible worlds as (largely) concrete universes, causally and spatiotemporally isolated from each other, but of the same kind as the world we are living in. The view was met with 'incredulous stares'; the literature provides a variety of arguments pro and, more often, against 'Lewisian modal realism'. A survey of this debate, provided in Chapter 11, is a must for an introduction to ontology. The debate on modal realism has been traditionally conducted within a standard largely Quinean metaontological framework. However, we will see in this chapter that non-standard metaontological views can provide fresh spin-offs to the discussion.

Another peculiar aspect of ontological debates emerges when one realizes that, as already hinted above in this Introduction, for prominent philosophers like Peter van Inwagen there are no such things as mid-size concrete, material objects like a banana or a table, but just subatomic particles arranged as so. According to other prominent philosophers, like David Lewis, there are such weird entities as the 'mereological fusion' (from the Greek *méros*, 'part') of one's head and one's father's body, i.e. that scattered thing whose parts are exactly one's head and one's father's body. For Lewis, given any two entities x and y, there always is a (possibly scattered) entity $x + y$, containing exactly them as parts. These views will be described in Chapter 12, devoted to the ontology and metaphysics of material objects. Other topics examined in that chapter include the issue of synchronic identity conditions for such objects (e.g., can more than one of them occupy one and the same place at the same time?) and the one of their diachronic identity (under which conditions do they *persist* in time in spite of their undergoing change?).

Yet another topic in modern ontologists' agenda has to do with the status of *fictional entities*: things referred to and described in works of fiction, like Sherlock Holmes, Anna Karenina or Gandalf. Chapter 13 is dedicated to them: we will see there how, while (neo-)Meinongians declare such things to be non-existent, and fictionalists apply to discourse on them their non-ontologically-committing techniques, *realist abstractionists* on such objects accept that they really exist, but treat them as metaphysically peculiar abstract objects.

Finally, Chapter 14 presents two challenges to the view that the world is nothing but a collection of particular things like this chair, this table, this apple and so forth. It seems that things share features, which make for their similarities. Two red apples are similar in virtue of sharing the feature of being red. Moreover, the world we live in is not boring and static: lots of things happen in it. New persons are born, philosophers debate about ontology, people go to parties. Does not this suffice to show that we should also include in our ontological catalogue *properties*, like the property of being red or that of being an apple, and *events*, like births, debates and parties? If so, what are these things? Some philosophers take both kinds of things as *universals*, that is, as things irreducible to particulars like individual apples and chairs, while others disagree.

The agenda does not end here. Other entries considered by ontologists include works of art, or social objects (things like mortgages, institutions and money), just to mention a few items. Surely, then, this survey of ours is not complete. As Bertrand Russell said at the end of his *Introduction to Mathematical Philosophy* (Russell 1919): 'there are innumerable unresolved problems in the subject, and much work needs to be done. If any student is led into a serious study ... by this little book, it will serve the chief purpose for which it has been written.'

Part I

Quinean Metaontology

1

On Denoting

Chapter Outline

In this short chapter we examine how Russell addressed the famous 'King of France' problem in his paper *On Denoting*. After a brief introduction in Section 1, we describe in Section 2 the problem. In Section 3 we explain what quantifiers are and how to express them in the canonical notation of elementary logic. In Section 4 we describe Russell's paraphrase strategy to eliminate definite descriptions. This strategy is important for us, because it pioneers an approach, popular in analytic ontology, to get rid of unwelcome ontological duties seemingly induced by our everyday language.

1 Language, thought and what is out there

> 'Just look along the road, and tell me if you can see either of them.'
> 'I see nobody on the road,' said Alice.
> 'I only wish I had such eyes,' the King remarked in a fretful tone. 'To be able to see Nobody! And at the distance too!' (Carroll 1871: 234)

Thus speaks the White King in Lewis Carroll's *Through the Looking-Glass*. There is something comically wrong in the King's last line. He is in all likelihood misled by language into taking 'nobody' as a name: an expression whose key semantic function consists in referring to an object. Then the King supposes there to *be* an object that the wannabe-name refers to: how could Alice's claim be meaningful otherwise?

The White King's mistake, trivial as it may appear, relates to a question at the heart of the foundation myth of contemporary analytic philosophy: To what extent do our representations of the world – language, thought – provide a bridge to the world itself? It is uncontroversial that our language in general, and many of our mental states, are *about* the world. But to what extent do language and thought reveal, rather than disguising and concealing, the structure and features of the world itself – that is, its ontology and metaphysics?

According to a philosophical tradition ranging back to Gottlob Frege and Bertrand Russell, examples not too different from the one of the King's little speech show that ordinary language can be ontologically fraudulent. For the logical positivist Rudolf Carnap 1932, of the famous Vienna Circle, Martin Heidegger's ontology was vitiated by a mistake very much like the White King's: the mistake of treating 'nothing' as a proper name. Hence came, for Carnap, Heidegger's views on the infamous (non-) object, Nothingness, and his uttering such alleged pseudo-sentences as 'Nothingness shows itself in angst.' We are tempted to take the semantics of our everyday language as modelled along the simple relation between names and the things they are to name – or, more generally, between referential expressions (those linguistic expressions whose main purpose is to hook up with objects in the world out there) and the things they supposedly refer to. When such referential expressions occur in intuitively true sentences, this leads us to posit the entities these expressions are to refer to: for if there *are* no such things, how can those intuitively true sentences be true, or even express a full-fledged *proposition*?

Propositions are themselves ontologically controversial, being accounted for in divergent ways by philosophers, and sometimes even rejected outright. We will speak about them directly in Chapter 10 in the third part of our book. For now, we will just mean by 'proposition' what is expressed by a sentence and is normally introduced in discourse by a that-clause, with no further commitment on what kind of things propositions are. So the English sentence 'Snow is white' expresses the proposition that snow is white, and the French sentence 'La neige est blanche' expresses that same proposition.

Now if we follow the simple-minded path that takes the relation between language and the world as modelled on the one between referential expressions and their objects, we easily get an overstuffed ontology. We may posit an entity for each seemingly referring expression of our language. And we may then find ourselves dealing with beings of bizarre and unwelcome kinds. At some point during his philosophical career, Bertrand Russell believed in such an ontology. He speaks thus in *The Principles of Mathematics*:

> Whatever may be an object of thought, or can occur in a true proposition, or can be counted as *one*, I call a *term*. … Every term has being, i.e. *is* in some sense. A man, a moment, a number, a class, a relation, a chimera or anything else that can be mentioned is sure to be a term; and to deny that such a thing is a term must always be false. … To mention anything is to show that it is. (Russell 1903: 43 and 449)

Russell's terminology is a bit misleading for us nowadays. Rather than speaking of the being of the term (qua linguistic item) itself, we may restate the essential point made by Russell here by claiming that, for any term or referential expression, there must *be* whatever the term refers to.

2 Descriptions and the current king of France

By the time of his 1905 essay *On Denoting* – one of the most celebrated works of contemporary philosophy – Russell had changed his mind. Here he dealt with the issue of providing a treatment of *definite descriptions*. What are these?

In English we ordinarily refer to things, not only via proper names like 'Aberdeen' or 'Barack Obama', or demonstratives like 'this' and 'that', but also via expressions that begin with a determinative article, of the form 'the *F*', with '*F*' a placeholder for some simple or complex predicate: 'the winner of the 2012 US presidential elections', 'the author of *Truth and Objectivity*', 'the second power of two'. These expressions refer to Barack Obama, Crispin Wright and the number four respectively. They do not refer to these things by calling them by name, though. They rather describe the relevant objects in a certain way, that is, by referring to some of their features (being the author of a certain book, being the result of a certain operation) – hence the label 'descriptions'. Furthermore, they are called 'definite' because, by using them, we aim at determinately referring to one and only one thing: the one complying with the description – hence the determinative article. The US presidential election singles out one winner at a time. Thus, by referring to a single election (the one that took place in 2012), we can single out a unique individual: its winner, Barack Obama. Definite descriptions are unlike *in*definite descriptions, expressions of the form 'an *F*' – like 'a chief Scottish city', which expresses a condition satisfied not only by Aberdeen but also by other cities, like Edinburgh and Glasgow.

Now in his paper Russell makes a celebrity for generations of philosophers of the following sentence, *prima facie* referring to another king:

(1) The current king of France is bald.

As France is (and was, in 1905) a republic, we are in trouble when we are to evaluate (1). *Prima facie*, (1) is true if the thing referred to by the term in subject position, the description 'the current king of France', has the feature referred to by the predicate 'bald', false otherwise. However, we can reasonably wonder whether the current king of France is bald or not only if *there is* such a thing to begin with. Thus, Russell says, (1) seems to defy the Principle of Bivalence – the principle according to which every (well-formed, declarative) sentence is either true or false:

> By the law of excluded middle, either 'A is B' or 'A is not B' must be true. Hence either 'the present King of France is bald' or 'the present King of France is not bald' must be true. Yet if we enumerated the things that are bald, and then the things that are not bald, we should not find the present King of France in either list. Hegelians, who love a synthesis, will probably conclude that he wears a wig. (Russell 1905: 48)

(Russell talks of the Law of Excluded Middle, but he actually formulates the Principle of Bivalence, and nowadays philosophers and logicians often introduce the caveat that the two principles can be considered equivalent only under certain assumptions; but this is not very important for our current purposes). Some philosophers we will talk about later on, called Meinongians (from Alexius Meinong, an Austrian philosopher active between the end of the nineteenth century and the beginning of the twentieth century), may address issues of this kind by claiming that, in fact, there *is* an object denoted by that description. Only that object does not exist given France's current political setting: the current king of France is a non-existent object, and (1) claims, of this object, that it is bald.

This solution, though, is unacceptable for the Russell of *On Denoting*. It would deliver, according to him, as congested an ontology as the one he himself subscribed to at the time of the *Principles*. In his 1919 *Introduction to Mathematical Philosophy*, he claims:

> It is argued, e.g. by Meinong, that we can speak about 'the golden mountain', 'the round square' and so on; we can make true propositions of which these are the subjects; hence they must have some kind of logical being, since otherwise the propositions in which occur would be meaningless. In such theories, it seems to me, there is a failure of that feeling of reality which ought to be preserved even in the most abstract studies. Logic, I should maintain, must no more admit a unicorn than zoology can; for logic is concerned with the real world just as truly as zoology, though with its more abstract and general features. (Russell 1919: 169)

3 Quantifiers and logical form

Russell's celebrated approach to the puzzle produced by (1) consists in saying that, in spite of grammatical appearances; 'the present king of France' does not make for a genuine singular term. Descriptions, for Russell, are 'incomplete symbols': their semantic role does not consist in autonomously referring to an object. Their meaning lies in their contribution to the truth conditions of the sentences within which they occur, but such a contribution is not the one of singular terms. Then (1), despite appearances, is not a singular sentence with a subject-predicate structure, which purports to refer to an individual and to ascribe it a property.

The general conception underlying such a Russellian approach is, roughly, the following. There is something like an authentic *logical form* of the sentences of our language, which lies below, and is sometimes concealed by, the surface grammar of language. Only at such a 'deep grammar' level can we address ontological issues effectively, for it's only there that the ontological underpinnings of language become transparent. Our natural language is ontologically deceptive insofar as its surface and deeply logical grammar diverge. For Russell, (1) is an example of such discrepancy. To make explicit the logical form of sentences containing descriptions, it is necessary to paraphrase them. A sentence whose grammatical subject is a definite description, such as (1), should be taken as having a more complex logical form. To understand what this more complex form consists in for Russell, we have to introduce the notion of *quantification*, which will be extremely important throughout this book.

In natural languages such as English, the quantifiers are expressions like 'all', 'some', 'every', 'most', 'many', etc. They often show up in the sentences traditional philosophy categorizes as *universal*, like the mournful but classic 'All men are mortal', and *particular,* like 'Some politicians are thieves'. The name 'quantifiers' comes from the fact that such expressions allow us to speak of quantities – to say of how many things does a certain condition or property hold. When we tell our students that everyone has passed the exam, we say how many of them have been successful with the assessment: all of them. When we say that nobody could believe Meinong's ontology, we express our view on how many things have the feature of possibly believing that theory: none ('nobody' and 'nothing' are just quantificational devices, not names, as believed by the White King and, possibly, by Heidegger). And when we say that some politicians are thieves, we talk – if in an undetermined way – of the amount of politicians who steal: what we claim is true if and only if there is at least one thing that is both a politician and a thief, not excluding that there be more than one.

In what is often called the canonical notation of elementary logic, two symbols are introduced to render quantificational constructions: the *universal* quantifier, represented by the symbol '∀' ('inverted-a'), corresponding to such expressions as 'all', 'for each', and used to formulate universal sentences; and the *existential* quantifier, represented by the symbol '∃' ('inverted-e'), corresponding to expressions like 'some', or 'there is', and used to express particular sentences (linguists usually do not call the

English expression 'there is' a quantifier, whereas logicians and philosophers usually do; but we don't need to bother with this).

Each of the two quantifiers can be dispensed with in favour of the other. Using '*F*' as a placeholder for an arbitrary predicate: to claim that everything is *F* (that is, using logical symbols: $\forall xFx$, to be read as: 'For every object *x*, *x* is *F*') is to claim that nothing is not *F* (that is: $\sim\exists x\sim Fx$; where '$\sim$' is the symbol for negation, 'not'). To claim that something is *F* (symbols: $\exists xFx$, 'For some object *x*, *x* is *F*') is to claim that not everything is not *F* ($\sim\forall x\sim Fx$). So we may just use one quantifier, if we wanted, given that either can be expressed by the other plus negation: $\forall$ can be defined as $\sim\exists\ldots\sim$, while $\exists$ can be defined as $\sim\forall\ldots\sim$.

4 Paraphrase

According to Russell, sentences of the form 'The *F* is *G*', of which (1) is an instance, are to be analysed precisely as complex quantificational constructions, along the lines of: (a) Something is *F;* (b) At most one thing is *F;* (c) Some *F* is *G* (one may also have 'Every *F* is *G*' for (c), with little difference for our purposes for it would leave the original Russellian analysis untouched, thereby allowing Russell's theory to have wider applications). Now (a) and (b) can be summed up into something like: 'There is exactly one *F*'. In particular, then, (1) becomes:

(2) There is exactly one present king of France, and some present king of France is bald.

Now for Russell, just as, we are about to see, for the majority of analytic philosophers, quantificational expressions like 'something', 'there is', etc., bear *existential* commitment. They commit those who employ them to assert declarative sentences to the existence or being of the things the quantifiers range over, in that what is claimed is true only if the relevant things exist. We will speak in detail of the notion of existential commitment in the following chapters, and we will see that such a notion involves many subtleties. For now, it is enough for us to appreciate how paraphrasing (1) into (2), for Russell, makes its logical form explicit – and thereby makes its existential commitment transparent. When one asserts that some politicians are thieves, what one says is true if and only if politicians who are thieves exist. Similarly, one assertively uttering (2) is claiming that exactly one thing satisfying a certain condition (i.e., presently being king of France) exists (and is bald). However, such a thing does not exist. Understood in the Russellian treatment as per (2), then, (1) is in the end false.

And now we have no violation of the Principle of Bivalence. The apparent violation was due, again, to a linguistic ambiguity – precisely, an ambiguity in the scope of negation. Consider:

(3) The present king of France is not bald.

This can be read in two different ways. One is as follows (with square brackets helping to visualize 'scope distinctions'):

(3a) It is not the case that [the present king of France is bald].

Here negation, rendered as 'it is not the case that', takes a wide scope over the description, that is, it applies to the whole sentence within the square brackets, description included. (3a) is true, being the contradictory of (1), a false sentence.

Another reading of (3) is as follows:

(3b) The present king of France is [such that he is non-bald].

Here the description takes wide scope over negation, which is confined to being a part of the predicate within the square brackets. And (3b) is false, for the same reason for which (1) is: in the Russellian analysis, (3b) actually claims that there is exactly one present king of France (and that some present king of France is non-bald). However, there is no present king of France. But in disambiguation (3b), no more does (3) contradict (1): they can bear the same truth value.

Whether definite descriptions actually count as autonomously referring singular terms, or should rather be analysed away as proposed by Russell, makes for a vast debate in the philosophy of language. Various philosophers have argued against the Russellian treatment. According to Strawson 1959, (1) does not *assert* the existence of a king of France, but rather *presupposes* it. In Strawson's theory of presupposition, sentence *P* is a presupposition of sentence *Q* when *Q* can have a truth value only if *P* is true. Since 'There is a current king of France' is a presupposition of (1), and is false, (1) itself is truth-valueless: it is neither true nor false – and we must limit the Law of Bivalence (we will meet a different theory of presupposition in Chapter 5). More than in this issue in the philosophy of language, though, we are interested in the general ontological spin-off of Russell's method. In *On Denoting*, Russell showed to analytic philosophers how apparently deep issues of traditional ontology could be approached and clarified via an analysis of ordinary language statements that resorts to minimal logical resources. He gave a concrete example of such an approach. He also substantiated the general view, to be found – in fact, in quite different forms – in Wittgenstein's *Tractatus Logico-Philosophicus* and in Frege's works, that the grammar of our ordinary language may be philosophically and in particular, ontologically misleading; and so much so that ontological investigation makes sense – if at all – only after logical analysis has properly reconstructed the 'hidden logical form' of our everyday statements. That we resort to certain linguistic expressions when we talk does not automatically entail the necessity to posit entities corresponding to those expressions. As we will see in the rest of our book, Quine and other contemporary ontologists made a lot of this Russellian insight.

Further Reading

For more on quantifiers, definite descriptions and the White King, look at the wonderful Chapters 3 and 4 of Graham Priest's *Logic: A Very Short Introduction* (Priest 2000), an engaging introduction to logic. For an advanced logical treatment of definite descriptions, see Chapters 11 and 12 of Fitting and Mendelsohn 1998. Ludlow 2013 is an excellent introduction to the topic of descriptions in general, and Neale 1990 provides a comprehensive defence of the Russellian account.

2

1948: On What There Is

Chapter Outline

For many authors trained in the analytic tradition, 1948 is the year ontology was (re)born. From that moment philosophers working in an environment that was hostile to traditional ontology started to take the investigation *on what there is* seriously again. They started to investigate whether things like the number 13, the virtue of modesty or the hole in my pocket really existed.

Doubtless, such an enterprise may still not look that serious to some eyes – also analytic philosophers' eyes (Yablo 1998: 230). It looked hopeless, for instance, to logical empiricists like Carnap. They thought such issues to be pointless because they were meaningless, and due to linguistic confusions. In 1948, Quine published his seminal paper *On What There Is* and, as for instance Putnam (2004: 78–9) remarked, he thereby changed such a general attitude. Quine thought that having to do with a meaningless question was a great thing: he was free to give it the meaning he preferred! (1966: 126). And so he proceeded: he defined the kind of debates ontology is concerned with, and stated the rules to conduct them. After Quine, philosophers confronted with ontological questions tended to be curious and to look for answers, rather than merely puzzled, doubting there being answers to be found.

We can summarize Quine's position into some pivotal theses, reviewed in the following Sections. Section 1 concerns ontology's fundamental question, which Quine identified with the question of what there is. Section 2 explains in which sense this question admits of a trivial answer and in which sense it does not. Finally, Sections 3 and 4 explain Quine's strategy to conduct debates about the existence of numbers, properties, propositions and other problematic entities, focusing respectively on his famous 'criterion of ontological commitment' and on his philosophical naturalism.

1 Thesis one: Ontology's fundamental question is 'What Is There?'

> A curious thing about the ontological problem is its simplicity. It can be put in three Anglo-Saxon monosyllables: 'What is there'? (Quine 1948: 4)

Thus begins Quine's essay. This may sound just like a terminological point, a kind of stipulation: ontology, as Quine inaugurated it, is *defined* as an attempt to answer the question of what there is. Still, there might be other candidates to the role of fundamental question for ontology different from the one Quine picked up. For instance, one could take ontology to be the investigation on what is real or fundamental, and not just on what is merely there. As we will see when we move on to alternative, non-Quinean metaontologies, some philosophers think that this initial choice of the ontological problem *does* make a difference – and sometimes dispute it directly. Some think that the question of whether there are numbers is trivial – obviously, there are lots of them: 1, 2, 3, 4, … . The tough question is, rather, whether numbers are fundamental and irreducible constituents of reality. For the moment, though, let us forget about this and focus our attention on the Quinean *answer* to the Quinean ontological question.

2 Thesis two: Everything exists

Ontology's fundamental question, in a sense, for Quine 'can be answered, moreover, in one word – "Everything" – and everyone will accept this answer as true' (Quine 1948: 4).

Really? Couldn't one provide lots of examples of things that do not exist: Santa Claus, Atlantis, the solution to all of life's problems? If these things do not exist, then something does not exist. So it is not the case that everything exists: doesn't this follow by elementary logic? The standard reply from Quine is that the fact that Santa doesn't exist cannot make one draw the conclusion that *there is* something which is Santa, and which does not exist. One should rather conclude that *there just is no* such thing.

Quine's point can be appreciated via an analogy. The claim that every Italian is a great chef would be taken by Quine as logically equivalent to the claim that there exists no Italian who is not a great chef. Then saying that everything exists should be logically equivalent to saying that there exists nothing which does not exist – the kind of claim everybody should agree with.

Quine also pursues another route to argue that everything exists. One cannot eat without eating something. Similarly, to exist, or to be, according to Quine, is to be something, i.e. to be identical with something. Now everything is identical with itself; so everything is identical to something (namely, itself); so given that to exist = to be = to be identical with something, everything exists (as we are going to see in Chapter 7, philosophers who reject this conclusion typically distinguish between *existing* and *being identical with something*).

Quine's conception of being or existence has its roots in a venerable ontological tradition. This stems from Kant's famous motto that 'Existence is not a (real) predicate'. The idea, to be found in Frege and Russell, too, is that unlike such ordinary predicates as 'runs', 'is red', or 'is a dog', 'exists' does not express a real, discriminating feature which some things have, and others lack. It makes sense to split the world into two via those ordinary predicates: some things are red, others are not; some are dogs, some others are not. But it doesn't make sense to split the totality of things into those that have the feature of existence and those that lack it. That would be for Quine tantamount to admitting that some things – those which lack that supposed feature – are non-existent, that is that there are things that do not exist, that is that there are things such that there are no such things.

This does not mean that the Quinean view of existence is *exactly* like the Fregean-Russellian one. Frege excluded that existence be a feature of individuals, but phrased his point by stating that 'Existence is a property of concepts' (Frege 1884: 53). The property at issue is a feature some concepts have, namely that of being *instantiated* or *exemplified*. Concepts are things that typically have instances, that is, things exemplifying them: Barack Obama exemplifies or instantiates the concept *man*, for he is a man. He does not exemplify the concept *horse*, for he is not a horse. Now, according to Frege, existential statements like 'There exist horses', or 'There do not exist unicorns' should be understood as claims about concept instantiation: the former should be equivalent to the claim that the concept *horse* has the property of being instantiated (at least once); the latter should be equivalent to the claim that the concept *unicorn* lacks such a property. This way, existential statements are closely connected to number statements: to say that there exist horses is to say that the number of horses, that is of things instantiating the concept *horse*, is one or more. To say that there do not exist unicorns is to say that the number of unicorns, that is of things instantiating the concept *unicorn*, is zero. For reasons we shall come to later on, Quine did not admit properties or concepts in his ontology; he therefore would not have phrased the Kantian point in these terms (more on these differences in Berto 2012: Ch. 2).

2.1 Easy and hard ontological debates

So there is a trivial answer to ontology's fundamental question. But there is a way to understand the question, such that no trivial answer can be given. Call 'ontological' a debate on whether things of certain kind exist. Although we (should) all agree that everything exists, for Quine 'There remains room for disagreement over cases' (Quine 1948: 1); for instance, 'disagreement on whether there are wombats, unicorns, angels, neutrinos, classes, points, miles, propositions' (Quine 1960: 233). So we can understand the question of what there is in such a way that there are non-trivial answers to it. When engaging in ontological debates about numbers or propositions, for instance, we want to know whether there really are such things as numbers and propositions – whether they should be included in the catalogue of the furniture of the world. And this is no trivial issue.

Now suppose you think that numbers or propositions exist and I think they don't. How are we supposed to *conduct* our debate, according to Quine? Let us compare two questions. First one:

(1) Are there numbers?

This seems to be a challenging question. It's the kind of issue philosophers should address, we are inclined to think. And they do: philosophers disagree about it, and they support their opposite views with sophisticated arguments. Second question:

(2) Are there Iraqi weapons of mass destruction?

This seems to be *philosophically* not so challenging. It may be hard, to be sure, to find hidden nuclear bombs or to ascertain that a certain geographical region is free from them. But firstly, it is easy to imagine cases in which question (2) could be settled on the basis of cogent empirical evidence. Secondly, and more importantly, there seems to be no theoretical or methodological issue for philosophy to address about how to proceed with (2): just send scientist, soldiers and inspectors to Iraq and let them investigate. This can involve extremely complicated diplomatic procedures, but governments do not consult philosophers on how to deal with such issues.

To summarize: we have an easy ontological debate and a hard one. We know how to settle the easy one, but with the hard one – with questions such as (1) – we may have serious doubts on how to proceed. Perhaps surprisingly, for Quine, the methodology we should apply to address questions such as (1) is not fundamentally different from the one we should apply to address questions such as (2). And this may sound encouraging: it may entail that question (1) about numbers' existence is not doomed to be pointless or in principle undecidable, since question (2) about Iraqi weapons certainly isn't. We *can* figure out whether there are numbers, just as we can figure out whether there are such weapons.

Philosophically hard ontological debates, according to Quine, are thus not substantially different in nature from 'mundane' ontological debates. The methodology to solve both is broadly the same. We will come back to what this Quinean methodological stance amounts to, after we introduce another key Quinean thesis.

3 Thesis three: Quine's criterion of ontological commitment (or, some ontological positions are inconsistent)

Quine sets up some methodological rules for ontological debates. Such rules are supposed to 'catch cheaters', i.e. people who are taking an inconsistent position. In general, being inconsistent means holding two things, which cannot be true at the same time. For instance, we would qualify as inconsistent somebody who claims that there are nuclear weapons in Iraq, but at the same time denies that there is any weapon of mass destruction in Iraq. You are taking an inconsistent position, in particular, if you say something that implies the existence of a certain kind of entities, and at the same time you deny that there is any entity of that kind (the phrase 'catching cheaters' comes from the Section 2.3 of Sider 2001, who used it in another context; Quine 1960: 242 spoke of 'philosophical double talk, which would repudiate an ontology while simultaneously enjoying its benefits').

How should we proceed in order to catch ontological cheaters? According to Quine, the answer is: look at the quantificational structure of discourses. Such a procedure is nowadays labelled as the Quinean 'criterion for ontological commitment'. Let us begin to see what this is about.

Quine presents his view as something completely uncontroversial, given that, according to him, it is little more than a stipulation on the meaning of the expression 'ontological commitment'. Not everybody agrees with him on this, as we will see. For now, it is worth noting that Quine's position breaks with much previous ontological tradition, and has some polemical targets. For instance, one may think that your commitment to a certain kind of entity is revealed just by your conferring a meaning to a certain word. 'Pegasus', for example, differs from 'biltri' in being a meaningful word. This means, one could argue, that it has meaning, so it must name something, so there must exist something it denotes. Not so, according to Quine: he stresses that 'there is a gulf between meaning and naming' (Quine 1948: 9), as witnessed by expressions like 'if', which is doubtless meaningful even though 'if' isn't anyone's name. The same goes for adjectives like 'red', which are meaningful without denoting (according to Quine) any such thing as the colour red, or the property of redness. They are adjectives and not names, after all. My red pullover and a red rose provide examples of red things, but again according to Quine, do not witness there being the property of redness in the world.

Next, recall from the previous chapter how Russell provided in *On Denoting* a simple logical technique to get rid of apparent commitment to such unwelcome objects as non-existent entities, apparently brought in by definite descriptions like 'the current king of France'. Quine subscribes to Russell's paraphrase technique in *On What There Is*, and believes it to be extendable to proper names like 'Pegasus' and 'Santa Claus'. We can rephrase such proper names into definite descriptions, like 'the old man dressed in red, who brings presents to children on Christmas' Eve'. We can even coin *ad hoc* predicates like 'pegasizes', if needed, turn 'Pegasus' into something like 'the *x* that pegasizes', and then apply the Russellian procedure from scratch.

Now having claimed that the use of adjectives or predicates does not commit us to the existence of properties, and that the use of singular terms like names and descriptions does not commit us to the existence of the items they were supposed to denote, Quine asks: is there *anything at all* that can be said that commits us to the existence of something? As it turns out, there is:

> We can very easily involve ourselves in ontological commitments by saying, for example, that *there is something* (bound variable) which red houses and sunsets have in common; or that *there is something* which is a prime number larger than a million. But, this is, essentially, the *only* way we can involve ourselves in ontological commitments: by our use of bound variables. The use of alleged names is no criterion, for we can repudiate their namehood. … Whatever we say with the help of names can be said in a language which shuns names altogether. To be assumed as an entity is, purely and simply, to be reckoned as the value of a variable. ... The variables of quantification, 'something', 'nothing', 'everything', range over our whole ontology, whatever it may be; and we are convicted of a particular ontological presupposition if, and only if, the alleged presuppositum has to be reckoned among the entities over which our variables range in order to render one of our affirmations true. (Quine 1948: 9)

The dictum 'To be is to be the value of a (bound) variable' summarizes the Quinean criterion of ontological commitment. Here, 'ontological commitment' has the same meaning as 'existential commitment', and the variables Quine has in mind are the variables of the canonical notation of elementary logic, which can be bound by quantifiers. Recall from the previous chapter how the logical symbol '∃', abbreviating such expressions as 'there is…', is named, not by chance, the *existential* quantifier. Given this reading of the quantifier, there is no room to doubt that 'existence is what existential quantification expresses. There are things of kind F if and only if $\exists xFx$' (Quine 1969b: 97, notation slightly modified; see also Quine 1981). You are ontologically committed to the Fs if and only if what you claim entails that $\exists xFx$.

The idea that '$\exists$', by abbreviating 'there is' – much in the same way as '+' abbreviates 'plus' – captures ontological commitment, can be further elucidated by looking at how Peter van Inwagen (1998: 238–9) explains the meaning of the idiom of quantification and variables by linking them to phrases of ordinary English. Following van Inwagen, call a *quantifier phrase* an expression of the form '$\exists x(x \ldots)$'. Our first step is to introduce third person pronouns which are free of any connotation of gender of personhood – say: 'it_x', 'it_y', 'it_z', etc. Our second step is to understand a quantifier phrase as an abbreviation of an English phrase of the form:

> It is true of at least one thing that it_x is such that…

If this is a correct account of the meaning of quantifier phrases, van Inwagen goes on, then:

> $\exists x(x$ is a dog)
>
> is an abbreviation for
>
> It is true of at least one thing that it_x is such that it_x is a dog.
>
> That is,
>
> It is true of at least one thing that it is such that it is a dog.
>
> That is,
>
> It is true of at least one thing that it is a dog.
>
> That is,
>
> At least one thing is a dog.
>
> That is,
>
> There is at least one dog. (van Inwagen 1998: 240–1, notation slightly modified).

When we want to ascertain the ontological commitments of a theory or of a group of statements in ordinary English, we then proceed backwards. One can just write down the sentences one subscribes to. One then translates them into a formal or semi-formal language, like the one of the canonical logical notation, i.e. (something close to) the standard quantifier-variable notation of elementary logic. The purpose of the translation is to capture and express the quantificational structure of the relevant sentences (this is why we can stick with semi-formal expressions like '$\exists x(x$ is a dog)' above, if we want: we can leave the English language predicate 'is a dog' there, without replacing it with a predicate letter of elementary logic, say 'D', getting something like '$\exists xDx$': what matters is that the quantificational structure of sentences be made transparent). Then one can check whether one's statements mean or entail that there are entities of a certain sort.

Now note that, according to Quine's criterion of ontological commitment, these claims just count as *inconsistent*:

(I1) Insects and spiders share some important anatomical properties, but there are no such things as properties. (Example by van Inwagen 2004: 114).
(I2) Some prime numbers are greater than 1,000, even though there are no such things as numbers.
(I3) My T-shirt and this rose are red, but there is nothing which is red.

On the other hand, it is not inconsistent to say:

(NI1) You are funny and I am funny, but we don't share any property: there is nothing which we have in common.
(NI2) Many are called, few are chosen, but there are no numbers.
(NI3) My T-shirt and this rose are red, but there is nothing like the colour red or the property of redness.

We will see plenty of examples of Quine's criterion in action. To get a feeling of where the notion of ontological commitment comes to bite, though, it is worth reminding that paradigmatic examples of inconsistent people, for Quine, were those who made such claims as 'There are numbers which are prime and greater than 1,000, but numbers do not exist'. Properly regimented, such a statement has a form like: 'Some *F*s are *G*s, but there are no *F*s', that is, '$\exists x(Fx \,\&\, Gx) \,\&\, {\sim}\exists xFx$' ('&' standing for conjunction 'and'). This is inconsistent, given that 'Some *F*s are *G*s' *entails* that there are *F*s: $\exists xFx$ follows from $\exists x(Fx \,\&\, Gx)$ in elementary logic. And that there are *F*s, $\exists xFx$, as we know, according to Quine is equivalent to the claim that *F*s exist.

The passage through canonical notation is crucial to Quine's perspective. We speak in natural language, but relations of implication can be precisely ascertained when we deal with sentences belonging to a formal language. In order to understand whether what we say commits us to a certain kind of entities we thus need to pass through a paraphrase of canonical notation. And this is not as simple as it may look from the previous examples. There is no easy road to uncover via such translation the quantificational structure of theories or (groups of) sentences, for we often cannot assume that every sentence belonging to natural language admits of just one correct translation into the formal language. Consider somebody claiming:

(O1) Red is a colour.

This sounds very true and, one may think, if red is a colour, then *something* (namely, red) is a colour. So (O1) would entail:

(O2) There is at least one colour.

The translation of (O2) into canonical notation would then be:

(O3) $\exists x(x \text{ is a colour})$.

Then following the Quinean criterion one would be committed, by asserting (O1), to the existence of things like colours: for (O2), that is (O3), appears to be entailed by (O1). Still, someone who accepts to play by the Quinean criterion of ontological commitment but, for whatever reason, does not want colours to be included in the furniture of the world, may take (O1) as nothing but an 'ontologically misleading' way to express the following claim:

(O4) All red things are coloured.

This can be rendered into canonical notation as:

(O5) $\forall x$ (if x is red, then x is coloured).

Now (O4), that is (O5), only involves quantification over (that is, ontological commitment to) things which are, if red, coloured: in order for it to be true there need be no such things as *colours* in the world.

Besides, sometimes there are things we say that seem not to admit of any translation into canonical notation. To borrow an example from John P. Burgess, think of somebody claiming:

(??) Iraqi weapons of mass destruction exist only in the mind of Dick Cheney.

Of course, people claiming (??) are not willing to commit themselves to the existence of Iraqi weapons of mass destruction. It is not easy though, to understand how to render (??) into canonical notation so as to maintain its intended meaning.

'Translation into canonical notation' denotes a complicated business. We are going to extensively discuss it in the next chapter. For the moment, let us just bring home these two points concerning Quine's approach to ontology. First, he took quantification over a certain kind of entities as the hallmark of one's commitment to the existence of such kind of entities. Second, as he was aware that translation into canonical notation by itself is not a fool-proof mechanical procedure, he came to consider ontology not a science that *reveals* pre-theoretical commitments to some kind of entities, but as the theoretical effort to get clear about what kind of entities we are disposed to admit by formulating our best scientific theory of the world. This leads us to the final key tenet of Quine's metaontology.

4 Thesis four: Naturalism

Physicists say that there are subatomic particles such as protons and electrons. One may think that it would be silly for a philosopher to contradict them. On what grounds may a philosopher seriously deny that such entities as subatomic particles exist? Who are you, *qua* philosopher, to tell scientists that they are wrong? (For nice variations on this rhetorical question, see Lewis 1991, 1993).

According to what Quine calls 'naturalism', such an attitude would indeed be preposterous. Philosophy cannot overrule the internal standards of scientific disciplines such as physics. Philosophers should rather take the findings of science on board, and reflect on them. They may, for instance, draw ontological morals from scientific explanations. Take subatomic particles again. Given the proper sense of 'seeing', nobody has ever *seen* an electron. In order to account for some phenomena, physicists postulate their existence. Such postulation is not, of course, gratuitous. Part of our scientific methodology seems to involve accepting what philosophers of science and epistemologist call *inference to the best explanation*: if the best explanation of why it is the case that *P* consists in supposing it to be the case that *Q*, we are justified in believing that *Q* is the case. We are legitimated by scientific standards to believe the explanation of a phenomenon say, heat, according to which heat just consists in the motion of subatomic particles. It seems plausible to suppose that, once we regiment into canonical notation such an explanation, it will turn out that it is ontologically committed to subatomic particles. Philosophers should abide by such a commitment.

We now have Quine's overall metaontological strategy in sight which addresses ontological disputes by combining naturalism with his criterion for ontological commitment (see Liggins 2008a for details on such an approach). The strategy may be summarized as consisting of three steps:

1. Paraphrase our best scientific theories into the canonical notation.
2. Take note of the ontological commitments of such paraphrase.
3. Accept these ontological commitments and just these.

Now two people can accept the same metaontological position, but disagree about what there is. A and B may both agree with Quine on how to conduct ontological debates; still, A may believe that there are numbers and B may think there are none. We will come back at length to ontological debates such as this in the third part of our book, but let us stick to the metaontological rules of debate for the moment. The most problematic of the three Quinean steps is perhaps the first. If A and B disagree about how to translate a given theory into canonical notation, there is no straightforward way for either to force the other to accept a certain paraphrase. Quine didn't attach too much weight to this. But people working within the mainstream Quinean metaontological approach have elaborated on this point. They have proposed various constraints on how translations into canonical notation should be carried out. By combining these indications with the original proposal by Quine, one gets what can be called the standard metaontological view. This is the topic of our next chapter.

Further Reading

The beginning of Yablo 1998 contains a vivid account of the attitude one can take with respect to ontological problems such as whether there really are such 'entities as the number nineteen, the property of roundness, the chance that it will rain, the month of April, the city of Chicago, and the language Spanish' (Yablo 1998: 230). On Quine's naturalism see Quine 1981. On naturalism in general see Papineau 2009; Williamson 2011a, 2011b. Our presentation of Quine's strategy to assess ontological commitments is inspired by those of van Inwagen 1998 and Liggins 2008a.

3

The Standard View

Chapter Outline

We saw in the previous chapter that putting the Quinean criterion of ontological commitment to work requires a rendering of the relevant sentences and, by extension, theories, into what has been called the canonical notation, with the aim of making their ontological commitments transparent. The twentieth-century development of this view has made clear that this is no fool-proof, algorithmic task. We start the chapter by expanding on this in Section 1. We explore a couple of dichotomies in the methodology of contemporary ontology and further examine how the Quinean criterion can be put to work as a methodological tool to conduct ontological debates.

Quine also provided substantive norms for the admissibility of kinds of entities in the ontological catalogue. In Section 2, we deal with his most famous negative norm, summarized by the motto 'No entity without identity.' We investigate what ontological *criteria of identity* are, distinguish them from epistemic *criteria of individuation*, and look at some sample identity criteria at work.

Section 3 deals with a venerable question of traditional ontology concerning the notion of being: is this notion *univocal*, that is, does it mean one thing only? Or is it true that, as Aristotle claimed, being is 'spoken of in many ways'? We focus in particular on how the question relates to the standard Quinean view in metaontology. At the end of this chapter we should have a good outline of the mainstream methodological tenets of contemporary ontology.

1 Paraphrase strategies

1.1 Descriptive vs. prescriptive ontology

In *The Method of Truth in Metaphysics,* Donald Davidson famously wrote: 'In sharing a language … we share a picture of the world that must, in its large features, be true.' He took this to entail that a good method for ontological and metaphysical inquiry was 'to study the general structure of our language' (Davidson 1977: 244). A 'picture of the world' was to be understood as a group of *intuitions* on the furniture and the most general structures of reality. What are intuitions? There is a growing literature on the subject. We take them, minimally, as something like shared beliefs, opinions or judgments: a plural declination of what one may call, with an easy-going mass-term, 'good old common sense'. We follow some trustworthy literature on this: 'Our intuitions are just opinions' (Lewis 1983: x); 'So-called intuitions are simply judgments (or dispositions to judgment)' (Williamson 2007: 3).

Taking the intuitions deposited in our ordinary language seriously is typical of a *descriptive* methodological stance in ontology. Descriptive ontology was theorized and endorsed by Peter Strawson in *Individuals* (Strawson 1959). The endorsement involved a two-stage argument of (sort of) a Davidsonian kind. First, to study the general structure of the world we need to look at the general structure of our thought whose essential feature consists in being about the world and which, by and large, must be capable of grasping its target. Secondly, the general structure of our thought shows up through our language. Thus, the philosophical examination of our ordinary language can give us access to a mostly true ontological picture. The worldly stuff we are looking for while in the business of writing the ontological catalogue must consist of what makes true the true sentences of our ordinary language or of what makes true our ('in their large features true') beliefs about the world, as expressed by those sentences. This is the world as it appears to us via our everyday concepts: a world made of chairs, newspapers, political parties and mortgages – things we refer to, and quantify over, all the time in our everyday businesses.

However, defenders of so-called 'ordinary language arguments' in ontology face immediate objections. One is that philosophy is not bound to common sense or shared beliefs any more than to argumentation or criticism, whatever these amount to in their turn. Philosophy's duty, on the contrary, has often been to overthrow shared beliefs and judgments not supported by persuasive reasoning or conclusive substantiation. Their being shared does not, after all, make them true: take the past banalities that, to quote Shakespeare, 'the stars are fire and the sun doth move'; or the gambler's mistaken idea that if a number has not been drawn in a long time, the chances that it will show up increase.

Two retorts to this objection, common in the literature and described in Matti Eklund's 2006a nice survey of metaontology, appeal to *a priori* intuitions and conceptual truths respectively. *A priori* intuitions are taken as beliefs we can form via armchair speculation, and are no less reliable than ordinary perception as a guide to the world's furniture. Supporters of conceptual truths in ontology, on the other hand, assimilate sentences like 'If there exist subatomic particles arranged table-wise, then there exist tables' to 'Bachelors are unmarried men'. It is fair to say, though, that the majority of modern ontologists agree that *some* revision of our ordinary language's apparent ontological commitments is due anyway, lest we end up committed to implausible, if not absurd, ontological kinds. In this sense, most philosophers nowadays agree that ontology cannot be naively descriptive.

For a *prescriptive* ontologist, we should unfold the basic categories of being independent of whatever picture of reality we may find intuitive or widespread, and even at the cost of radically resetting any such picture. It is generally agreed that such a revision will be costly – a quick conclusion from the claim that belief revision is costly in general. We highlighted that 'some' in the previous paragraph, however. Description and prescription come in degrees, with several intermediate positions allowed, and actually explored: twenty-first- century metaontology has evolved into an industry of subtle cost-benefit analyses aiming to determine which revisionary prices are worth paying.

To refer back to our initial chapter: no philosopher would follow the White King in taking Alice's famous answer as bringing commitment to an object called Nothing. Russell felt the need to dig underneath the surface grammar of sentences apparently entailing commitment to non-existent French kings. And Quine himself was a largely revisionary or prescriptive ontologist. According to him, we are bound to revise the ontological commitments brought by our ordinary language and beliefs, when these would lead us to posit entities we may find unacceptable for various reasons, ranging from lack of clear identity criteria (what these are, we will soon see), to dispensability in the light of our best scientific theories.

We will now explore a sample ontological debate between two hypothetical philosophers, one more inclined to descriptivism, the other to prescriptivism. Both play strictly by the rules of the mainstream Quinean view in metaontology, which we explored in the previous chapter. However, their debate quickly becomes tricky. The story draws on a beautiful paper by David and Stephanie Lewis 1970.

1.2 Argle and Bargle on holes

Argle is a materialist philosopher. He does not believe in 'entelechies or spirits of auras or deities or other things unknown to physics' (Lewis 1986: 1). In his ontology, there is only room for material objects: concrete, spatiotemporally located things with a mass (when we come to the relevant chapter in the third part of our book, we will see that defining the notion of material object is not that straightforward; but we can rest with a rough intuitive characterization for now). This seems to entail that, for him:

(0) There are no holes.

Being immaterial, massless things, holes don't meet the criteria for inclusion in Argle's parsimonious ontological catalogue. However, in his everyday talk he is likely to utter such sentences as:

(1) There are holes in that piece of cheese.

Now Bargle steps in, and claims that Argle is in for an ontological predicament. If Argle accepts to play the game of the Quinean criterion of ontological commitment, then by assertively uttering (1) he is committed to the existence of holes: (1) can only be true if there exist holes in that piece of cheese, thus only if holes are in the range of that quantifier, 'there are' (one can, of course, semi-formalize (1) as: $\exists x$(x is a hole & x is in that piece of cheese)). But this is inconsistent with (0) (that is, $\sim\exists x$(x is a hole)).

Is Argle the kind of 'ontological cheater' we referred to in the previous chapter – one whose inconsistent commitments can be exposed via the Quinean strategy? Argle can reply that his *prima facie* quantification over holes in (1) should not be taken seriously. As Russell and Quine taught us, issues of ontological commitment can be seriously addressed only after the appropriate logical analysis of our claims. In particular, (1) should be paraphrased along the following lines:

(1a) That piece of cheese is perforated.

Now (1a) is not inconsistent with (0): it commits one who asserts it only to there being pieces of cheese, and these are legitimate material beings. (1a) is true just in case there exists pieces of cheese that are perforated, that is, so-and-so shaped (one may semi-formalize this as: '$\exists x$(x is a piece of cheese & x is perforated)'). The agreeable fellow that he is, Argle wants to speak with the vulgar, so he keeps uttering such sentences as (1). However, he means *nothing but* (1a).

Bargle has a strategy to fight back. Argle is committed by his ontology to dispense with quantification over holes, in principle, in all *prima facie* holes-committing sentences. In other words, Argle needs a systematic paraphrase strategy. One may claim:

(2) There is a hexagonal hole in that piece of cheese.

In (2) we seem not only to quantify over holes, but also to ascribe them properties, such as being hexagonal. Argle will need to turn (2) into something like:

(2a) That piece of cheese is hexagonally perforated.

In (2a), we dispense with holes and we turn (what, in (2), appeared to be) reference to a property of the (wannabe-)things we wanted to dispense with into an adverb modifying the shape-predicate 'perforated'. Consistency with (0) seems preserved.

But Bargle may come back with a more complicated claim, apparently involving the number of holes in a certain cheesy state of affairs:

(3) There are as many holes in my piece of cheese as in your cracker.

Argle may now resort to something like the following:

(3a) Either both my piece of cheese and your cracker are singly perforated, or both are doubly perforated, or both are triply perforated. … And so on.

The *ad hoc* adverbs 'singly', 'doubly', etc., are again shape-predicate modifiers. The sequence from (1)–(1a) to (3)–(3a) seems to exhibit something like a pattern. Argle's ontology looks simple, neat and parsimonious: it only allows objects of a single general kind, namely material beings. Argle pays the price for simplicity in ontology, though, in the coin of logical form complications: each paraphrase (#a) looks more convoluted than its counterpart (#). Will Argle manage to provide paraphrases of all true ordinary language sentences involving *prima facie* quantification over holes? Bargle can, of course, easily cook up more troublesome apparently holes-committing sentences (you may think about some yourself).

Also, we quantify over massless things of all kinds in our ordinary talk – from scandals to mortgages, iPhone apps, and even more ethereal entities like numbers, concepts and propositions. A parsimonious ontologist like Argle, who accepts to abide by the Quinean criterion, seems compelled to give systematic translations of apparently true ordinary language statements involving surface grammar quantification over such unwelcome things (though calling them 'translations' may sound a bit strange, since they don't require switching from, say, English to French or Japanese). This paraphrase dialectics is made even more complicated by the consideration of *what* such paraphrases are supposed in general to achieve in ontological debates – and to this we now turn.

1.3 Hermeneutic vs. revolutionary paraphrases

Suppose Argle manages to complete his translation handbook, or to provide a recipe allowing him to dispense, in principle, with all the potentially infinite quantifications over ontologically unwelcome stuff. What has he accomplished, philosophically speaking?

One may assume that the task of an adequate paraphrase is to preserve the truth-value, intuitive content, and entailments of the paraphrased sentence. Then if sentence (#), in which we seemingly quantify over unwelcome things, is successfully paraphrased into sentence (#a) in which such quantification is avoided, then the translation can be read backwards as well. We can say that (#a) expresses the true ontological commitments of (#), but we may as well say that it's the other way round. Perhaps the right way to come to grips with sentences to the effect that pieces of cheese are *n*-perforated is by accepting that there are *n* holes in them. This is how good (meaning-and-entailments-preserving) translations work, one may claim: they are symmetric. *Ceteris paribus*, one can read them in either direction. The privilege of one direction over the other, as providing an ontologically justified reduction, should be argued for *independently* by our Argles, on pain of begging the question against less parsimonious ontologists at the Bargles' party: simply providing a translation does not by itself settle the issue.

However, it is even controversial that paraphrases of this kind ought to preserve meanings. The paraphrase strategy can in fact be understood in two rather different ways, following a distinction due to Quine 1960 and developed by John Burgess and Gideon Rosen 1997, which has become widely accepted in contemporary ontology (the following exposition is indebted to Carrara and Varzi 1997).

According to a *hermeneutic* reading of the paraphrases proposed above, what Argle is about when he translates (#) into (#a) is making explicit the ontological commitment of (#) *in the mouth of* competent speakers of English. We can keep speaking of the number and shape of the holes in that piece of cheese, but what *we* really mean is … and there follows the paraphrase. The ontological commitments of our natural language are to some extent opaque to ourselves, and the paraphrase is supposed to get rid of such opacity. This way of understanding paraphrases may still be to some extent compatible with a descriptive approach to ontology (one can take Ryle 1932 as a classic example of the hermeneutic strategy). Of course, we cannot take all the apparent ontological commitments of our everyday talk at face value. Our careful paraphrases are to reveal ontological commitments, which are to some extent already there, implicit in the way we talk, whether we realize this or not.

According to a *revolutionary* reading of the paraphrase strategy, Argle is rather into illustrating what he takes to be the real furniture of the world, independently from what laymen or philosophers mean when they talk of holes in the cheese. There exist no holes for him, whether or not people or other philosophers believe the opposite. He can utter sentences like (1)–(3) to make communication easier, but we should take them as abbreviations for what he really means, in conformity with his ontology, as per (1a)–(3a). In the revolutionary understanding of paraphrases, these are more like amendments than like explications.

Suppose that Russell acted as a revolutionary ontologist when he claimed that 'The current king of France is bald' ought to be turned, against surface grammar, into a complex quantified statement. Then he was not trying to uncover the real ontological commitments of that sentence in the mouths of everyday speakers, by translating it into an ontologically less misleading synonym. Rather, he had an antecedent ontological conviction: that we should not admit in our ontological catalogue such things as non-existent or merely possible kings, incompatible with that 'feeling of reality which *ought* to be preserved even in the most abstract studies' (our emphasis). We may or may not be committed to such things given how we ordinarily talk. But we *ought* not to commit ourselves, for there are independent reasons for believing that there are no such things.

The meaning-preservation requirement for good translations may be relaxed for revolutionary paraphrases, more than for hermeneutic paraphrases. Revolutionary ontologists may only grant a loose connection between the original sentence (#) and the corresponding paraphrase (#a). As stressed by Carrara and Varzi 1997, if the ontologist's aim is not to clarify the real ontological import of speakers' ordinary talk, but to reform it so that it better sticks to what is out there, she may not need her paraphrases to do what we ordinarily expect from good translations.

1.4 The Quinean criterion as a strategy

The Quinean criterion of ontological commitment, as we have seen, is a methodological (contrast substantive) yardstick for ontology. Methodologically careful ontologists like Peter van Inwagen have suggested that we take the label 'criterion of ontological commitment' as naming, rather than a fool-proof procedure, a heuristic strategy to conduct ontological disputes. The view that we can mechanically, or almost-mechanically, (a) turn the sentences composing our theories into the canonical notation; (b) list the sentences that begin with an existential quantifier and (c) read the ontological commitments of our theories off these sentences – is an oversimplification. Theories are not easily identifiable objects. Even if they were, according to van Inwagen it is controversial whether there is something like a unique, objective, logical form, lurking below the deceptive surface grammar of language. He grants that 'sometimes, in simple cases involving little or no creativity, a refusal to accept the obvious proposal for the introduction of quantifiers and variables can border on the unintelligible' (van Inwagen 1998: 28–9). However, there can often be competing and equally plausible translations of the same sentence into the canonical notation, uncovering incompatible ontological commitments.

Besides, according to some ontologists the commitment of theory T, even once all parties have agreed upon a single translation into the quantifier-variable idiom, may well go beyond what is explicitly asserted in translated-T, or logically deduced from it. It will extend to commitments entailed by the translated claims, not by way of plain logic, the relevant entailments being a further possible source of controversy. Can one deny, for instance, that '$\exists x$(x is a black swan)' brings commitment to concrete objects, or that '$\exists x$(x is a prime number larger than 100)' brings commitment to abstract beings? In *The Ways of Paradox*, Quine claimed that one cannot: by asserting that there are black swans and prime numbers larger than 100, we commit ourselves to physical objects and abstract entities (see Quine 1966: 128). But such commitments themselves are not logical entailments: they depend on one's background metaphysical theory of the entities at stake (as stressed, for instance, by Chihara 1968 and Chateaubriand 1971). The mainstream position on them is that prime numbers are abstract entities, while black swans are *concreta*. But non-standard metaphysicians may have non-standard views: they may admit black swans as being out there in the world, but reduce them to bundles of properties or universals, therefore, to (even more) abstract aggregates of abstract objects; or, they may advocate reductions of all mathematical statements to sentences ultimately about *concreta*. They may also retain quantification over swans and numbers in their everyday talk, and maintain, with (revolutionary) Argle, that they speak with the vulgar, but think with the wise: 'Lo, I do keep saying that there are numbers to make your life easier, but what I really mean is …' and there follows a suitable acceptable paraphrase.

2 No entity without identity

Quine also had substantive (contrast methodological) proposals on how to answer the ontological question. One had to do with the indispensability of the kinds of entities we quantify over in our *best* theories – which for Quine meant, consistently with his naturalism, which we have met in the previous chapter: the best scientific theories, with physics standing at the forefront. He had another substantive proposal – this time, a negative one: a proposal to the effect that some putative kinds of things ought *not* to be admitted in a safe and sane ontology. This is summarized by another famous Quinean motto, making for the title of this section. The motto expresses the idea that we should not allow putative objects lacking clear-cut identity conditions, or identity criteria. We therefore need to say something on what identity criteria are. We will then look at some examples of how the motto was put to work by Quine himself.

2.1 Identity and individuation

An identity criterion is normally taken as something of the following form:

(CI) If a and b are things of kind F, then $a = b$ if and only if …

The identity of the identity criterion is fixed by the condition that is to replace the dots. The 'if and only if' between the identity statement and the relevant condition says that a criterion is supposed to provide necessary and sufficient conditions for the identity of *a* with *b*. But of course, it is the *sufficiency* condition that matters, that is, the entailment from right to left in the consequent of (CI). The other direction, the necessity condition, simply follows from the *Indiscernibility of Identicals*, also often called Leibniz's Law: the principle according to which, if *a* is identical with *b*, then *a* and *b* are indiscernible: any property or feature of *a* is also a property or feature of *b* and vice versa (of course: 'they' actually are one and the same thing. How could *that* thing have a property *it* lacks?).

The idea of identity criteria is usually traced back to Frege's *Grundlagen der Arithmetik*. However, the way Frege puts the point there has produced some confusions in ontology, of which we must get rid straightaway:

> If we are to use symbol *a* to signify an object, we must have a criterion for deciding in all cases whether *b* is the same as *a*, even if it is not always in our power to apply this criterion. (Frege 1884: §62)

The first thing to clarify is that, while Frege oscillates between talk of symbols signifying things and talk of the things themselves, it is the latter reading that matters for ontology. What we need is a criterion for the identity of the given objects *a* and *b*, not for whatever linguistic expressions we use to refer to them, say, '*a*' and '*b*'. These are ostensibly different as symbols. The problem is whether we have one thing or two, when what may or may not be one single thing comes forth in two different guises – say, as what is referred to by '*a*', and as what is referred to by '*b*'.

To pick a famous example, also due to Frege: the ancients did not know that Hesperus just is Phosphorus. They did not know, that is that the celestial body they called 'Hesperus' (the first star showing up at sunset) is the same as the celestial body they called 'Phosphorus' (the last star disappearing at dawn), namely planet Venus. The ancients had no doubts, of course, on the difference between the two names. But those two names – unbeknownst to them – happened to name one and the same thing. (The puzzle produced by situations of this kind is thus sometimes called *Frege's Puzzle*, or the puzzle of informative identities; it has generated an enormous amount of discussion in contemporary philosophy, having to do with the difference between trivially *a priori* true and uninformative identity statements like 'Hesperus is Hesperus', and statements like 'Hesperus is Phosphorus', which can make for substantive *a posteriori* discoveries).

Secondly, Frege speaks of a criterion for 'deciding' when we are dealing with a case of identity, which must be there even though we may be unable to apply it in specific cases. However, it is one thing to wonder about the conditions under which *a* and *b* are the same; it is another thing to wonder how we can ascertain or decide whether *a* is the same as *b* or not. The latter topic belongs to epistemology in a broad sense, that is, to issues concerning how we know about things. The former topic only belongs to ontology or metaphysics properly, that is, to issues concerning the things themselves.

To put the tracked distinction another way: criteria of identity are not criteria of *identification* or *individuation*. The latter are procedures by applying which we may come to decide whether we have a case of identity. Such procedures may involve practical methods allowing us to single out objects in the context of our experience or to re-identify them across time (think of policemen checking the fingerprints of suspect *a*, in order to find out whether he is the same as much-wanted criminal *b*).

Criteria of identity, on the other hand, are properly metaphysical or ontological principles. They are to specify the conditions under which *a* and *b* are the same thing, independently of our being in a position to establish whether they are. Identity criteria may play important roles in the individuation of worldly stuff, but the two issues should be kept distinct. Some ontologists hold that animals have their identity conditions fixed by their causal source and the gametes that originated them. However, we wouldn't normally identify an animal by checking which gametes it comes from. According to some ontologists, a good criterion for things of kind *F* captures what it means to be an *F* or, at least, tells us something about the identity of objects of kind *F*, also when individuating them is cognitively complicated, or even unfeasible for us.

2.2 Identity criteria at work

With this clarification out of the way, let us put identity criteria to work via a couple of examples. Quine's motto 'No entity without identity' summarizes a prescription to the effect that, while in the business of writing down the ontological catalogue, we should never admit kinds of entities for which we lack clear criteria instantiating (CI). To understand the prohibition, let us start with a couple of positive cases – cases in which, for him, we do have good criteria.

Quine believes that we have a good instance of (CI) for K = material object. We can again take material objects as things located in space-time: things which occupy some space, are involved in causal interactions, and are subject to change and motion, generation and decay in the flow of time. Such are things like cats, trees, statues and tea-cups. For these, Quine subscribes to something like the following criterion (Quine 1975):

(CI_{MO}) If a and b are material objects, then $a = b$ if and only if a has the same spatiotemporal location as b.

Material beings are identified by their address in space-time. One immediate consequence of (CI_{MO}) is that there cannot be two numerically distinct material objects occupying the same place at the same time. As we will see in the third part of our book, some ontologists disagree with Quine on this. The Quinean view entails, for instance, that a given statue and the lump of bronze it is made of count as one and the same thing (after all, one is exactly where the other is) – which seems counterintuitive to some. This is not our issue now, however. What matters for our purposes is that, if something like (CI_{MO}) arguably counts as a good criterion of identity for material objects then we are allowed to include them in our ontology. Or, more precisely, the Quinean motto does not put a ban on them: for we have a principle specifying when, once we stumble upon objects of this kind, we should count one thing out there in the world, rather than two.

Some abstract objects, namely *sets* or *classes,* also have clear identity criteria for Quine. As it is the first time we mention these things, we need to say something on the terminology and notation adopted for them in our book. Throughout it we are using 'set' and 'class' interchangeably, even though some set-theoretic approaches employ the two terms differently. Sets or classes are collections of things: for instance, the set of human beings is the collection of all and only the things which are human beings; the set of red chairs is the collection of all and only the things which are both red and chairs. Human beings are said to be the *members* of the set of human beings, and red chairs are said to be the members of the set of red chairs.

We will occasionally use the standard notation to name sets, which consists in listing (the names of) their members within curly brackets: '{*a, b, c*}', for instance, is a term denoting the set or collection of things *a, b, c*. {Socrates} is the set whose only member is Socrates (it should not be confused with Socrates himself: Socrates is a paradigmatically concrete object, {Socrates} is a paradigmatically abstract object). This notation properly works only for sets with a finite number of members: we cannot list all the members of the set of natural numbers (0, 1, 2, 3…) between brackets, for the list is endless; however, we can still refer to the set (we just did).

Now the so-called Extensionality Principle of set theory can, in fact, be understood as delivering identity conditions for sets:

(CI_{Sets}) If *a* and *b* are sets, then $a = b$ if and only if *a* has the same members as *b*.

This makes of sets or classes purely *extensional* entities: things whose identity is fully determined by their extension, that is, by the objects which are their members (so much so that sets are usually identified with the extensions themselves). (CI_{Sets}) tells us, for instance, that the set of all houses is the same as the set of all habitations, given that each house is a habitation and each habitation is a house. Anything which is a member of the first set is also a member of the second and vice versa; by (CI_{Sets}), this entails their identity. So sets are respectable entities. Again, 'No entity without identity' expresses a merely negative guideline: that things of kind *F* comply with it may not, by itself, give us sufficient motivations for admitting *F*s in our ontology.

For Quine we have positive reasons for accepting sets: they are indispensable insofar as we need to quantify over them when we do mathematics, and mathematics is, of course, embedded in our best scientific theories. So Quine combines the permission to have sets granted by (CI_{Sets}) with positive and, for him, naturalistically based reasons for admitting them – a topic we will return to when we speak of 'indispensability arguments' for the admission of abstract objects later on in our book. But other ontologists with a more parsimonious attitude may want to reject sets even though we have an identity criterion for them, on the basis of their rejection of abstract objects of any kind.

(CI_{Sets}) also marks the distinction between sets and their intensional cousins, namely properties. In general, entities of a kind *F* are called *intensional* when they can be intuitively distinct even though they are associated with the same actual extension. For instance: sameness of extension is not sufficient for the identity of properties, for there are intuitively distinct properties whose extensions coincide. One famous example due, again, to Frege: the property of being a *renate* (an animal with kidneys) and the property of being a *cordate* (an animal with a heart) are intuitively distinct. Having kidneys is not quite the same thing as having a heart. However, all (normally endowed) animals with kidneys also have a heart and vice versa. Thus, the set of all animals with kidneys and the set of all animals with a heart, by (CI_{Sets}), are one and the same set.

That we cannot have anything like (CI_{Sets}) for properties does not, by itself, entail that there are no plausible identity criteria for properties. But Quine is sceptic: according to him, intensional objects like properties (and propositions, too) just lack clear identity conditions. If we don't quite get what it takes to assert, or to deny, that property or proposition *a* is the same as property or proposition *b*, then the very identity of objects of these putative kinds is obscure. Quine calls them 'creatures of darkness' – another one of his rhetorical expressions. We ought not to admit them in a safe and sane ontology.

The same holds, according to Quine, also for the putative objects admitted by prodigal ontologists like Meinong, whom we mentioned two chapters ago: things like mythical and fictional objects (Sherlock Holmes, Pegasus), and *possibilia*, that is, things which exist in merely possible situations or circumstances, distinct from the actual one (Wittgenstein's oldest daughter, for instance: Wittgenstein died childless but he certainly could have had a daughter; so it looks like there's a possible circumstance in which Wittgenstein has a daughter, and a prodigal ontologist may want to infer from this that there is something like Wittgenstein's merely possible oldest daughter). As we have seen in Chapter 1, Russell already objected that such things upset the 'feeling of reality' we should stick to even in our most abstract investigations. Indeed, this was the main motivation for developing his eliminative strategy in the analysis of definite descriptions.

Quine follows Russell on this. When *a* and *b* are fictional or merely possible objects, for instance, there is no clear criterion in sight, specifying when *a* counts as identical with *b*. Here is a notorious passage from *On What There Is*, where 'Wyman' names a fictional (!) philosopher, a straw man playing the role of the prodigal ontologist:

> Wyman's slum of possibles is a breeding ground for disorderly elements. Take, for instance, the possible fat man in that doorway; and, again, the possible bald man in

> that doorway. Are they the same possible man, or two possible men? How do we decide? How many possible men are there in that doorway? Are there more possible thin ones than fat ones? How many of them are alike? Or would their being alike make them one? Are no two possible things alike? Is this the same as saying that it is impossible for two things to be alike? Or, finally, is the concept of identity simply inapplicable to unactualized possibles? But what sense can be found in talking of entities which cannot meaningfully be said to be identical with themselves and distinct from one another? These elements are well-nigh incorrigible. … I feel we'd do better simply to clear Wyman's slum and be done with it. (Quine 1948: 16)

The adjective 'possible', occurring within the definite descriptions in play, 'the possible fat man in that doorway' and 'the possible bald man in that doorway', speaks for the *existential* situation of the (wannabe-)object(s) at issue. This qualification is not trivial. Barack Obama is a possible bald or fat man in the doorway, in the following sense: Obama, a real man, is neither bald nor fat (at the time of our writing), nor is he in the doorway (we assume Quine had in mind a specific, real doorway). But Obama is such that he *could* be fat and/or bald, and in the doorway. Thus, he is an object endowed with the modal features of being possibly fat, possibly bald and of being possibly in the doorway. According to Quine, however, Obama has crystal clear identity conditions given by (CI_{MO}): he is identical with whatever is his spatiotemporal roommate, and with nothing else. This is not what Quine has in mind when he speaks of possible such-and-so's. His targets are (wannabe-)things that lack being in the actual world: (wannabe-)things that do not exist, like Pegasus, mentioned a few lines before in the paper.

So one may phrase the Quinean point as follows. Let 'Fx' abbreviate 'x is a man and x is fat and x is in the doorway and x is non-existent'. Let 'Bx' abbreviate 'x is a man and x is bald and x is in the doorway and x is non-existent'. Suppose, as prodigal ontologists like Wyman may do, that 'the x such that Fx' denotes some object satisfying the description – call it f: f is a non-existent (merely possible, lacking actual existence) fat man in the doorway. Ditto for 'the x such that Bx' – and call the relevant thing b: b is a non-existent (merely possible, lacking actual existence) bald man in the doorway.

Now Quine asks: Is it so that $b = f$ or not? There is no reply to this. We have two characterizing conditions, Fx and Gx, which are certainly distinct, but of which we just cannot tell whether they characterize the same object, or two distinct ones. In fact, for Quine that's a rhetorical question just like the other ones he asks in that passage. We have no causal interactions with non-existent (wannabe-)objects, purely fictional objects like Pegasus, *possibilia* lacking actual existence like a merely possible current king of France, etc. We are given, at most, descriptive conditions by which they are characterized; and these usually give no clear picture of the identity of the involved (wannabe-)objects. These putative ontological categories make for further 'creatures of darkness': non-well-defined kinds of things we had better expunge from a safe and sane ontology. Hence comes Quine's final rhetorical expression:

> Wyman's overpopulated universe is in many ways unlovely. It offends the aesthetic sense of us who have a taste for desert landscapes. (Quine 1948: 16)

3 The meaning(s) of being

As we have seen since the Introduction, part of what metaontology is about is the very notion of being or existence: the concept whose extension we aim to capture by providing our universal ontological catalogue. But is there *one* such concept? Or does being split, rather, into a plurality of irreducible notions? In the latter case, how – if at all – are these notions related to one another? For assume that there are no relations between the supposedly distinct concepts at issue. Then how can we aim for a unique science of being *qua* being? How can ontology be a single discipline? If the word 'being' is equivocal, that is, standing for different unconnected things, as the word 'dog' does (meaning, say: a kind of animals; a constellation; a bad actor; or a part of a gun), then a single science of being *qua* being is as impossible as a single science of dogs *qua* dogs.

The issue is a venerable and tangled one in Western philosophy. We will browse very quickly through some landmarks of its history, before moving on to the mainstream solution proposed for it within the standard view.

3.1 Aristotle vs. Plato on being

In the dialogue called *The Sophist*, Plato proposed to take *being* as one of the five largest genuses: one of the five all-encompassing concepts applying to reality as a whole, the other four being *identity, difference, motion and rest*: see *Sophist* 254b-258e. Since everything is identical with something, namely itself, and different from anything else, the two former concepts are good candidates for being universal notions. The two latter notions, motion and rest, can be taken as jointly exhaustive and mutually exclusive: everything is either in motion or at rest. Plato may have understood these two in a very broad sense. Being at rest may count as something like being unmovable, eternal, not subject to change – typical features of Plato's realm of Ideas. Then being in motion means something like being subject to movement, change, generation and corruption, as the world of material objects is.

What matters most for ontology is that *being* counts for Plato as a *single* genus. This may be understood as meaning that the concept of being is univocal. There is but one thing for 'being', so understood, to mean. The extension of such a concept (as we would say today) seems just to be *everything*, the totality of things, that is, of beings – none excluded.

Aristotle disagreed. According to a famous catchphrase of his, 'being is spoken of in many ways'. For instance, Socrates *is*, and so *is* his skin colour. Both are something, that is, both are beings. But being an individual man and being a colour are for Aristotle distinct and irreducible ways of being. This immediately raises some questions: If there are many ways of being, how many of them are there, and what are they? Next, we have the issue mentioned above: How, if at all, are these different ways of being related to one another?

Aristotle addressed the first, twofold question both in his logical writings and in the *Metaphysics*. He spoke there of what he called the 'categories' (*kategorémata*), and he spoke of them in both venues for these had, for him, both a logical-linguistic and an ontological-metaphysical aspect. In their linguistic guise, the categories are the most general kinds of predication; in their ontological guise, they are the most general kinds of being. Sometimes Aristotle listed eight of them, sometimes ten. The list includes *substance, quality, quantity, relation, place,* and others yet. But we don't need to enter into details. What matters is that, though any being belongs to some category or other (they are supposed to be mutually exclusive and jointly exhaustive), none of the categories is *being*. Socrates *is*, as a *substance* (we will soon say something, though not that much, on what the notion of substance may amount to for Aristotle). The colour of Socrates' skin *is*, as a *quality* of Socrates. And these are irreducibly distinct ways of being. Consequently, unlike for Plato, for Aristotle there is no such thing as the genus or category of being in general. The Medieval ontologists following Aristotle called being a 'transcendental', meaning that it, together with other most general notions like *one, true, good*, transcended the division into categories, being applicable to items falling under each category. No transcendental notion, according to Aristotelians, can be univocal: each is split into different and irreducible ways of being (being one, being true, etc.).

Then Aristotle faced our aforementioned question: how is something like a science of being *qua* being – something like general ontology, as we would say today – possible, if *being* is spoken of in irreducibly different ways? Aristotle's reply was that there is some connection between the different ways of being, which makes them all amenable to a unified treatment by a single discipline. The notion of being is not univocal, but neither is it merely equivocal: it is an *analogical* notion. Analogy is supposed to be something between univocity and equivocity. And the analogy at issue is one of reference, dependence, and fundamentality. All the other notions of being, captured by the other categories, somehow refer to or depend on a single category, the most fundamental: the notion of substance.

The doctrine of substance is exposed in a very convoluted part of Aristotle's *Metaphysics*. To begin with, the very word 'substance' has a tangled history. Aristotle used the Greek word *ousìa*, which is almost untranslatable to us. The

Latin philosophers of the Middle Ages rendered it via the Latin word *substantia*, meaning something like 'that which lies under', or 'that which *grounds* (something else)'. The idea behind such a translation is that the category of substance makes for the fundamental kind of being, grounding beings of any other kind. As we will see in Chapter 8, the notion of *grounding* has made an important comeback in contemporary analytic ontology, and some grounding theorists nowadays are directly inspired by Aristotle.

According to a mainstream interpretation of Aristotle, to which we will stick, Socrates counts as a paradigmatic substance in Aristotelian metaphysics. So do human beings in general, the other animals, trees and plants, and, in some versions of Aristotelianism, also artefacts like chairs and boats. Substances, Aristotle remarked, exist, so to speak, on their own or autonomously, in a way things belonging to the other categories cannot. There could not be colours, or weights, or shapes or relations, if there were no substances which *are* coloured, related, which have certain weights, shapes, etc. Thus, Socrates' being as a substance is more fundamental than the being of his qualities, like the colour of his skin: if there were no Socrates, there would be no colour of Socrates' skin.

The other categories embed in their notion some (implicit) reference to the notion of substance: they are qualities *of* substances, quantities *of* substances, relations *between* substances, etc. The being of what falls under the other categories is grounded in the being of the respective substances. Thus, Aristotle claimed, if there were no substances, there would be nothing at all. Then even if being is not a univocal notion, 'being' does not mean unrelated things, like 'dog': the category of substance provides enough unity underlying the various ways of being to allow for a unified science of being *qua* being. Aristotle claims that (what we now call) ontology is first of all '*ousiology*': the science of *ousía*, substance.

3.2 The univocity of being

The view that being is spoken of in many ways was challenged already in the Middle Ages, for instance, by the theologian and philosopher Duns Scotus. It remained popular also in contemporary philosophy. According to Martin Heidegger, for instance, the being of the *Dasein* (continental ontologists out there will forgive us for translating this, simplifying, as 'human being') is irreducibly distinct from the being of things like animals, plants and – even more – artefacts. The difference is so big that only of human beings can we rightly say, for Heidegger, that they *exist*, whereas of the other kinds of things we can say, at most, that they live, or that they plainly *are*. We need not enter into issues of Heideggerian terminology: it is enough for us to notice that this position amounts to the admission of irreducibly distinct ways of being.

The claim that being is not univocal had supporters also in the analytic community. One famous proponent of the view was Gilbert Ryle:

> It is perfectly proper to say, in one logical tone of voice, that there exist minds and to say, in another logical tone of voice that there exist bodies. But these expressions do not indicate two different species of existence. ... They indicate two different senses of 'exist', somewhat as 'rising' has different senses in 'the tide is rising', 'hopes are rising', and 'the average age of death is rising'. A man would be thought to be making a poor joke who said that three things are now rising, namely the tide, hopes and the average age of death. It would be just as good or bad a joke to say that there exist prime numbers and Wednesdays and public opinions and navies; or that there exist both minds and bodies. (Ryle 1949: xx)

The mainstream position on the meaning of being in analytic ontology, however, is opposed to Aristotle as well as to Ryle. The supporter of the standard view who has most clearly made the point, we think, is Peter van Inwagen 1998.

Recall again that, for Quine, the notion of being or existence is captured by the quantifier. Thus, as Frege already spotted and as we have also seen in the previous chapter, the notion of being or existence is closely allied to the notion of number. Thus van Inwagen notices number words like 'four', 'fifty-six', 'one thousand, nine hundreds and five', etc., used to answer the Fregean question 'How many *Fs* are there?' (*Fs* being entities of some kind), cannot have different meanings depending on the kind *F* of things we want to count. 'The very essence of the applicability of arithmetic is that numbers may count anything' (van Inwagen 1998: 17). Theorems and musicians may be things of extremely different kinds. But if you proved four theorems while I was listening to the Fab Four, then the number of theorems you have proved *is* the number of historical members of the group I've been listening to. We cannot say that 'four' means different things when used to count theorems and when used to count musicians.

Now consider that intimate connection between existence (as captured by the quantifier) and number, characteristic of the standard view in metaontology. To say that there are horses is to say that the number of horses is one or more. To say that there are no unicorns is to say that the number of unicorns is zero. In fact, 'There are *Fs*', expressing ontological commitment to the *Fs* in the Quinean view, is just a way of speaking of the number of the *Fs*: it amounts to claiming that the *Fs* are one or more. Then if number words like 'four', 'fifty-six' or 'one thousand, nine hundreds and five' are univocal, then 'exists' must be univocal too. Theorems and musicians may have very different *natures*, says van Inwagen: they vastly differ in *what* they are; but this doesn't mark a difference in *being*.

This powerful argument for the univocity of being, thus, seemingly stems directly from the conception of existence underlying the Quinean metaontological approach we examined in the last chapter. This is why it has been included here, as part of what makes for the standard Quinean picture of metaontology. However, the argument has not remained unchallenged in contemporary ontology, as we are just about to see in the following chapter.

Further Reading

The hermeneutic/revolutionary distinction was first introduced by Burgess and Rosen 1997. For some advanced discussion, see Carrara and Varzi 1997; see Stanley 2001 for the hermeneutic approach and Daly and Liggins 2010 for the revolutionary one.

Holes are a fascinating subject for ontological inquiry. Lewis and Lewis 1970 is the wonderful dialogue about the existence of holes we reviewed in Section 1.2 and a highly recommended reading. See Casati and Varzi 1994, 2014, for a more in-depth analysis. The literature on Aristotle's ontological pluralism and substantialism is immense; a good starting point is Cohen 2012.

Part II

Alternative Metaontologies

4

Ontological Pluralism and Neo-Fregeanism

Chapter Outline

When one introduces the standard view of ontology explained in the previous chapters, it often takes time to convince people that tables and numbers exist in the same sense of 'to exist'. They could in fact be right to resist this suggestion! As we saw in the previous chapter, Aristotle thought that 'Being is spoken in many ways', and versions of this view have also been subscribed to by such important philosophers as the early Russell, Ryle, and Heidegger. *Ontological pluralism*, the doctrine that there are various ways of being or existing, is regaining some popularity in recent work on metaontology. After introducing the view in Section 1.1, we put forward in Section 1.2 some objections to it, and review the strategies devised by supporters to reply to them.

Another approach to metaontology that departs to some extent from the traditional Quinean methodology is that of the Neo-Fregeans, to which Section 2 is dedicated. After explaining the link between the neo-Fregean view and the so-called *linguistic turn* of twentieth-century philosophy in Section 2.1, we focus on what neo-Fregeans take to be their central metaontological tenet (Section 2.2), briefly discuss some of its problems and finish by comparing the approach with the Quinean metaontological set up (Section 2.3).

1 Ontological pluralism

1.1 Ways of being

As McDaniel 2009 nicely puts it, we all agree that tables and numbers are different kinds of beings, i.e. different kinds of things, entities, objects. But according to the standard view – clearly exemplified for instance, by the van Inwagen of the previous chapter – this does not mean that they also enjoy different kinds of *being*, i.e. that they *exist* in different ways. To say that there exist tables, according to the standard view, is just to say that something is a table; to say that there exist numbers is just to say that something is a number: and 'something' means the same in both cases. The standard view is ontologically monist: it admits just one way of being. To borrow a metaphor from Jason Turner (2010), the ontological monist's picture of reality is that of a big pegboard. Pegs correspond to entities, and there are rubber bands of different colours indicating which objects have a given property (say, via a band around the peg) and which objects stand in a given relation with which (say, via a band stretching from an object to another).

Ontological pluralists think that this picture is misleading. Reality is best represented by multiple pegboards, each representing a kind of thing together with its associated mode of existence. It makes perfect sense to say – in one breath, so to speak – that there are singers who play soccer in Italy and that there is a soccer team of Italian singers. But an ontological pluralist can add that the Italian singers' soccer team and the people who play in it exist in two very different ways (the example comes from Panza and Sereni 2013). And maybe both the cheese on my plate and its holes exist, and even the number of those holes does, but these things enjoy different kinds of existence.

Existence is captured and expressed by quantification: on this, ontological pluralists are aligned with Quine and van Inwagen. They think, however, that we need different quantifiers to express the different kinds of existence of beings which exist in different ways. Consider the distinction between abstract and concrete objects, to which we resorted many times already in our exposition. What the distinction amounts to exactly is a complicated business, as we will see in Part III of our book. In any case, many have the strong intuition that abstractness and concreteness are exclusive, exhaustive, and intrinsic features of objects: everything is either abstract or concrete, nothing is both; nothing belonging to one category is allowed to trespass into the other in any possible situation (think about kissing the number four). It may be reasonable for two so vastly different kinds of things to have different modes of being. We will take this as our sample form of ontological pluralism in the following: supposing that concrete and abstract objects exist in irreducibly different ways, we can have '$\exists_a$' to mean *exist abstractly* and '$\exists_c$' to mean *exist concretely*.

It is important to correctly appreciate the significance of the move. One way to understand multiple quantifiers is to think of them as more parochial versions of the familiar, unique existential quantifier dear to Quine and van Inwagen – technically: as 'restrictions' of it. One employs restricted quantifiers not to talk of all there is, but only of a fraction of what there is. What the restriction amounts to is often understood contextually. To use a famous example by David Lewis: when one claims that all the beer is in the fridge, we should interpret that quantifier 'all', as (implicitly) restricted. One does not mean, of course, that all the beer of the world is in the fridge. Probably, one means something like: quantifying only over a small part of the world – say, home – all the beer available there, at home, is located in the fridge. Restricted quantifiers are ubiquitous. In our ordinary talk we rarely aim to speak, as Lewis liked to say, 'with our quantifiers wide open'. We normally, if implicitly, focus on just a part of the pegboard: 'We sold everything' (whatever was on sale in the shop today); 'There are no dolphins' (at the zoo of Berlin).

One could think that this is just what is going on with our quantifiers $\exists_a$ and $\exists_c$. One could read '$\exists_c xFx$' ('Some concrete existent is *F*') as '$\exists x(Cx \;\&\; Fx)$', with '*C*' standing for the feature of being concrete ('Something is both concrete and *F*'). However, according to the ontological pluralist for whom to exist abstractly and to exist concretely are different ways of existing, this would be deceptive. Such a reading would make of concreteness a property some things have, rather than a way of being. The multiple existential quantifiers should be taken as primitives. The notions they express are irreducible.

The pluralist may even admit that generic quantification makes sense. Take a pluralist for whom the only two ways of being are being abstractly and being concretely. The pluralist may accept that one can define a disjunctive, generic, existential quantifier by saying that to generically exist is either to exist abstractly or to exist concretely. But it is the generic quantifier that has to be understood in terms of the multiple quantifiers, not the other way round. A language that fails to have the multiple quantifiers as primitives fails to be ontologically perspicuous.

It is worth spending some words on this point. The core idea is that a language containing just one quantifier fails to represent an important aspect of the way the world is structured. A language with the appropriate multiple quantifiers, instead, can let this aspect of reality reveal itself. To use an example adapted from Sider 2011, consider a simple world made of just two coloured regions, one white and one black:

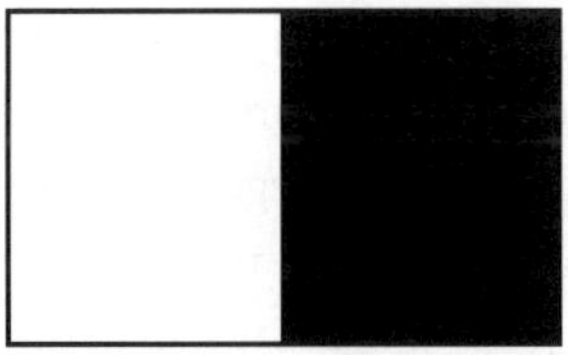

Figure 4.1 Natural carving of the black/white world.

Now imagine people using a language with just two basic predicates: 'whack' refers to the region on the top-left of the dashed line below, while 'bhite' refers to that on the bottom-right:

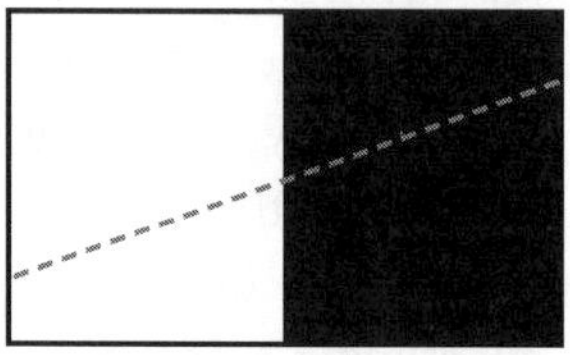

Figure 4.2 Unnatural carving of the black/white world.

There is a sense in which this simple language misrepresents the simple reality. To use a nowadays popular expression, it fails to 'carve reality at the joints'. Notice: this is not to say that people using it say *false* things thereby. They don't need to: they may only say that something is bhite, when it is indeed bhite (it is the bottom-right portion with respect to the dashed line). But their language obscures the way reality is structured: in particular, it being divided into *white* and *black* stuff. According to a tradition stemming from the work of David Lewis (see for instance Lewis 1986: 60–1), a class of things, as well as a predicate whose extension is that class, are more or less *natural* depending on how similar the members of the class are to each other (Lewis took the notion of *similarity* to be itself primitive). Now, black things *qua* black, or white things *qua* white, resemble each other much more than whack or bhite things, *qua* whack, or *qua* bhite. This makes 'is black' and 'is white' much more natural predicates than 'is whack' and 'is bhite'.

Lewis distinguished between more and less natural *predicates*, but the distinction may be applied to other kinds of expressions. In particular, Sider 2011 applies it to quantifiers, so that one can distinguish between more and less natural meanings for the quantifiers. Now the adoption of this framework can help us to make intuitive sense of the ontological pluralist's position. The framework as such leaves open the issue of which quantifiers have the most natural meaning. Sider himself, for instance, thinks that the single-generic existential quantifier has a perfectly natural meaning. On the other hand, an ontological pluralist of the aforementioned kind will hold that $\exists_a$ and $\exists_c$ have much more natural meanings than a disjunctive generic quantifier defined in terms of them: the multiple quantifiers carve being at the joints, the single-generic quantifier does not.

A parenthetical note on terminology is needed at this point: in his nice survey of metaontology, Eklund 2006a labels 'pluralists' those deflationary ontologists who deny that there is a metaphysically privileged language. We can understand this to be denial that there are more or less natural meanings for the quantifiers: meanings that carve or fail to carve at the joints of reality's structure. The ontological pluralists we are discussing in this chapter are not pluralists in Eklund's sense. Ontological pluralists in our terminology claim that there is a metaphysically privileged language, and that it employs multiple quantifiers.

Now this view can be developed in different ways. Let us stick to our division between abstractness and concreteness as a sample basic dichotomy of ways of being. One form of pluralism was championed by Gilbert Ryle, whose pluralistic inclinations on being we already met in the previous chapter. For Ryle, we mean two different things with such words as 'there are' and 'exist' when we make claims like:

(1) There are tables/Tables exist.
(2) There are numbers/Numbers exist.

Moreover, there is no sense in which one could say:

(1 + 2) There are tables and numbers/Both tables and numbers exist.

According to a simple Ryle-style pluralism, 'exist' or 'there are' can mean either of two things but not both:

(Ex_1) concretely exist/there are concrete things, such that.
(Ex_2) abstractly exist/there are abstract things, such that.

If quantificational-existential expressions have (Ex_1) meanings, then to say that some things exist in a way and other things exist in another way is to say that some things exist concretely in a way and some other things exist concretely in a different way, which would just be false. The situation is symmetrical if we give (Ex_2) meanings to our quantificational-existential expressions.

So according to this form of ontological pluralism, it makes no sense to say that things exist in different ways! Rather, we should just say that 'exist', 'there are' and cognate terms have a plurality of meanings. They are ambiguous. There is another form of ontological pluralism, defended by McDaniel and attributed by him to Heidegger, which acknowledges a generic sense of existence, but goes on to say that the generic quantifier that expresses it is much less natural, in a sense akin to the one explained above, than the multiple quantifiers used to represent different modes of existence. These two versions of ontological pluralism deal in different ways with standard arguments for the univocity of being, which we are going to review in the next session.

1.2 Arguments for ontological monism and rejoinders to them

Quine 1960: 242 considered the view that there are many kinds of existence as nonsense. He seemed to take this dismissive attitude as a consequence of his doctrine that existence is expressed by quantification. As we have seen in the previous chapter, van Inwagen made explicit the connection between the Quinean view and ontological univocism or monism.

However, as we have also seen, the ontological pluralists we are dealing with in this chapter have no problem in agreeing with Quine and van Inwagen on the idea that quantification captures being or existence. They just add that there is more than one way of being or existing, thus more than one meaning for quantificational expressions. They are *quantificational* pluralists. And this ontological pluralism can rejoinder in refined ways to considerations that seem to undermine it, as Turner 2010 shows. Consider again van Inwagen's 'counting argument', explained in our chapter on the standard view above. Claiming that there are *F*s is a way of speaking of the number of the *F*s: it means that the number of *F*s is not zero. Now numerals, i.e. number words ('one', 'two', etc.) must be univocal: they can be used to count anything. Numbers themselves are abstract objects while US presidents are concrete, but we can say that the number of even primes just *is* the number of the US presidents. Existence claims, for a Quinean, are just like number claims – so existence must be univocal.

Turner's 2010 reply is straightforward: numerals have just one meaning. This accommodates van Inwagen's intuition that numbers can be used to count beings of any kind. But what the predicate '*x* is the number of *F*s' denotes is different when we consider things that exist in different ways. The first part of the phrase 'The number of *F*s is not zero', i.e. 'the number of', can have different senses.

McDaniel 2009, on the other hand, grants that expressions like 'the number of' can have a generic sense. This just corresponds to the sense of existence expressed by the generic existential quantifier, which he does accept as meaningful, as we have seen. This kind of ontological pluralism can grant to van Inwagen that there is an all-encompassing or blanket sense of the quantifier; but will reject that this is the only sense, and will also add that this sense is ontologically less fundamental than that of the relevant plural quantifiers.

Let us go back to this idea once again: one proposes to define a disjunctive generic quantifier, say $\exists^*$, starting from our usual sample quantifiers, $\exists_a$ and $\exists_c$:

($\exists^*$) $\exists^* xFx$ if and only if either $\exists_a xFx$ or $\exists_a xFx$.

To somebody claiming that $\exists^*$ is the real existential quantifier whereas $\exists_a$ and $\exists_c$ are just restricted version of it, as we know from the previous Section, a pluralist *granting* that $\exists^*$ is meaningful may reply that it is much less natural than each of the original multiple quantifiers. However, a pluralist following Ryle will claim that $\exists^*$ is not even a quantifier (see Turner 2010 on this). In order for $\exists^*$ to be a legitimate quantifier, an expression like '$\exists^* xFx$' should have the following truth conditions: it is true if and only if *there is* something that is *F*. But according to Ryle-style ontological pluralism the expression 'there is' and its cognates are ambiguous and can mean one of two things: *there abstractly is*, or *there concretely is*. Now it is not the case that '$\exists^* xFx$' is true if and only if there is something that is *F*. This is so because that 'there is' in the sentence you just read can just mean one of two things: *there abstractly is*, or *there concretely is*. And, by definition, '$\exists^* xFx$' is not true just in case there abstractly are *F*s, or just in case there concretely are *F*s.

Another objection to ontological pluralism is conjunctive rather than disjunctive. It seems that it makes a lot of sense to say:

(Mix) The world is very vast: there are tables, and electrons, and numbers, and functions that map them, and …

But according to Ryle-style pluralists this cannot work for the usual reason: 'there are', for them, is ambiguous (say) between $\exists_a$ and $\exists_c$, and any way to disambiguate it, taking it to mean $\exists_a$ or $\exists_c$, would make (Mix) false. Yet (Mix) sounds very true. Ryle-style ontological pluralists can accept that their doctrine conflicts with this intuition, but argue that it arises out of conceptual confusion about the nature of existence. Heidegger-McDaniel-style ontological pluralists can make their usual move again: grant that (Mix) makes sense and is indeed true, but remind us that it obscures the important ontological fact that the things it refers to exist in different ways.

2 Neo-Fregean metaontology

Another approach to the methodology of ontology different from that of Quine develops insights coming from the work of Frege. We will first give a sketch of the neo-Fregean conception of ontology; then we will turn to a comparison with the Quinean metaontology.

2.1 The linguistic turn

In his *The Foundations of Arithmetic* Frege wonders how one may come to know anything about numbers, given that nobody has ever seen or touched or had any kind of contact with them. His answer comes in what Michael Dummett 1991: 111 has called 'the most pregnant philosophical paragraph ever written':

> How, then, are numbers to be given to us, if we cannot have any ideas or intuition of them? Since it is only in the context of a proposition that words have meaning, our problem becomes this: To define the sense of a proposition in which a number word occurs. (Frege 1884: §62)

Although it need not be apparent at first sight, what Frege says here may be important for the nature of debates about what there is. Two crucial ideas are put forward: (i) To know about numbers one must look at the meaning of number words. (ii) To know about the meaning of numbers words, one should look at the meaning of the sentences in which number words figure.

Idea (i) is interesting from the metaontological viewpoint because, on one reading, it suggests that the answers to some ontological questions – e.g., questions about the ontology of numbers – can come from an analysis of language. That philosophical questions in general are essentially linguistic questions has been a popular slogan of the so-called 'linguistic turn' of twentieth-century philosophy. Some philosophers engaging in ontological inquiry in this spirit followed Frege in believing that we should approach metaphysical and ontological questions like 'What are numbers?', or 'Are there numbers?', by first asking such linguistic questions as 'What is the meaning of number words?', where number words are terms like 'one', 'two', 'the number of Martian Moons', etc. (you may recall from Chapter 1 how Russell proposed to eliminate descriptions via paraphrase in *On Denoting;* this was not Frege's view: for him, descriptions like 'the number of Martian Moons' were genuine singular terms).

A general ontological spin-off of the linguistic turn has been the idea that the ontological notion of *object* should be explained in terms of the linguistic category of *singular term*. This is what Crispin Wright 1983: 53 called the 'syntactic priority thesis': an object is what may be denoted by a singular term. It is an undisputed fact that words belonging to this syntactic category ('Bill Gates', 'the oldest son of Brad Pitt', etc.) have the function of referring to, or denoting, an object. Other kinds of words, like connectives, predicates or quantifiers ('some', 'because', 'runs', 'is red', etc.), do not have this function. But a substantive idea behind the syntactic priority thesis is that our grasp of the notion of object is mediated by our grasp of the notion of singular term. Linguistic notions, in an explanatorily relevant sense, come first. We understand what an object is because we know what it is to be the possible referent of a singular term.

The next question, of course, is how singular terms are to be defined. To reply by saying that a singular term is one that denotes, or purports to denote an object, would be unacceptably circular. Neo-Fregeans think it is possible to characterize singular terms by looking at their grammatical, or more technically, at their syntactical and inferential role. This means looking at how singular terms interact with other words, and at the kind of inferences they allow. How to do this is a matter of some delicacy, but for our introductory purposes we need not get into the details. A syntactical feature of singular terms is that it makes sense to have them on the two sides of an identity statement, i.e. a statement of the form '$t_1 = t_2$'. For instance, it makes sense to say: 'Batman is Bruce Wayne', because 'Batman' and 'Bruce Wayne' are singular terms, whereas other kinds of words, like connectives or verbs, do not fit well into identity statements. Neo-Fregeans generally do not think that the possibility of occurring in the aforementioned way in identity statements gives a *definition* of the notion of singular term (see Hale and Wright 2001: Essays 1 and 2). Their proposal is to define singular-termhood inferentially. We need not enter into this either. However, to see how one could come to understand the meaning of an expression by looking at the inferential patterns it is involved in, think about explaining to someone the meaning of the connective '&', also known as 'and'. Instead of just saying that '&' means *and*, one could say something like: 'This is what "&" does: when *P* and *Q* are sentences, it allows you to infer *P*, or *Q*, from *P* & *Q*; and from *P* and *Q* taken together, it allows you to infer *P* & *Q*'.

This tells us how to discriminate between singular terms and other kinds of words. It does not tell us much on how to establish whether there is something a singular term succeeds in referring to, and what kind of entity it might be. However, Frege's *other* key idea, idea (ii) above, suggests us to start by looking at how the meanings of such singular terms as number words contribute to the meaning of the sentences of which they are part.

This may sound obscure, but there is a commonsensical way of looking at the proposal. We don't assign names to objects just for the sake of it. Denotation is just part of a larger enterprise, that of representing reality through language. And this is not done by just crying out a name, but by asserting sentences. A mainstream tradition in philosophical semantics, starting from Frege and Wittgenstein, gives privilege to sentences as the fundamental semantic unit. And the simplest sentences are composed of a name, which picks up an object, and of a predicate, which is used to say something of that object. Representing a situation via a sentence is the basic linguistic activity. Referring to an object with a singular term is just part of this. This is a rough version of what often goes under the name of 'Frege's context principle'. The crucial application of this idea here is that in the case of the simplest sentences involving singular terms, like basic identity claims ('2 + 3 = 5'), the singular terms involved need to refer in order for those sentences to be true. That's their contribution to the meaning of the whole sentences. We may then formulate the principle:

(NF1) If atomic sentences – like '2 + 3 = 5' – are true, then there are numbers denoted by number-words.

The conditional in (NF1) expresses a direction of explanatory priority from its antecedent to its consequent. It's not that in order to show that basic arithmetical statements are true we must first assure that there are numbers that can serve as denotations for the number words occurring in such statements. It is the other way round. This is why Frege's point (ii) is so important. If we are able to show that (NF1)-like statements are true, then, according to neo-Fregeans, the ontological issue about the existence of numbers is settled. There is no room for:

> The possibility of some sort of independent, language-unblinkered inspection of the contents of the world, of which the outcome might be to reveal that there was indeed nothing there capable of serving as the referents of … numerical singular terms. (Wright 1983: 13–14)

2.2 The 'Central Ontological Idea'…

Still, one could ask, *how* do we know that basic identity statements such as '$2 + 3 = 5$' are true? Another crucial Fregean idea comes into play here. In paragraph 64 of the *Foundations of Arithmetic,* Frege shifts from numbers to the concept of *direction*:

> The judgment 'line *a* is parallel to line *b*', or, using symbols,
>
> $a//b$
>
> can be taken as an identity. If we do this, we obtain the concept of direction, and say: 'the direction of line *a* is identical with the direction of line *b*'. Thus we replace the symbol // by the more generic symbol =, through removing what is specific in the content of the former and dividing it between *a* and *b*. We carve up the content in a way different from the original way, and this yields us a new concept. (Frege 1884: §64)

Frege is presenting here a way to introduce concepts, which nowadays goes under the label of *abstraction principle*. The example he considers is (read '*dir*' as 'the direction of', '$a//b$' as 'line *a* is parallel to line *b*'):

(DIR) $dir(a) = dir(b)$ if and only if $a//b$.

Now (DIR) is taken as a kind of implicit definition for a new concept: we introduce the concept of *direction* by giving the conditions under which direction-statements are true – their truth conditions – in a way that is perfectly understandable for anyone who is already familiar with the old concepts of *line* and *parallel to*. Nothing more is involved in the direction of line *a*'s being identical with that of line *b* than the two lines' being parallel. The situation that makes true one statement is the same that makes true the other. Using the nice terminology of Rayo 2013: for two lines to have the same directions 'just is' for them to be parallel. Compare: To say that there is a deck of cards on the table *just is* to say that there are 52 cards of a certain kind on the table. Or, for someone to be a sibling *just is* for him to share parents with someone else.

This has an epistemological moral: we may now have a simple answer to the question, 'How do we know that there are directions?'. The simple answer is that we know that line *a* is parallel to itself, $a//a$; and we know, via the (DIR) equivalence, that this means that the direction of line *a* is identical with itself, $dir(a) = dir(a)$. Therefore, there is a direction of line *a*. Therefore, there exist directions.

But this also has an ontological moral. We can answer the epistemological question because we are in a position to answer the ontological question, 'How must the world be like in order for there to be directions?'. The simple answer is that a world in which there are directions is just a world in which there are lines (and they are parallel to themselves). A world like this:

Line a

We may now appreciate what neo-Fregeans Bob Hale and Crispin Wright call their 'central ontological idea', the idea:

> ... that it is permissible to fix the truth-conditions of one kind of statement as coinciding with those of another – 'kind' here referring to something like logical form – in such a way that the overt *existential* implications of the former exceed those of the latter, although the *epistemological* status of the latter, as conceived in advance, is inherited by the former. (Hale and Wright 2009: 180–1)

(DIR) is just one possible abstraction principle. The general form of abstraction principles is this (read '$\leftrightarrow$' as a biconditional, as 'if and only if'):

(AP) $\Sigma(x) = \Sigma(y) \leftrightarrow E(x, y)$.

An abstraction principle states an equivalence between its two sides. In the schema (AP), we have a placeholder for an operator to form new terms Σ, which associates to the objects that are in the range of the variables x, y (newly introduced) objects which are also in the range of those variables. And we have a placeholder for a relation E, which needs to be an *equivalence* relation, that is, a relation which is reflexive (every x is E-related to itself), symmetric (if x is E-related to y, then y is E-related to x), and transitive (if x is E-related to y and y is E-related to z, then x is E-related to z). You can check the requirement that the relevant instance of E be an equivalence relation is met in (DIR), for *being parallel to* is precisely that (each line is parallel to itself; if line a is parallel to line b, then line b is parallel to line a, etc.). Note that abstraction principles are tailor-made to satisfy Quine's 'No entity without identity' motto: his request, which we saw in the previous chapter, of providing identity criteria for the objects admitted into one's ontology (in this respect, neo-Fregean ontology is in line with the standard view).

As an anticipation of what we will see in the third part of our book: neo-Fregeans propose a very important instance of (AP) for the concept of *number*. This the so-called Hume's Principle:

(HP) The number of *F*s = the number of *G*s if and only if the *F*s and *G*s are 1-1 related.

(Very roughly: to say that the *F*s are one-to-one related to the *G*s is to say that *F*s and *G*s can be matched like the right shoes with the left shoes: each right shoe is related only to its left mate and vice versa; no shoe is left alone; we will meet a more precise definition in Section 5.2 of Chapter 9). We will see that Hume's Principle brings with it some problems, due to the way it is formulated. Discussing them here would distract us, so we just stick with the general shape of Hale and Wright's 'central ontological idea' behind the method of abstraction. This is the idea of *re-carving content*: that the truth conditions of a statement with terms standing for a certain kind of objects (directions, numbers: instances of the left side of the biconditional schema (AP)) can be stipulated to be equivalent to those of statements that do not mention numbers or directions (the corresponding instances of the right side of (AP)).

2.3 ... And its problems

Let us go back to (DIR) as our sample instance of an abstraction principle. A first problem with taking (DIR) as an implicit definition of the concept of direction was already spotted by Frege. (DIR) gives us an identity criterion for objects of a certain kind: directions. It tells us when things *a* and *b* of a kind *F* are the same object rather than two different ones. But it seems that (DIR) does not give us a criterion telling us what kind of things can be classified as *directions*. It does not tell us, for instance, that people or nations cannot be directions. However, it seems that such a criterion is needed in order to distinguish, for instance, the direction of the Earth Axis from England. 'Of course', Frege writes, 'nobody is going to confuse the direction of the Earth Axis with England; but this is not thanks to our definition' (Frege 1884: §66).

Shifting from directions to numbers, Frege also says that the problem of taking Hume's Principle as a definition of the concept of number is that (HP) doesn't tell you that, and why, Julius Caesar is not a number. Hence this difficulty goes under the name of the 'Julius Caesar problem'. Neo-Fregeans attach a lot of weight to the issue (see Hale and Wright 2005), but spelling out their proposal to address it in detail would take us beyond the limits of our book. The basic idea is something like this: that the identity criterion for numbers is very different from that for people means that numbers are not people, and therefore Julius Caesar is not a number.

One other qualm with the neo-Fregean approach to ontology has to do with the very idea of re-carving content. There is a feeling of pulling an ontological rabbit out of a linguistic hat in the thought that the existence of directions can be ascertained by just noting that there is a line and it is parallel to itself (the metaphor comes from Yablo 2000: 275). How can the truth of a claim that refers only to lines guarantee the existence of abstract objects like directions? One neo-Fregean answer comes from distinguishing between what a statement refers to and what it ontologically commits to. If I say that I am an uncle, I don't explicitly talk about parents, but in order for my claim to be true there must be someone who is a parent and who is my brother or sister (the example is from MacBride 2003).

Maybe there is something deeper going on in the qualm. As MacBride puts it, neo-Fregean abstractionism may be based on the rejection of a certain conception of the relation between language and reality. The resistance to the method of abstraction seems in part to lie in the idea that two sentences having different logical form, as it happens with those on the right and left hand side of the biconditional an abstraction principle consists in, cannot be used to represent the same situation. This thought may be rooted in the conviction that the structure of reality is crystalline, as MacBride puts it, 'fixed independently of our language' (2003: 126), so that (at most) only the structure of *one* kind of statements can mirror the structure of reality. It is this metaphysical conception that neo-Fregeans must reject. There is nothing like *the* structure of a state of affairs, which our language can either correctly represent, or fail to.

This tells neo-Fregeans apart from other approaches to metaontology. Interestingly, the idea that there cannot be any meaningful question about the degree to which the logical form of statement mirrors the ontological structure of the reality it is about echoes a thought Quine himself had:

> The fundamental-seeming philosophical question, How much of our science is merely contributed by language and how much is a genuine reflection of reality?, is perhaps a spurious question which itself arises wholly from a certain particular type of language. (Quine 1953: 78)

There are points of contact between the Neo-Fregean and the standard Quinean metaontology. One is the stress on the importance of identity criteria, which as we have seen complies with Quine's 'No entity without identity' motto. There is also (at least) one important difference. When it's about ascertaining the ontological commitments of our language and theories, the Quinean view gives pride of place to quantification over singular reference. Besides, as we know, Quine's own specific approach aimed at dispensing with singular terms *tout-court* by extending to names the Russellian eliminative treatment of descriptions. On the contrary, neo-Fregeans take reference via singular terms to be the key bridge between language and reality. For them, we may say, 'To be is to be the potential referent of a singular term'.

Further Reading

McDaniel 2009 and Turner 2010 are two important recent defences of ontological pluralism. For a first illustration of the idea of metaphysical structure, see the introduction to Sider 2011. For an overview of Neo-Fregean meta-ontology, see Wright 1983, the introduction of Hale and Wright 2001 and also Linnebo 2012b. For more advanced discussion, see Eklund 2006b and Hale and Wright 2009. On the context principle, there is a nice lecture by Linnebo, available online: https://www.youtube.com/watch?v=l_g44OP-6UU.

5

Carnap's View of Ontology and Neo-Carnapians

Chapter Outline

In this chapter we deal with challenges to the standard Quinean meta-ontology, whose core ideas go back to the work of Quine's master, Rudolf Carnap. According to Yablo 1998, the philosophers who deal with the prospects of ontology divide in two camps: those who are sceptical about the meaningfulness and depth of ontological questions, and those who are curious to find an answer to them. The first group has a hard time making sense of how questions about the existence of numbers, or properties or propositions, can be properly answered. These philosophers think that progress can only be made in ontology by clarifying the *meaning*, if there is one, of these questions. Curious philosophers on the other hand think that ontological questions are not hard to *understand*: they are hard to *answer*, but the answers are to come from the usual methods of theory-choice, whatever they are. Carnap can be presented as the champion of the sceptical party, whereas Quine is a champion of the curious party.

In Section 1 we introduce and elucidate two key views that Carnap held about ontology: his famous distinction between *internal* and *external* questions, and his idea that philosophers seeking answers to traditional ontological questions are not clear about what they are looking for. We then present two recent approaches to metaontology inspired by Carnap's work: the *quantifier variance* view defended by Eli Hirsch (Section 2), and Thomas Hofweber's approach, based on the distinction between two roles of the existential quantifier (Section 3). Finally, in Section 4 we review other broadly Carnapian approaches.

1 The original Carnap: Internal vs. external as meaningful vs. meaningless

Carnap's deflationary attitude towards ontology can be seen as flowing from his distinction between internal and external questions (a nice overview of Carnap's metaontology is in Eklund 2013). Let us illustrate the distinction by considering two groups of questions. First group:

What is the number of planets in the solar system?
Do spiders and insects share interesting anatomical properties?
Are there Iraqi weapons of mass destruction?

Second group:

Are there numbers?
Are there properties?
Are there material objects?

Questions in the first group are ordinary or scientific questions. Whether they are hard to settle or not, that's not for philosophical reasons. But the questions in the second group look philosophical *and* hard to settle. As we saw in Chapter 2, Quine maintained that the appearance of a specific difference was somewhat misleading. The two kinds are not, according to him, radically different; they differ, we may say, in their degree of generality. On the other hand, Carnap thought the difference between the two groups to be radical. He labelled questions of the first kind as *internal*, questions of the second as *external*.

What are these questions internal or external *to*? The short answer is: to what Carnap called a *framework*. The long answer begins by illustrating with some examples what a Carnapian framework is. Suppose we ask whether there currently (in mid-2014) are tennis players capable of beating Rafael Nadal on clay. It is natural to hear our question as not addressing the issue whether there really are macro-physical objects, such as tennis players. When asking such a question, we are taking for granted that there are ordinary material objects like tennis players, tennis rackets, courts, etc. In Carnap's terminology, we take for granted the framework of material objects. Something like this goes for numbers: when asking what the number of planets in our solar system is, we are taking for granted the number framework.

Carnap characterizes frameworks in linguistic terms:

> If someone wishes to speak in her language about a new kind of entities, she has to introduce a system of new ways of speaking, subject to new rules. We may call this the construction of a *linguistic framework* for the new entities in question. (Carnap 1950: 206)

The phrase 'framework of entities' appears in Carnap's first publication (Carnap 1950). It is replaced by 'linguistic framework' in the version reprinted in *Meaning and Necessity* (Carnap 1956). Once the framework is in place, claims about the relevant entities can be evaluated. In Carnap's own words, a framework provides 'rules for forming statements and for testing, accepting or rejecting them' (Carnap 1950: 208).

The characterization of frameworks, thus, is directly connected with the issue of the meaningfulness of ontological questions. According to Carnap, only when a term's meaning has been defined by laying down the appropriate rules for its usage does a question containing that term make sense. Thus, such questions as whether there are things of kind *F* (Carnap considered numbers, material objects, propositions as candidate *F*s) only make sense within a framework that gives a meaning to the term '*F*'. The framework will give the rules to use the newly introduced terms. For instance, in the number framework there will be a rule that allows one to transform a claim like:

(Alpha) I have eaten two bagels.

Into:

(Omega) The number of bagels I have eaten is two.

Such a step is for Carnap as straightforward as that which allows one to pass from saying that one has eaten twelve bagels to saying that one has eaten a dozen of bagels. As soon as one is clear about the meaning of 'dozen', one will just treat the two claims as equivalent. Similarly, the rules of the property framework establish that if something is red, then that thing has the property of redness.

Once these transformation rules are laid down, there are easy answers to questions about the existence of numbers, or properties, etc. From the (empirical) fact that I have eaten two bagels it follows that there is a number of bagels I have eaten, namely two. So if we ask whether there are numbers within the number framework, the answer is, trivially, in the positive.

But questions about whether there are *F*s are often taken as external to the *F*-framework. They are supposed to be something difficult, not just a trivial consequence of empirical facts plus linguistic or conceptual stipulations. For Carnap, on the contrary, questions about the existence of *F*s can hardly make sense when so understood, given that only a framework confers a meaning to the terms of the *F*-language. One can, to be sure, discuss whether speaking the *F*-language is useful or not. But that's a practical rather than a theoretical question. It is not a question about how the world is like, but about the ins and outs of the ways in which we choose to describe it.

Given all this, according to Carnap questions about the existence of *F*s can be understood in different ways. To begin with, they can be taken as factual questions asked in an internal vein. Carnap uses the framework of material objects to illustrate the point. The concept of reality occurring in these internal questions is an empirical, scientific and eminently non-metaphysical concept. To recognize something as a real thing or event in the material objects framework means to succeed in incorporating it into the system of things with a particular space-time position, so that it fits together with the other things as real according to the rules of the framework.

Now internal questions can be easy to answer, but they are unlikely to be what traditional metaphysicians take themselves to be into. 'There are numbers', understood in an internal vein, is, as Carnap acknowledges, rather trivial (as opposed to a statement like 'There is a prime number greater than a million'): it does not say more than that the number framework is not empty. One who understands the question 'Are there numbers?' in the internal sense will not even seriously consider a negative answer. So it is plausible that

> those philosophers who treat the question of the existence of numbers as a serious philosophical problem, and offer lengthy arguments on either side, do not have in mind the internal question. (Carnap 1950: 209)

Secondly, questions about the existence of *F*s can be taken as practical questions about the adoption of certain kind of language: is talk about *F*s, *F*-language, useful? So understood, they are for Carnap meaningful, but again unlikely to be what traditional metaphysicians are interested in. The philosophers who raise the issue of the reality of the material objects world itself don't seem to have in mind a practical question. If they were, we would be dealing with a matter of decisions concerning the structure of our language: we would be asked to choose whether or not to accept and use the forms of expression in the framework in question (see Carnap 1950: 206).

Thirdly, questions about the existence of *F*s can be seen as factual and, Carnap says, 'theoretical' questions asked in an *external* vein. Now external-vein questions about the reality of a framework are likely to be what metaphysicians are asking, but so understood they are just confused, if not meaningless: they are not real questions, rather pseudo-questions. An ontological question of this latter kind cannot be solved because it is just framed in a wrong way:

> To be real in the scientific sense means to be an element of the system; hence this concept cannot be meaningfully applied to the system itself. (Carnap 1950: 207)

Philosophers taking ontological questions as factual in an external vein have so far not given formulations in terms of the common scientific language, and for Carnap they have not succeeded in giving to the external questions and to the possible answers any cognitive content. We are justified in believing that their questions are pseudo-questions, disguised in the form of theoretical questions while in fact they are not (see Carnap 1950: 209).

Carnap's original view lost popularity, mainly due to its connecting the distinction between internal and external issues with that between *analytic* and *synthetic* truths. Carnap thought framework rules to be analytic, i.e. true in virtue of meaning. One famous and paradigmatic example of analytic statement is: 'All bachelors are unmarried' – which, as a traditional view of analyticity has it, is true due to the fact that 'bachelor' just means 'unmarried man'. Analytic truths are opposed to synthetic truths, like 'George Clooney is a bachelor', which are true in virtue of how the world is like.

Now Quine criticized Carnap in his famous 1951a sustained attack to the analytic/synthetic distinction, which he called a 'dogma of empiricism'. The core of Quine's view, roughly put, is that there are always two factors responsible for any sentence's truth: the meaning of the terms that figure in it, *and* worldly facts. There is no way to tell these two factors apart. Quine argued that all attempts to precisely define the notion of analyticity turn out, on close examination, to form a circle with other notions, such as the notion of synonymy, which themselves call for explanation in terms of analyticity.

Quine's critique of the analytic/synthetic distinction has been highly influential and, as Yablo 1998 notes, this had a repercussion on the assessment of Carnap's view of ontology. Carnap was held to have lost the debate with Quine about ontology because he had lost the debate about analyticity. Many believed that, given Carnap's pairing of the internal/external distinction with the analytic/synthetic one, dismissing the latter entailed dismissing the former. If the analytic and the synthetic are intermingled in any meaningful sentence, then no basis remains for the contrast stressed by Carnap between the internal and the external.

Recent developments suggest this line of thought may have been too quick. Although Carnap's views about analyticity may still be discredited, his approach to ontology has been revived. Many contemporary philosophers working on metaontology are grouped under the label of *deflationists*, meaning that, for them, many or most ontological questions are somehow shallow or unsubstantial and we should devalue their importance (see Eklund 2006a; Hawthorne 2009, and references therein). Carnap is often cited as a source of inspiration for such philosophers. There have been recent proposals to understand the notion of framework and in particular the internal/external distinction, in such a way that the latter can be disentangled from the troubles of the analytic/synthetic distinction.

2 Quantifier variance: 'It all depends on what you mean by ...'

We saw that one role assigned by Carnap to frameworks was that of defining the meaning of ontological questions. A similar position is held by advocates of the so-called *quantifier variance* doctrine. Imagine a politician who, asked whether he had sex with a member of his staff, replies: 'It all depends on what you mean by "sex"'. This may be taken as a sneaky way to disentangle oneself from an uncomfortable question, by shifting attention from the facts (Did they have sex?) to language use (What is meant by 'sex'?).

Now suppose the politician is asked a different question, this time an ontological one. Suppose he is asked whether there exists an object composed exactly by his nose plus the White House. This seems uncomfortable, too, albeit for very different reasons. It turns on what ontologists call the *Special Composition Question*, which asks under which conditions objects x and y constitute a further object: their so-called 'mereological sum' $x + y$ (we will come back to this in the chapter devoted to material objects, in the third part of our book). According to some philosophers, if the politician replied: 'It all depends on what you mean by "exists"?', he would now have a point indeed. Putnam draws just this moral from his discussion of the problem of the Special Composition Question: 'the notions of object and existence have a multitude of different uses rather than one absolute "meaning"' (Putnam 1987: 19; see also Putnam 1994). Inspired by passages like this and by the Carnapian conception of ontology we discussed above, Eli Hirsch (2011) has defended the doctrine of quantifier variance, according to which:

> The world can be correctly described using a variety of concepts of 'the existence of something'. ... Different concepts of an 'object' might be employed in different conceptual schemes, schemes that are all adequate for describing the world. ... We reject as unintelligible the idea of a metaphysically privileged concept of 'a thing'. (Hirsch 2011: 60, 139, 143)

Hirsch frequently combines the doctrine of quantifier variance with the idea that many ontological disputes are only apparently factual, but actually merely verbal:

they give the impression of being about how the world is, but they are about language and language use (we follow Hirsch's own way of presenting the doctrine of quantifier variance and the verbal dispute claim together, but as Eklund 2006a, 2011b argues, they are to some extent separable). For instance, Hirsch (2011: 229) sees the dispute between three-dimensionalism (the view that material objects are only extended in the three dimensions of space) and four-dimensionalism (the view that they are also extended in time and have temporal parts), which we will also discuss in our chapter on material objects, as a paradigm case of this phenomenon (see in particular 'Durran's dilemma', the philosophical parable that closes Hirsch 2009).

Hirsch also offers a vivid illustration of what a merely verbal dispute boils down to:

> Look at your hand while you are clenching it, and ask yourself whether some object called a fist has come into existence. ... The first thought that must come to mind when we ask this question is this: There can't be anything deep or theoretical here. The facts are, so to speak, right in front of our eyes. Our task can only be to remind ourselves of relevant ways in which we describe these facts in our language; to 'command a clear view of the use of our words', as Wittgenstein put it, that is, a clear view of how the relevant concepts operate. (Hirsch 2011: 90)

The issue of verbal disputes is a slippery one (see Eklund 2006a; Manley 2009). The good answer to a question depends, of course, upon the meanings of the words employed in the question. Suppose that Martians speak a language, MartEnglish, which is identical to English save for the fact that in MartEnglish 'grass' means snow. If a Martian asks you in MartEnglish, 'Is grass green?', the right answer is 'No'. It is uncontroversial that sentences need to be meaningful in order to be true/false. It is also uncontroversial that the same sequence of words, understood as meaningful sounds or inscriptions, can have different meanings in different languages. In this sense, the correctness of the sentences we utter depends on the language we are speaking. But that doesn't make an ordinary question like that about the colour of grass a merely verbal dispute. If we ask you whether grass is green, it would be a lame excuse for your reluctance to point out that it all depends on what we mean with 'grass', with 'green', or with 'is'. Wittgenstein's 'I mean what you mean' would be a good rejoinder. We speak a public language, English. The possibility of different languages doesn't imply that you are free to choose to answer our question using any language whatsoever. Now, 'there is' is also an expression of English. So why couldn't somebody reply to the quantifier variantist's suggestion that in ontological disputes it all depends on what one means by 'there is', 'I mean what you mean'?

Let us go back to our hypothetical politician's reply to the first uncomfortable question: 'It all depends on what you mean by "sex"'. Suppose there are at least two admissible interpretations of the word 'sex' and, that according to one, a certain oral practice counts as sex while, according to the other, it doesn't. The answer to that first question depends on which interpretation is in play. Both are admissible in the sense that language use does not settle which one is correct. There are questions whose meaning is clear enough that we don't need to make them more precise in order to answer, and there are questions which are more ambiguous. The latter needs to be made precise before we can answer them. That in some trial a judge may ask for a precise definition of the meaning of 'sex' supports the idea that the word has a relevantly ambiguous meaning. Couldn't the same hold for the expression 'there is'?

One problem with exporting suggestions of this kind to the quantifier variance view can be illustrated via an example by Cian Dorr 2005. Consider a language – call it 'astronomically impoverished English' – where 'there is' is used in such a way that one can only quantify over things that are within a certain distance from us. Imagine two philosophers discussing whether it is ontologically better to stick with astronomically impoverished English or to adopt regular English. They are not discussing whether one language is more convenient than the other for practical purposes. They debate on a theoretical issue: whether one language is, in some sense, more faithful to reality, or better suited to represent its structure.

One could reply, in Putnamian fashion, that the theoretical question makes no sense, insisting that whether something exists or not depends on the meaning of the existential quantifier. But this is not the way many feel about the choice between English and astronomically impoverished English. It is hard not to think that somebody who speaks astronomically impoverished English is just *restricting* the range of the existential quantifier. 'There are galaxies outside our light cone' turns out false in astronomically impoverished English; but this is just *because* in that language people don't quantify over that kind of entities. 'There are galaxies outside our light cone' is true in English because there are such galaxies.

The point generalizes. Given two interpretations of the existential quantifier, a case can be made to always assess the broader as superior. Call interpretations such that the existential quantifier ranges over some kind of entities *F inclusionists* and interpretations such that the existential quantifier does not range over the *F*s *exclusionists*. Now an inclusionist interpretation seems to win by default: if there is the possibility of quantifying over the *F*s, then there are *F*s to quantify over! This is, *in nuce*, the main idea behind the position presented by Eklund 2007, which he labels *maximalism*.

A theorist of quantifier variance may say something in reply to these worries. In order for two interpretations of the existential quantifier to be both admissible they must belong to two equivalent languages – languages that have the same expressive power, that are capable of representing and describing the same situations, albeit with sentences having different logical forms. More technically (see Hirsch 2011:

Introduction), the two languages must be *truth-conditionally equivalent*: given any sentence of one language, there is a sentence of the other which is true under the exact same conditions of the first sentence, and vice versa. Take a language like ordinary English, which quantifies over mid-size objects like chairs and tables, and another language, call it 'English*', which only quantifies over subatomic particles. Whenever it is correct to say, in English, 'There is a chair in front of me', it is correct to say, in English*, 'There are particles arranged chair-wise in front of me', and vice versa. Hirsch stresses that such equivalence provides the speakers with a way to interpret each other. When an English speaker truthfully says something entailing the existence of chairs, an English* speaker can translate the relevant statement into her own language of so-and-so arranged particles in such a way that the English* speaker's counterpart comes out true.

Then English* may not be an impoverished version of English in the sense in which astronomically impoverished English is. It is not clear that English* is inferior to English, even from a theoretical point of view, and this seems to give some credit to the idea that the choice between the two languages is an ontologically shallow issue. It is not clear whether this is really a successful reply to the maximalist, though. The maximalist is not concerned with the superiority of one language over another. Her worry is just that there must be *F*s for the quantifier of a given language (be it superior or not to other languages) to range over them. However, see Hirsch 2009: 249–52 for an advanced discussion of this topic.

Even if the supporters of quantifier variance do not claim that the inclusionist always wins over the exclusionist, they refrain from claiming that the former never wins. This is so for the reason noted above: there can be cases where a language that does not quantify over the *F*s just is expressively impoverished with respect to a language that does quantify over the *F*s. One case could be that of the comparison between ordinary and impoverished English, but there are others. Take the debate in the philosophy of mathematics between platonists, who believe there really are abstract mathematical objects, and nominalists, who do not. As we will see in the third part of our book, there are cases where it is difficult to translate claims that involve quantification over abstract mathematical entities into claims that do not. Hirsch 2009 takes this a reason to think that platonist languages are not equivalent to nominalistic ones, which leads him to side with platonists.

The possibility of languages which are truth-conditionally equivalent albeit displaying very different logical forms raises an intriguing issue. Burgess 2005, drawing on work by Quine, presents a language which can be shown to be equivalent to what Quine called 'English in canonical notation', but is such that it completely dispenses with quantification. In fact, this unusual language contains no variables! To understand how such a variable-free language works, think about the fact that some English sentences have a merely pleonastic subject. When we say 'It rains', the pronoun 'it' does not denote any object: it appears in the sentence just to fill a syntactic gap. In *predicate functor calculus*, all verbs behave like 'rains' in English: they do not need a subject, nor do they need an object. This is pretty close to a formal counterpart of a language imagined by Borges:

> There are no nouns in Tlön's conjectural Ursprache, from which the 'present' languages and dialects are derived: there are impersonal verbs, modified by monosyllabic suffixes (or pre- fixes) with an adverbial value. For example: there is no word corresponding to the word 'moon,' but there is a verb which in English would be 'to moon' or 'to moonate.' 'The moon rose above the river' is *Hlör u fang axaxaxas mlö*, or literally: 'upward behind the on-streaming it moonated'. (Borges 1962: 23, cited in Burgess 2005)

Quine showed how to turn a regimented version of English into a regimented version of a variable-free language in a paper with a telling title: *Variables Explained Away*. That's telling because, if you combine this result with Quine's motto that 'To be is to be the value of a variable', you get the title of Burgess' paper: *Being Explained Away*. *Predicate functor calculus*' equivalence with English regimented into canonical notation may show that it is indeed possible to make a very radical 'quantifier variation': it may be possible not to quantify over anything. This would correspond to a kind of Nihilist language: a language where nothing exists, in the sense that such a language lacks the resources to express the existence of anything (apart maybe from The Absolute, which we can think of as the object implicitly denoted by the pronoun 'it').

The philosophical significance of Quine and Burgess' results is a delicate issue (we just refer to Turner 2011 for careful discussion). Still, note that the technical result generalizes. If one's language has different variables for concrete and abstract objects, it is possible to get rid of quantification over the latter ones by using the techniques described by Burgess 2005 and obtain a language equivalent to the one that we started with. Then Hirsch's claim that there is no nominalistic language truth-conditionally equivalent to a platonist one should be qualified in order for a language obtained by just eliminating variables for abstract objects not to count as a genuine nominalistic language.

Finally, a word on the relation between the doctrine of quantifier variance and Carnap's position. Carnap was a verificationist: very roughly, this means that he thought the meaning of sentences to be given by the methods via which we can in principle ascertain whether they are true or false. A consequence of Carnap's verificationism was that metaphysical claims, for which we lack a method of verification, are meaningless. Verificationism is not part of the doctrine of quantifier variance. Nor are parts of the doctrine such idealistic views as that there is no reality outside language, or that language creates reality. Quantifier language just rests on the view that, when we are confronted with two truth-conditionally equivalent languages, there is no reason to prefer one over the other. In the intentions of its supporters, this is compatible with maintaining that the world is what it is independently of the way we choose to think about it or describe it (Hirsch 2011: xvi, makes such remarks to distinguish his position from that of Putnam).

3 Internal vs. external role of the quantifier

We know that for Quine ontological questions are quantificational questions, i.e. questions of the form 'Are there *Fs*?', where *Fs* = numbers, propositions, properties, etc. Carnap believed that quantificational questions could be asked in two very different spirits, in an internal or in an external vein. If so, then the identification of ontological and quantificational questions should be qualified. Properly conceived, ontological questions are quantificational questions asked in an external vein.

Theorists of the *double reading of the quantifiers*, like Thomas Hofweber 2005a, 2005b, 2006, 2009, think that Carnap's insight about the two readings of ontological questions was a good one. Nonetheless, their reasons are slightly different from Carnap's. Hofweber claims that quantified statements can be read in two different ways because the quantifiers have different meanings in different contexts. Consider for instance a typical utterance of:

(E) There is some beer in the fridge.

Clearly, somebody uttering (E) wants to communicate some piece of information about what the world (in particular, the fridge) contains: (E) has some implications for which kinds of entities exist in the real world. When the existential quantifier is used in this way, we can say that an *external* reading of the quantifier is in play.

Contrast this with the case where two children talk of their favourite cartoons. Having noticed that they both like Batman, they report to their parents that:

(I) There is someone we both like.

In such a case, Hofweber claims, the quantifier is used in a different way. Roughly: it is used to point out that there is a way to fill in the dots in the following, so that it turns out true:

(I*) Child *a* likes … and child *b* likes … .

Does (I) tell us something about what exists in the world? Not necessarily. Although not every philosopher will agree (see our chapter on fictional objects in the third part of the book), we can here say that Batman does not exist, that is, there is nothing like

Batman in reality. (I) is used just to keep track of the fact that there is a way to fill the blanks in (I*) with a term in such a way as to obtain a true statement.

Now it is true that the term we fill the blanks with must be a meaningful one. In general, this does not mean that there must exist an object denoted by the term in question. Remember what we learned from Russell and Quine: there's a lot of difference between having a meaning and denoting an object (witness such terms as 'but', which are arguably meaningful without denoting anything). In the case of (I*), we can fill in the dots with 'Batman', which slightly complicates matters: how can a name be meaningful without naming something? We can stick with the view (see Kripke 2011: Essay 3) that, even granted that the key semantic function of a name is to refer to an object, there must be room for the possibility of names not fulfilling their function. The function of a pen is to write and that of a name is to refer to an object. Just as there can be defective pens which fail to write, so there can be defective names which fail to refer. Something's being a name does not guarantee that it does a good job at referring, any more than something's being a pen guarantees that it does a good job at writing.

As 'Batman' is such a defective piece of language, in the context sketched above (I) does not imply that something of a certain kind exist. The 'there is' in (I) just marks the possibility of filling the blanks in the corresponding (I*) with an expression that turns (I*) into a true statement, even if the expression may fail to refer. This Hofweber calls the *internal* or *inferential* use of the quantifier. Why 'internal', we will soon see. As for 'inferential', this is because we can infer the conclusion that there are *F*s (e.g., 'There is something which both child *a* and child *b* like') by noticing that for some term *t*, '*Ft*' is true (let 'Batman' be the relevant term; then the instance of (I*), 'Child *a* likes Batman and child *b* likes Batman', is true in our context above). This view is also close to what some call the substitutional reading of the quantifier: 'substitutional', because term *t* is what we substitute for the variable in '*Fx*' in order to get a true sentence.

Both the internal and the external use of the quantifier are present in ordinary language, so for Hofweber there is no point in asking which is the correct one. It all depends on context. Now we see why Quine's Thesis 2 from Chapter 2 needs to be qualified in the light of the two roles quantifiers can play. That everything exists is uncontroversial only insofar as, in that 'every-', we have the external role of the quantifier in play. Of course, any of the things that exist exists. But things are different if that 'every-' has the inferential role of the quantifier in play. It is not the case that, no matter what term you fill in the dots with in '… exists', you always get a true claim. For instance, 'Batman exists' is not true given our assumption above.

Accepting the doctrine of the double reading of the quantifiers may help to solve a puzzle about apparently uncontroversial inferences connected to highly controversial ontological issues (see Hofweber 2005b). These are inferences that start with premises like:

(Alpha*) There are two pens on my desk/Both Matteo and Francesco are philosophers/I claimed that I like porridge yesterday and I claim that I like porridge today.

It seems we can safely infer from them that:

(Pi) The number of pens on my desk is two/There is something Matteo and Francesco have in common/There is something I claimed yesterday which I also claimed today.

But from (Pi) it seems to follow that:

(Omega*) There are numbers / properties / propositions.

While the premises may be uncontroversially true and the inferences seem logically unobjectionable, the conclusions may be unwelcome to many ontologists. But whether the conclusions in (Omega*) are controversial or not depends on the role the quantifier is playing throughout the inference. If the quantifier is used according to its internal role, then the inference is correct (it's the *inferential* reading!), and the conclusion is uncontroversial. But we did not settle the ontological question. The ontological question is framed with the external reading of the quantifier in mind. And under that reading, the inference is no longer uncontroversial.

We now see a motivation for the terminology of 'internal' vs. 'external'. *Within* mathematics – that is to say, from a viewpoint internal to the discipline, which does not consider 'external' ontological issues – a conclusion such as that there are even prime numbers is uncontroversial. It can be safely inferred from the true claim that 2 is both prime and even. The inferential/substitutional role of the quantifier is that which is internal to our scientific as well as ordinary (as opposed to philosophical) talk of numbers.

And we also get the connection between this view and Carnap's. Quantificational questions as questions internal to our scientific or everyday talk are easy to settle. External questions are a different story. However, unlike Carnap's, in no way does Hofweber's proposal classify ontological questions as traditionally understood as meaningless. They are perfectly significant, and can be addressed (see Hofweber 2009). We cannot get into the details here, but the key step to address ontological questions, according to Hofweber, is to figure out whether some kinds of terms are referential or not. Whether there are numbers, for instance, will turn on the question whether expressions like 'the number two' are indeed referential. This can be answered, according to Hofweber's metaontology, by looking at the syntactic and semantic behaviour of number words. So ontology is a legitimate enterprise, for it has a domain of questions to answer to: external quantificational questions. Also, it has a methodology to answer them: for the most part, research in the philosophy of language and mind.

4 Other Carnapian approaches

Other positions in the current literature can be broadly characterized as Carnapian. For instance, Yablo's 1998 version of fictionalism (we devote to fictionalism our next chapter), called *figuralism*, was put forward as a way to spell out the Carnapian internal/external distinction via games of make-believe playing the role of frameworks. More recently, Yablo 2006, 2009, 2010, 2014 has replaced games of make-believe with *presuppositions*. In Yablo's view, very roughly, a presupposition is something we take for granted in the process of evaluating some claim. If we ask you whether you picked up your guru at the airport, we are assuming as the background of our question that you do have a guru (the example is from Yablo 2006). Yablo's view of presupposition is different from that of Strawson, which we encountered in Chapter 1. In Yablo's account it may happen, even though *P* presupposes *Q* and *Q* is false, that *P* is nonetheless evaluable as true or false.

Now Yablo's idea is that what internal/external questions are internal/external to are sets of presuppositions. If we ask you: 'Is the number of planets in the solar system bigger than 5?', we are taking for granted that there are numbers, and focusing on planets. On the other hand, when we ask you: 'Are there numbers?', we are clearly not presupposing that there are numbers; otherwise, our question would look as something like: 'Taking for granted that there are numbers, are there numbers?' – which is too trivial to be what we mean when we ask such ontological questions. We need not get into the details of this intriguing position, but we mentioned it to show yet another way to develop the Carnapian internal/external distinction.

Two other approaches that echo points made by Carnap are the one of the so-called *easy approaches to ontology* in the style of Thomasson 2009, 2014, and the neo-Fregean approach we discussed in the previous chapter. In both cases, the idea is that the existence of allegedly disputed kinds of things, like numbers, properties, or propositions, can in fact be easily inferred from undisputed empirical claims like those presented in (Alpha)-(Alpha*) (see Sections 1 and 3 above in this chapter). The inference is taken as licensed by 'conceptual truths', such as that whenever something is *F*, something has *the property of* being *F*; or that whenever it rains, it is also the case that *the proposition that* it rains is true; or that whenever one eats two bagles, the *number of* bagels one eats is two.

In the case of Neo-Fregeans, a Carnapian flavour is combined with two pieces of Fregean wisdom: in the first place is a stress on the importance of abstraction principles, which may play a role similar of that of frameworks in conferring a meaning to mathematical expressions. Secondly, the resort to Frege's context principle, that we also met in the previous chapter, and for which in order to figure out whether a given expression is referential we need to look at the contribution it makes to the truth conditions of the sentences in which it appears.

Further Reading

Eklund 2006a is an excellent critical survey of the metaontological approaches discussed in this chapter. Maurin 2013a contains sections on Carnap and neo-Carnapian approaches to metaphysics. On Carnap's meta-ontology, see also Eklund 2013. 'Quantifier variance and realism', reprinted as the fifth essay in Hirsch 2011 and the one that gives the title to the collection, is a good place to start exploring Hirsch's deflationism, while Eklund's 2011b review of Hirsch 2011 is a good critical discussion of its central themes. 'Durran's dilemma', the philosophical parable that closes Hirsch 2009, is also highly recommended reading. A readable introduction to Hofweber's analysis of ontological problems can be found in Hofweber 2009.

6

Fictionalism

Chapter Outline

It does not seem to be literally true that 221b Baker Street is Sherlock Holmes' home, and few people believe that. Still, sometimes it is appropriate to say that Sherlock Holmes lives in Baker Street: after all, the claim does seem to hold, if not in actual reality, at least *within* Conan Doyle's fictional stories. *Fictionalists* in ontology hold that something similar happens when we say that modesty is a virtue, or that there are prime numbers greater than one million: we are not speaking the literal truth, but only the truth according to a certain fiction. And such talk can have its virtues.

Section 1 of this chapter introduces the main idea behind fictionalism in ontology and explains how the approach requires us to modify Quine's methodology for conducting ontological debates. Section 2 presents some applications of the fictionalist strategy to ontological debates about possible worlds, numbers and properties. Section 3 gives an account of how and why fictional discourse can be useful. A model is offered of how and why saying things that are not literally true can help to convey valuable information about the world. Section 4 discusses other kinds of fictionalist accounts. While one immediate motivation for adopting fictionalism in ontology is that it allows you to reduce your ontological commitments, more sophisticated – and possibly more interesting – motivations are reviewed in Section 5. Finally, Section 6 is dedicated to the most prominent objections to fictionalism and to ways for fictionalists to deal with them.

1 Are we serious?

Like all respectable fathers, Quine may have told his sons some story from time to time. He may have said things like: Once upon a time, there was a magic kingdom. In such a kingdom there lived a beautiful princess named Cinderella. Suppose one of his students caught him while he was pronouncing these words and told him: 'Wait a minute, professor Quine! You just said "There was a magic kingdom": how should I translate this into canonical notation? That looks like quantification over magic kingdoms, committing you to the existence of pretty mysterious entities. Didn't you say somewhere (Quine 1948) that you prefer desert landscapes to Meinongian jungles?'

Most of us would find the student's remark pretty dull. Still it is interesting to ask, what exactly would make such behaviour stupid? An answer can be found in a passage Quine himself wrote:

> One way in which a man may fail to share the ontological commitments of his discourse is … by taking an attitude of frivolity. The parent who tells the Cinderella story is no more committed to admitting a fairy godmother and a pumpkin coach into his own ontology than to admitting the story as true. (Quine 1953: 103)

Could something similar be going on in our talk about numbers, moral values, properties and so on? Some philosophers believe that, when engaging in mathematical or moral discourse or in property-talk, we are putting forward our claims in 'a fictional or make-believe spirit' (Yablo 2001: 74). Like a parent who tells the Cinderella story, we in a sense 'fail to share the ontological commitments of' our discourse. This is the gist of fictionalist strategies in ontology. Such strategies see an analogy between fictional discourse and discourse about problematic entities. As Yablo 2001 presents it, it is to begin with an analogy in the *attitude* we display towards the claims we put forward in both kinds of discourse – that 'attitude of frivolity' Quine spoke about.

Were this correct, it would affect the third thesis of Quine's metaontology, presented in Chapter 2. Quine told us that if we assert *P*, and the proper translation of *P* into canonical notation entails that there are *F*s, then we are committed to the existence of *F*s. To assert *P* while at the same time denying that there exist *F*s would be to hold an inconsistent position – the kind of inconsistency Quine aimed at exposing via his ontological commitment strategy.

But fictionalists make a lot of the distinction between a sentence's commitments and the commitments of a speaker uttering the sentence. We can utter *P* without committing to the literal content of *P*. This means that we are not committing ourselves to every implication of the literal content of *P*. In particular, we may fail to share all the ontological commitments of *P*. Then it may not be inconsistent to utter *P* while also claiming that there are no *F*s, even though *P*, taken literally, entails that there are *F*s.

An example. It may sound inconsistent to jointly say that:

(1) Sherlock Holmes lives in Baker Street.
(2) Sherlock Holmes does not exist.

For – one may claim – (1) logically entails that there is something that is Sherlock Holmes (and lives in Baker Street), and this is inconsistent with there being no Holmes, as per (2). But the impression of inconsistency vanishes when we consider that, normally, one uttering (1) does not really believe, and does not want to assert, that *literally, strictly speaking* Sherlock Holmes lives in Baker Street. A speaker uttering (1) is normally indulging in a pretence. What she says should therefore not be taken at face value: even if the literal content of (1) entails that there is Sherlock Holmes, one may utter (1) while failing to share the relevant ontological commitment.

A parenthetical remark: in the chapter on fictional objects in the third part of our book, we will meet *realist abstractionists* – ontologists who maintain that, *qua* fictional character, Sherlock Holmes really exists, but as an abstract entity, i.e. as something in a sense more similar to the number seventeen than to a flesh-and-blood human being. Even according to realist abstractionists though, Sherlock Holmes, being an abstract entity, has no spatiotemporal address. In particular, he does not really live in 221b Baker Street in London. So even these philosophers do not accept sentences such as (1) as literal truths.

The obvious question now is: what *is* someone who puts forward a claim in fictional spirit actually asserting? Granted that she is not committing to the literal truth of the sentence, is there any content at all she is committing to and, if so, which one? Before we deal with this important question, it is useful to speak in more detail of the analogy between philosophical discourse and fiction.

2 Philosophy-Fiction

If you are wondering how there could ever be a real connection between fictional discourse and serious theoretical philosophy, consider this passage:

> There are countless other worlds. … The worlds are something like remote planets; except that most of them are much bigger than mere planets, and they are not remote.

> Neither are they nearby. They are not at any spatial distance whatever from here. They are not far in the past or future, nor for that matter near; they are not at any temporal distance whatever from now. They are isolated: there are no spatiotemporal relations at all between things that belong to different worlds. Nor does anything that happens at one world cause anything to happen at another. Nor do they overlap; they have no parts in common. … The worlds are many and varied. There are enough of them to afford worlds where (roughly speaking) I finish on schedule, or I write on behalf of impossibilia, or I do not exist, or there are no people at all, or the physical constants do not permit life, or totally different laws govern the doings of alien particles with alien properties. There are so many other worlds, in fact, that absolutely every way that a world could possibly be is a way that some world is. (Lewis 1986: 1)

Doesn't this sound a bit like science fiction? Should we call it a philosophical fiction? Not so, according to the author of the passage.

We will talk at length of *possible worlds* in a chapter in the third part of our book, but we can give a rough anticipation here. The notion of possible worlds is highly serviceable in most branches of contemporary philosophy. One mainstream way to understand talk of modal notions like possibility and necessity, for instance, is by resorting to possible worlds. One can express the truth conditions of sentences of the form 'It is possible that *P*' as follows:

> (Poss) It is possible that *P* if and only if there is some possible world *w* such that *P* is true at *w*.

But this biconditional, on the face of it, quantifies in its right hand side over things called possible worlds. So (Poss) raises the obvious ontological and metaphysical issue of whether there really exist such things, and of what kinds of entities they are. Now in his book *On the Plurality of Worlds*, from which the above quotation comes, Lewis advocates the view that, for every way the world could be, there really exists a (often largely concrete) possible world in which things are that way: a world which is causally and spatiotemporally isolated from ours, but of the same kind, and just as real. This view is often called, for obvious reasons, *modal realism* (or, *genuine* modal realism: we will see in our chapter on possible worlds why the qualification 'genuine' may be in order). *On The Plurality of Worlds* therefore includes a story that, taken literally, commits its subscribers to the existence of concrete, real worlds different from the one we are part of.

Lewis' story, taken literally, has had little success. Almost nobody believes it and most people react to it with what Lewis called an 'incredulous stare': they definitely refuse to share its ontological commitments and to believe in the existence of real, concrete possible worlds. However, things can change if we understand Lewis' story in a different way. Believing in a plurality of real concrete worlds may be crazy, but speaking *as if* there were such worlds has proved useful to handle claims about what is possible and what is necessary. Then we may take Lewis' theory not as literally true, but, in Yablo's 2005 terms, as a useful *representational aid*.

This phenomenon seems not to be limited to possible worlds. Aren't numbers very useful to handle counting, i.e. to figure out how many things of a certain sort are there? As we are going to see in Chapter 9, it may be convenient for various purposes to pretend that, if there are *n* things of the sort *F*, then there is a number that counts them. Talk of properties may be similarly useful. Supposing that the White House is white in virtue of having the property of whiteness, or that Bill Gates is smart in virtue of possessing the property of smartness, and in general that something is *F* in virtue of having the property of *F*-ness, provides us for instance with a powerful way to describe change: we say that something changes whenever it loses or gains some property across time. An alternative way would be to list the possible cases of change: something changes if it is earlier white and later not white, or if it is earlier young and later old, or. ... But this may be too cumbersome and impractical, or just unfeasible (see Yablo 2014).

An ontological fictionalist may go for the view that Lewis' theory of possible worlds, as much as mathematics, the theory of properties, or that of moral values, need not be taken as holding literally of the world in order to be useful. To use Hartry Field's 1989 famous phrase: they can be 'good without being true'. The corresponding theories can play a role as representational aids, although possible worlds, numbers, properties or moral values are not really part of the furniture of the world. We don't need to believe in the existence of such entities, or in the truth of these theories, to enjoy their benefits. We can have 'all the benefits' of number/possible worlds/property-discourse 'without the ontological costs' (Rosen 1990: 330). This makes of it an attractive strategy for those who care about ontological economy, but do not want to reduce their expressive powers.

We know that, within the standard metaontological view, somebody uttering a sentence *P* apparently bringing ontological commitment to the *F*s, but refusing to admit the *F*s in her ontology, is in for predicament. She ought to either:

- **a** Stop uttering *P*; or
- **b** Accept the *F*s in her ontology; or
- **c** Paraphrase away all talk about the *F*s.

Calling this 'Quine's menu', Yablo 2001: 72 points out that one can see fictionalism as the offer of an additional option: we can continue to utter *P* and keep rejecting that there exist *F*s even in the absence of a strategy to paraphrase away talk of the *F*s, *provided* we are clear about the attitude we are taking when putting forward such statements as *P*. This further menu choice may sound very liberating. Still, it needs to address a number of issues.

3 How does fictional discourse work?

Fictionalism pivots on the idea of discourses that are 'good without being true'. But how is this possible? What's the point of not speaking the truth? If you tell us that there is a man in the closet when there is none, you have made a mistake: it would be very hard to see how your claim could help us. Why is the situation different when we turn to talk of controversial entities like numbers or properties? A path to the answer comes from developing Yablo's claim above: talk of numbers, possible worlds, moral values, etc., is useful as providing representational aids. Here are some quotations focusing on the number-case:

> Numbers enable us to make claims which ... we ... would otherwise have trouble putting into words. (Yablo 2002: 230)

> Mathematics is used in science simply in order to make more things sayable about concrete objects. (Melia 1998: 70–1)

> In short, mathematics appears in our empirical theories as a mere descriptive aid: by speaking in terms of the real number line ... or of some other mathematical structure, we simply make it easier to say what we want to say about the physical world. (Balaguer 1998: 137)

Exactly how does this work, and how does it relate with *fiction*? A general account of fiction is called for. We will consider the one offered by Walton (1990, 1993), which was applied to fictionalism in ontology by Yablo in a series of essays (collected in Yablo 2010). We will then consider alternative accounts of the utility of fictional discourse.

On Walton's account, a fiction or pretence is a particular kind of game: a game of *make-believe*. A game is a rule-governed activity. The point of the rules is to discriminate between legitimate and illegitimate moves in the game. In a game of make-believe, we pretend that something is the case. Children play games in which they pretend that trees are bears, or that certain pieces of mud are cakes, etc. The rules that govern make-believe games are called (after Walton 1990) *principles of generation*. Such principles tell us what we should pretend to be the case, or what we should take as true in the fiction, in the given circumstances. For instance, some principles of generation for a vampire make-believe game could be the following:

(PG1) It is true according to the vampire-fiction that x is a vampire if and only if x is wearing sunglasses after dusk.

(PG2) It is true according to the vampire-fiction that x is dead if and only if x is lying on the ground.

Suppose it's midnight, we are playing the vampire game and we encounter another player who is lying on the floor. On closer inspection, we notice she is wearing sunglasses.

What should be our next move? Given (PG1) and (PG2), we should pretend that a vampire is dead. This shows one way in which principles of generation can be used: they tell us how to behave in order to respect the content of the story we are pretending to be true.

But principles of generation can in principle be used also to gain information about the actual world. Suppose some people are playing a Sherlock Holmes game (call it 'Holmes-today'). They walk though London and act as if Conan Doyle's novels were true. One principle of generation of their game is:

(PG+) It is true according to the Holmes-today fiction that *x* is close to Holmes' house if and only if *x* is in Baker Street.

Suppose we are in London and we meet some people who we know are playing the Holmes-today game. We want to figure out where we are, so we ask them. They tell us we are close to Holmes' house. We know we cannot take them literally: even assuming they are sincere, we know they may tell us what is true according to the Doyle stories rather than what is really the case. Still, we can use the piece of information they gave us to figure out where we really are. Being aware of (PG+) we know that, in order for it to be true in the fiction that we are close to Holmes' house, we must be in Baker Street. So, assuming our interlocutors were sincere, we can infer that we are in Baker Street.

It seems that, by knowing what is fictionally true, we can gain knowledge about what is really the case, via principles of generation. In Walton's theory, *props* are those real-world conditions that make such moves in make-believe games legitimate. Walton 1993 calls 'prop-oriented make-believe' those games where our engagement is not motivated by our interest in the content of the story (i.e. in what is true according to the fiction), but in the real world conditions that make something true according to the story. Metaphorical talk provides good cases. To use Walton's classical example: you ask someone where Crotone is and she tells you that it is at the arch of the Italian boot. Your interlocutor is speaking metaphorically, pretending that Italy is a boot. This is not literally right, but by so talking she is able to convey information about reality. When we say that Crotone is at the arch of Italian boot, we are communicating something about Crotone's geographical position: we point to the real-world conditions that make it correct to make that claim, within the Italy-is-a-boot pretence.

Principles of generation give us a clue to understand how fictional discourse works, which can be extended to cover discourse about controversial entities. Yablo 2001: 78 gives the following analogues of generation principles for talk of numbers, properties, and possible worlds:

There are zero (or one, or two…) things of kind *F* if and only if, according to the number-pretence, the number of the *F*s is zero (or one, or two…).

x is a *Q* if and only if, according to the property pretence, *x* has the property of *Q*-ness

> It is possible that *P* if and only if, according to the possible world pretence, there is a world at which *P*.

(This is not an exact quote: we paraphrased Yablo for the sake of exposition). Suppose we want to tell you that object *x* has undergone change, but we do not want to say exactly how it changed. We can indulge in the property fiction and tell you that object *x* has lost or gained some property *Q*. Then you will know, through generation principles, that object *x* was sooner cold and later hot, or sooner young and later old, or one of the alternatives. Applying Walton's account of fiction to discourse involving controversial entities yields an account of the utility of fictional talk.

4 Varieties of fictionalism

Fictionalists will typically claim that, when we utter ontologically disputed sentences, we do not need to literally mean what we say and we do not need to believe it. The truth of such disputed sentences would commit us to the existence of disputed entities whereas, according to fictionalists, the content that we want to convey by uttering those sentences does not (this sets fictionalists apart from some paraphrase theorists, who think that the literal meaning of disputed sentences does not commit to problematic entities).

What *do* speakers mean and believe, then, when uttering disputed sentences? Borrowing the terminology of Yablo 2001, who presents and defends a version of fictionalism he calls *figuralism*, we should distinguish between the literal content of a disputed sentence, which is not asserted in ordinary utterances, and the *real* content, which is. For Yablo, when uttering a fictional claim *P* we really assert what makes *P* pretence-worthy. This is the real-world condition in virtue of which *P* is the right thing to be pretended in the relevant fiction. Crotone's geographical location for instance, is what makes it correct to say, when speaking as if Italy were a boot, that Crotone is at the arch of the Italian boot. It is plausible that, when we say that Crotone is at the arch of the Italian boot, what we really assert and believe is that it is in such-and-such location. By indulging in pretence, we convey information about the real world: that such a real-world condition obtains. According to figuralism, when one claims that the number of starving people is increasing, one's concern is not the content of the game or fiction – rather, it is the real world. Hence we speak of prop-oriented make-believe: we are not merely interested in what is true according to the fiction, but rather in the features of the real world that make it so.

Not all fictionalisms are of this kind. An example of a fictionalist of a different sort is Field 1980. Field sees mathematics as just a 'theoretical juice extractor' (cfr. Hempel 1945: 391): a pure instrument to speed up deductions, itself devoid of content. There seems to be no role here for talk of numbers working as representational aid (see Yablo 2005: fn. 11, for some subtleties). When we utter a sentence infused with mathematics, according to this account, we do not convey *any* content. Our utterance is just like a move in a game of chess. Chess moves can be correct or incorrect, but they have as such no truth-evaluable or representational content: there is nothing true you are conveying when correctly moving chess pieces on the board (or when pressing buttons on a calculating machine, etc.). Following Yablo 2001 we can label this version of fictionalism *instrumental fictionalism*: uttering a fictional claim *P* is just a move in a useful game.

According to yet another version of fictionalism (Field 1989; Woodward 2012), when we speak within a fiction we are really speaking about the content of the fiction. This is *meta-fictionalism*: by uttering a fictional claim *P* we really say that *P* is true according to the fiction. Meta-fictionalism is thus different from the figuralist account inspired by the idea of prop-oriented make-believe we presented above. Anyway, all versions of fictionalism mentioned so far agree that we should neither believe nor assert the full content of ontologically disputed sentences. We should put them forward with another attitude, or force, different from assertion, and sometimes called quasi-asserting (Yablo 2001). In the terminology of Eklund 2011a, they all qualify then as versions of *force* fictionalism. Unlike instrumental fictionalism, meta-fictionalism and figuralism also qualify as versions of *content* fictionalism, in that according to them utterances of disputed sentences do have a content.

While discussing paraphrase strategies in Chapter 3, we have introduced the distinction between hermeneutic and revolutionary approaches by drawing on Burgess and Rosen 1997. According to authors like Stanley 2001, the distinction can be applied also to fictionalist views. Hermeneutic fictionalism focuses on how to interpret speakers who utter disputed sentences. It is a thesis about the content of our utterances of disputed sentences and our attitude towards that content, according to which, when we mention problematic entities like numbers, we do not literally mean what we say. The real content of our utterances, which is believed and asserted, does not commit us to the existence of such entities. Revolutionary fictionalism on the other hand, claims that we *should* just stop believing the disputed sentences. It is thus a prescriptive view about the attitude we ought to have, not a descriptive view about the attitude we actually have, nor a thesis about the actual content of our disputed claims.

5 Other motivations for fictionalism: Oracles and paradoxes

The most obvious motivation for revolutionary fictionalism has already been surveyed: if one wants to avoid commitment to some kind of disputed entities, fictionalism offers a promising way, alternative to paraphrase strategies. One is inspired by considerations of ontological economy, or one thinks that problematic entities are unacceptable because they are somehow obnoxious. In the case of numbers, propositions and other abstract entities, for instance, many raise classical epistemological worries: they wonder how we could get knowledge of them, given that we cannot see them, touch them, or have any form of causal interaction with them (see e.g. Field 1989; Liggins 2010a and the discussions on abstract objects in the third part of our book, Chapters 9 and 10).

Hermeneutic fictionalism may meet other needs, though. A typical hermeneutic fictionalist may be Yablo. He does not think that we should *find a way* to avoid commitment to problematic entities. He just thinks that the existence of entities like numbers or similar is already irrelevant for the truth of the real content we wish to convey when we engage in discourses that involve such entities. One can see the point by engaging in a thought experiment. Were an oracle (Burgess and Rosen 1997: 3) to tell you that there are no numbers, Yablo 2005 wonders, would you go around asking mathematicians as well as ordinary people to stop saying things like '2 + 2 = 4', or 'There are prime numbers greater than 1000'? Would you find such a behaviour reasonable? If you were a mathematician who has just proved a beautiful conjecture of number theory, would you retract your claim were somebody to convince you that there are no abstract objects like numbers and sets?

And we don't need to take only pure mathematics into account. Consider an astronomer claiming that 'star formation is an exponentially decreasing function of time elapsed since redshift 2' (Yablo 2010: 3). Would you consider the claim as taking a stance in the platonism vs. nominalism debate? If the astronomer were to confess later that he doesn't believe in the existence of such mathematical entities as functions, he wouldn't sound as somebody who has changed his mind. He was talking about stars earlier – an astronomical issue. Now he is talking about the existence of abstract objects, an ontological issue. The two belong to different subject matters. People uttering math-infused claims are usually not concerned about the existence of mathematical objects. They don't care about them and they are not talking about them when using math-infused sentences. So, the argument goes on, they shouldn't be *interpreted* in a way that commits them to the existence of the problematic entities. In schematic form (see Yablo 2001: 102):

(P1) Taken literally, disputed sentences commit to some kind of problematic entities.
(P2) People normally uttering disputed sentences take themselves not to be committing to the existence of the problematic entities.
Therefore:
(C) People uttering disputed sentences shouldn't be taken literally.

Another motivation for the view is that there seems to be a mismatch between two questions like the following:

(Q1) Are Matteo and Francesco both Italians?
(Q2) Are there properties?

(Q1) is philosophically uninteresting, while (Q2) is hotly debated by philosophers. However, it seems that by answering the first question we thereby answer the second one, given that we move from:

(A1) Matteo and Francesco are both Italians.

Into:

(A2) There is a property that Matteo and Francesco share: that of being Italian.

And (A2) just seems to answer (Q2). It seems strange that we can derive the existence of properties or other problematic entities from claims that look unproblematic and that don't seem to have anything to do with ontological issues. We seem to have a 'something from nothing transformation' (see Schiffer 1996). Yablo 2000 calls this problem the 'paradox of existence': how come that hard existential questions are so easy to solve? A hermeneutic fictionalist diagnosis of the tension would be as follows: inside a fiction ruled by some generation principles, such transformations can be taken for granted; but outside the context of the fiction, the principles that allow such transformations are highly contentious.

6 Problems with fictionalism: Philosophical authority, autistic children and bombs

Various philosophers are not happy with fictionalism. Revolutionary fictionalism has been accused of *philosophical immodesty*. The issue can be illustrated by taking the example of Hartry Field 1989, a meta-fictionalist of the revolutionary kind about mathematical discourse. Field thinks that mathematical claims, taken literally, are not true although lay people and scientists commonly take them to be true. We believe and assert that 2 + 2 = 4 and that some classes can be mapped one-to-one to some other classes but, according to Field, we should change our attitude. We should stop believing that 2 + 2 = 4 and rather believe that, according to standard mathematics, 2 + 2 = 4. We should do so because we have *philosophical* reasons (to be discussed in section 9) to doubt that such claims are literally true.

Confronted with a position entailing something of this kind, David Lewis' reaction was the following:

> If there are no classes or numbers, then our mathematics textbooks are works of fiction, full of false 'theorems'. Renouncing classes means rejecting mathematics. That will not

> do. Mathematics is an established, going concern. Philosophy is as shaky as can be. To reject mathematics for philosophical reasons would be absurd. If we philosophers are sorely puzzled by [the entities] that constitute mathematical reality, that's our problem. We shouldn't expect mathematics to go away to make our life easier. Even if we reject mathematics gently – explaining how it can be a most useful fiction, 'good without being true' – we still reject it, and that's still absurd.
>
> That's not an argument, I know. But I laugh to think how presumptuous it would be to reject mathematics for philosophical reasons. How would you like to go and tell the mathematicians that they must change their ways, and abjure countless errors, now that philosophy has discovered that there are no classes? Will you tell them, with a straight face, to follow philosophical argument wherever it leads? If they challenge your credentials, will you boast of philosophy's other great discoveries: that motion is impossible, that a being than which no greater can be conceived cannot be conceived not to exist, that it is unthinkable that anything exists outside the mind, that time is unreal. … (Lewis 1993: 14–15)

Revolutionary fictionalists ask us to reject claims that are acceptable according to the internal standards of scientific disciplines for philosophical reasons. Lewis doubts that philosophers have credentials to overrule such internal standards. His complaint has been echoed by such authors as Burgess and Rosen (see Burgess 1983; Burgess and Rosen 1997, 2005), and is usually seen as just a corollary of Quine's naturalism, which we met in Chapter 2. However, in recent times some authors have defended revolutionary fictionalists from Lewis' charge. Liggins 2007 and Daly and Liggins 2011 distinguish between the reasonable demand of respecting science's internal standards, as requested by naturalism, and the less reasonable demand to defer to science for resolving the dispute about the existence of problematic entities.

Hermeneutic fictionalism has been criticized too. A first objection stems from a phenomenological remark. Consider fictionalism in the philosophy of mathematics. Doing mathematics seems to be a very different kind of intellectual activity with respect to playing make-believe games like those described by Walton (Stanley 2001: 47ff.) Doing maths does not seem to involve pretence the way playing Cowboys and Indians does. Rather the opposite: speakers will typically tell you, after introspection, that when they utter a mathematical claim they really believe what they are saying, whereas in case of claims clearly put forward in a make-believe spirit, they do not. If you say that Sherlock Holmes lives in Baker Street and somebody, incredulous, ask you: 'Really?' – you will probably reply that, well no, not really. If somebody asks you whether you really believe that $\sqrt{2}$ is irrational, things will go differently. And this difference can be very important: autistic children are able to perform arithmetical computations but, Stanley remarks, they have variously limited ability to engage in make-believe games.

To evaluate the objection one needs to get clear about the notion of pretence involved in fictionalist accounts of mathematical discourse or of discourse involving ontologically disputed entities in general. Yablo (2001, Appendix) suggests to replace 'making believe' with 'being as if one believed' when describing the kind of state people involved in fictional discourse are in. Now 'being as if one believed' might not express a conscious activity: dreaming (a case considered by Walton) may be a case in which fictional truths are generated by something like a game of make-believe, but without any conscious effort to engage in such an activity. Mathematical discourse could be a case of unconscious rather than conscious make-believe game as well (see also Liggins 2010b).

Another problem stems from a crude way of interpreting the link between what is true in the fiction and what is true in reality. Considering mathematical discourse, for instance, it is tempting to think that the following schematic equivalence holds for fictionalists (see Yablo 2001):

(N) 'The number of the *F*s = *n*' is true according to the number fiction if and only if there are *n* *F*s.

But unqualified endorsement of (N) would bring trouble. It is part of the content of the number fiction that the number of even prime numbers is one (the only prime number being the number two):

(Intra-N) According to the number fiction, the number of even prime numbers = 1.

But then we have, in virtue of (N) + Intra (N), that:

(Extra-N) There is one even prime number.

... Which fictionalists don't want to assert. In its most famous form the objection (known as the Brock-Rosen objection) is presented with reference to a view called 'modal fictionalism' (Rosen 1990). We will speak of this in the chapter on possible worlds in the third part of our book but for now, the following coarse characterization will do. In spite of its misleading name, the view is not fictionalist about *modality*: it does not consist in the claim that modal notions like possibility or necessity are fictional, not real. Rather, the view is fictionalist about possible worlds. Its key claim is that talk of (and quantification over) possible worlds ought to be understood as literally false. Now the objection arises by considering the modal fictionalist schema:

(P) *P* is true at all possible worlds according to the possible worlds fiction if and only if *P* is necessary.

Problems arise because the following is commonly taken to be part of the content of the possible world fiction:

(Intra-P) According the possible worlds fiction, at all possible worlds it is true that there is a plurality of worlds.

By combining (P) and (Intra-P) one gets to the conclusion that:

(Extra P) It is necessary that there be a plurality of possible worlds.

Assuming that what is necessarily true is true, this means that modal fictionalists accepting (P) would end up committing themselves to the existence of possible worlds.

To see one way in which this objection can be accommodated, we have to deepen our understanding of the relation between what is fictionally true and what is true *simpliciter*. When speaking of the conditions in virtue of which *P* is the right thing to be pretended in the relevant fiction, we did not assume that this condition *always* had be a real-world condition. What makes true in the number fiction that the number of apples on the table is two is the real-world fact that there are two apples on the table. But what makes fictional that the number of even primes is one is not a fact about the natural world: it is a fact about the way numbers are imagined to be. So what makes it fictional that *P*, in the case of mathematical fiction, need not be a fact about the real world: it could be a fact about the way numbers are to be conceived.

If this is the case then, as Yablo's 2002 strategy goes, we could limit the original (N) and add to it a distinct principle. When the relevant *F*s are a plurality of concrete objects, (N) can still hold. But when the *F*s include abstract objects as well, we need another schema. Read '*…*' as 'It is to be pretended that…'. The schema is:

(N*) 'The number of the *F*s = *n*' is true in the fiction if and only if *there are *n* *F*s*.

Fictional truths can be generated not only from truths about the real world, but also from other fictional truths. So we cannot always rely on principles like (N) and (P) to find the real content of claims belonging to fictional discourse. We may have to look the way numbers (or possible worlds, etc.) are to be imagined.

Another complaint against hermeneutic fictionalism, due to Stanley 2001, is that it offers an inadequate semantics for sentences belonging to fictional discourse. The mainstream semantic view has it that semantics for a given area of discourse should specify the conditions under which sentences belonging to that area of discourse are true. It is widely accepted that this should be done in a *systematic* way, i.e. by providing a finite set of rules from which the truth conditions of a potentially infinite number of sentences can be recursively generated, starting from the meanings of the words that figure in such sentences. This is taken as the only plausible way to account for the following fact: ordinary language speakers like us can understand the meanings of a potential infinity of sentences even though they only have a finitely specifiable linguistic competence. We only know the meanings of a finite number of words, and a finite number of grammatical rules. But we can potentially understand indefinitely many sentences we hear for the first time, provided they are composed, according to those grammatical rules, by words whose meanings we know. As Stanley puts it:

> Speakers have an extraordinary ability to understand the real world truth-conditions of novel utterances, that is, utterances of sentences they have never heard before. But in order to explain this ability, there must be a systematic relationship between the real world semantic values of the parts of the sentences, and the real world semantic values of the whole sentences. (Stanley 2001: 41)

But 'fictionalist semantics' provides nothing adequate for this. There is no fictionalist account of how the meanings of constituent expressions within fictional discourse generate the meaning of whole sentences.

However, this may not perforce be a bug of the view. Fictional discourse is compared by Yablo 2001 with metaphorical discourse. It seems that we do not get the actual content of a claim like 'Crotone is at the arch of the Italian boot' by putting together the metaphorical meanings of words like 'Crotone', 'arch' and 'boot'. These words do not have a special meaning when they are used in a piece of metaphorical discourse. Rather, we get what that claim means because we know the generation principle that makes it correct to say that Crotone is at the arch of the Italian boot only if Crotone is located at such-and-such a position. Of course, generation principles are specific to games of make-believe: there is no *single* account of how the real content of an utterance is related to its literal content (Yablo 2001: 96).

Fictional discourse has also been considered by Yablo as akin to hyperbolic discourse. When we speak hyperbolically ('Lady Gaga must have one billion pairs of shoes') we do not mean what we literally say. How do we manage to get the real content of what we are saying out of the literal content? It seems that the real content – in the case: that Lady Gaga has a huge number of shoes – is somehow part of the literal content. We obtain the former by somehow reducing the full content of our assertion. Providing a precise account of how this works may be difficult; but the ability to understand hyperbolical talk certainly is part of our ordinary linguistic competence.

The parallel with hyperbolic talk brings us to a suggestion by Joseph Melia 2000. In hyperbolic talk we 'say less with more'. This suggests to get the real content by starting with the literal content and taking something back. Melia submits that it is sometimes possible to withdraw an implication of what we assert in a practice he calls 'weaseling'. Somebody tells you that everybody came to the party just to later add that John did not come. It seems obvious that you should not interpret this as if one made the inconsistent statement:

(W) For all x, x came to the party, but there is an x that didn't come to the party.

But rather as:

(W*) For all x such that $x \neq$ John, x came to the party.

Weaseling is close to what linguists call 'logical subtraction', i.e. the practice of scaling down part of the content of an assertion. Yablo himself has recently (2012, 2014) worked on the topic. It is important to appreciate that logical subtraction sometimes makes sense, but sometimes does not. Suppose somebody tells you that snow is white and it's hot, but later retracts and asks you to subtract the part about the hotness of the snow. It is clear what part of her assertion remains: that snow is white. Suppose then someone tells you that Quine is a philosopher and later asks you to subtract the implication that someone is a philosopher. This would hardly make sense: *no part* of the original claim is left as remainder of such a subtraction. The first task of one willing to apply logical subtraction techniques to an account of fictional discourse is to distinguish between cases where logical subtraction is possible and cases where it is not. This will be relevant for the discussion of Melia's nominalistic account of mathematics in our first chapter on abstract objects, in the third part of our book.

Further Reading

Liggins 2012 is an extensive commented bibliography on fictionalism in metaphysics. Our presentation of fictionalism has been inspired by the beginning sections of Yablo 2001. See also the introduction to Yablo 2010. Eklund 2011a is nice presentation of fictionalist approaches in ontology, their motivations, and problems. On fictionalism in mathematics, see Balaguer 2011. For the original presentation of the Brock-Rosen objection, see Brock 1993 and Rosen 1993. In presenting the objection we followed Eklund 2011a: 4.7, and Divers and Hagen 2006. See also Liggins 2008b; Woodward 2008, and Nolan 2011. On prop-oriented make believe, see Walton 1993. On the 'autism objection' to hermeneutic fictionalism, see Stanley 2001 and Liggins 2010b.

7

Meinongianism

Chapter Outline

In this chapter we delve into *Meinongianism:* a non-standard (meta-) ontological view according to which the notion of existence is not captured by the quantifier. Existence is, rather, a full-fledged, non-trivial feature which some things have and others lack. Against Quine's second metaontological thesis, then, it is not the case that everything exists. Section 1 introduces and briefly motivates the view. Section 2 explains how quantifiers work according to Meinongians. Section 3 explores which kinds of things may count as candidates for nonexistence, while Section 4 addresses the key problem: what is existence, if not what Kant, Frege, Russell and Quine believed it to be? Section 5 introduces the issue of the Comprehension Principle for Meinongianism: a principle answering the question of what non-existent objects there are. We examine how a simple reply brings trouble to so-called naïve Meinongianism, and we glimpse at more sophisticated Neo-Meinongian answers in Section 6.

1 Introducing Meinongianism

We already met Alexius Meinong, *en passant*, in previous chapters. We are now giving a closer look at the position of some non-standard (meta-)ontologists, called 'Meinongians' after this Austrian philosopher (or, at times, 'neo-Meinongians': we will soon come to the reasons for the prefix 'neo-').

Meinongians believe that some objects do not exist, but we can generally refer to them, quantify over them, and make true claims about them (see e.g. the characterization in Sainsbury 2010: 45). The view denies the second of Quine's pivotal metaontological theses from Chapter 2 – in fact, it disagrees with the very opening of Quine's *On What There Is*: according to Meinongians, not only is it not obvious that everything exists, but it is also untrue. Following Meinong, they distinguish the *Sein* of objects – their existential status – from their *Sosein*, their having certain features or properties (which properties? This is a key issue to be addressed later). Meinongians believe that things can be there to bear properties, and to make some statements true, even when they do not exist. This Meinong called the 'Principle of Independence' (of *Sosein* from *Sein*) in his most famous work, the *Gegenstandstheorie* or Theory of Objects (Meinong 1904).

Meinongianism can be motivated as a commonsensical, intuitive theory, or family of theories, and matches fairly well with a broadly descriptivist approach to ontology. It is usually agreed that one methodological advantage of the view (some say: the only advantage) is that it dispenses with paraphrases of various kinds, in which ontologists who play by the Quinean criterion of ontological commitment have to engage. We appear to refer to actually and/or currently non-existent objects via names and descriptions: we meaningfully and, at times, truthfully make such claims as that Sherlock Holmes is more famous than any existing detective, that tomorrow's dawn is expected to be cloudless, that Heraclitus is still misunderstood and that Atlantis is believed by some to have existed even though it most certainly hasn't. The general Meinongian attitude here is that what appears to be the case is indeed the case. The view sticks to ordinary language, and the intuitions deposited in it, better than most of its rivals.

What can be said about language can similarly be said about thought. Representing non-existent objects seems to be a pervasive feature of our mental activity, and philosophers like Tim Crane 2013 have recently defended the view that we will not have an adequate account of *intentionality*, that is, of the representational capacities of our thoughts, unless we admit non-existent objects, against the Quinean mainstream metaontology.

2 Meinongian quantifiers and ontological commitment

We also seem to quantify in complex ways over objects that lack existence. Such quantification, for Meinongians, should again be generally taken at face value:

> There is something which has been sought by many, namely the site of Atlantis, but it does not exist. (Wolterstorff 1961)
>
> Some of the gods are tempestuous, but of course no gods exist. (McGinn 2000)
>
> I thought of something I would like to give you as a Christmas gift, but I couldn't buy it for you because it doesn't exist. (Priest 2005)

Meinong expressed the general moral we are supposed to get out of such examples by claiming: 'There are objects of which it is true that there are no such objects' (Meinong 1904: 49). Looking at this claim with Quinean glasses, it certainly looks like a *contradictio in terminis*. In the canonical notation of elementary logic, '... there is no such object (say, x)' becomes $\sim\exists y(y = x)$. Then 'There is some object, x, such that there is no such object' becomes $\exists x\sim\exists y(y = x)$. This is tantamount to $\exists x\sim(x = x)$: something is not self-identical. To avoid such blatant logical absurdity, Meinongians need to give a non-standard treatment of quantification.

Let us use 'Λ' and 'Σ' for two Meinongian quantifiers, to be read 'for all' and 'for some' respectively. The former is the universal quantifier. The latter we will call the particular quantifier: a natural name, as 'particular', not 'existential', expresses the dual of 'universal'. Like the standard quantifiers, these are inter-definable: Λ is $\sim\Sigma \ldots \sim$, while Σ is $\sim\Lambda \ldots \sim$; we can get rid of either by substituting it with the other plus negation. Both are devoid of existential commitment: against the Quinean motto, there are things that can be values of variables despite failing to be.

But is there not an 'is' in 'there is'? 'For a thing to have *being* is for there to *be* such a thing as it', van Inwagen 2006: 39 objected to Meinongians. We may call this the Argument from Italics: If there *are* such things, how can they fail to have *being*? Some Meinongians reply to the Argument from Italics by advocating a distinction between being and existence (Zalta 1988: 103–4). They grant that quantification brings commitment to the being of the things one quantifies over, but claim that some things lack the full-fledged form of being we ordinarily call existence: they only have an impoverished or watered-down form of being, expressed by the 'is' in 'There is such a thing as x'. Matti Eklund calls this position 'modes-of-being Meinongianism', and notices that Meinongianism is understood in this way 'typically when the view is discussed by its foes' (Eklund 2006a: 328). Modes-of-being Meinongianism is a partial retreat in the face of Quinean – or Inwagenian – backfiring. It grants to quantification (watered-down) ontological commitment, commitment to the (watered-down) being of what one quantifies over. So it looks close enough to (a watered-down) Quineanism.

Other Meinongians accept that being is the same as existence, but declare that some things just lack being, that is, existence. And if being is spoken of in many ways, that is, if there are different ways or modes of being, namely existence, then such things have none of them. Eklund (Eklund 2006a: 328) calls these 'non-commitment Meinongians': Routley 1980; Priest 2005; Berto 2012, and Crane 2013, certainly are among them. As the non-commitment variety seems to be more popular among Meinongians, and more clearly anti-Quinean, we will stick to this version of the view in the rest of our exposition.

How do non-committed Meinongians deal with the Argument from Italics? The short answer, summarizing what is claimed by Berto 2012 and Crane 2013, is the verb 'to be' is accidental to quantification. Its showing up in some of the quantificational expressions we use lends thin linguistic support to the thick metaontological conclusion of the Argument. English uses 'some', where 'to be' does not appear. German often uses '*es gibt*', but we would hardly infer that Germans ascribe *giving*, or *being given*, to anything they quantify over. In French one says '*il y a*': '*être*', again, it does not show up. We wouldn't claim that the French are ascribing *having*, *avoir* (?) to the things they quantify over. Besides, we use 'there is' in locative constructions where 'exists' is nonsensical. 'There was a guy at the door this morning, looking for you' makes sense. That's not so for the claim that a guy was existing at the door this morning and, while he existed there, he was looking for you: a bad result for a presumed always-substitutable synonym.

We saw in Chapter 2 how in *On What There Is* Quine claimed that terms like 'man' or 'red' don't commit us to the existence of universals (the universal *man*, the universal *red*). Even proper names, for Quine, fail to commit us to the existence of their bearers, for by extending the Russellian technique for definite descriptions we can eliminate them: we can replace a given name, like 'Pegasus', with a description supposedly synonymous with it (even one coined *ad hoc*, like 'the pegasizer'), and then we apply the Russellian procedure from scratch.

For the Meinongian, too, names don't commit us to the existence of their bearers, but for quite a different reason: these may be there, but just lack existence. And for her, even the quantifiers don't commit us to the existence of what we quantify over. Does *anything* at all commit us to the existence of something, then? The fast Meinongian answer is, Yes: to state that it exists. One is explicitly committed to the existence of something by asserting of the thing a normal existence predicate, say, '*E!*', applicable to individuals. Sentences like 'Lady Gaga exists' (true) and 'Batman exists' (false) are translated into the canonical logical notation as what they appear to be: simple subject-predicate sentences in which a property is ascribed to an individual: *E!g*, *E!b*.

The existence predicate can also be used to define the universal and particular existentially loaded quantifiers – say, '∀' and '∃', to adopt the usual symbols. 'All existing things are such that *F*', is (read '$=_{df}$' as 'is equal by definition to'):

$$\forall xFx =_{df} \Lambda x(\text{if } E!x, \text{ then } Fx).$$

And 'There exists something such that *F*' is:

$$\exists xFx =_{df} \Sigma x(E!x \text{ and } Fx).$$

Some claim that Meinongians have two couples of quantifiers, the existentially neutral and the existentially loaded ones. But this is misleading: the existentially loaded couple is just defined, thus always dispensable, via the Meinongian quantifiers and the primitive existence predicate. The Meinongian quantifiers should really be called just quantifiers. When one says '∀*x*...' or '∃*x*...' one is excluding from the domain of things one is quantifying over those that do not exist. Existentially committing quantification is just quantification – restricted to a sub-domain of the totality of things. We already spoke of the phenomenon of restricted quantification in previous chapters. Quantification is, in fact, restricted in various context-dependent ways in everyday talk. To use the Lewisian example again: when I claim that all the beer is in the fridge, I don't need to explicitly declare that I am quantifying only over beer that is in the house; this is easily understood by sensible speakers.

Now Meinong explained our 'prejudice in favour of the actual' (by which he meant: of the existent) as due to our 'lively interest in reality which is part of our nature', and which leads to the 'exaggeration which finds the non-real a mere nothing' (Meinong 1904: 79). Even if 'the totality of what exists, including what has existed and will exist, is infinitely small in comparison with the totality of the Objects of knowledge' (Meinong 1904: 79), this smaller totality is the set of things that usually matter in our lives. When we say 'there is', or 'for some', we usually mean to deal only with things that exist. Rather, we often contextually deal only with some of the things that exist. Or rather, we often deal only with some of the things that exist now (English quantifiers are typically existentially loaded, restricted and presentist). Default restrictions, though, can be abandoned: we say that some orcs from *The Lord of The Rings* look really ugly, or that some of the cities described by Kafka are purely imaginary. Few would consider us committed to the real existence of these things.

3 Candidate non-existents

Suppose Meinongian quantification makes sense, and that we can truthfully claim that there are non-existent objects. In which kinds and shapes do they come forth? The most straightforward candidates to non-existence usually presented by Meinongians are *fictional objects*: things mentioned and described in tales, novels, fantasy stories, operas, and so on – Sherlock Holmes, Gandalf, Jessica Rabbit, Gregor Samsa, Phlebas the Phoenician and Alice in Wonderland (these will have a chapter devoted to them, in the third part of our book).

Other candidates for non-existence are provided by *possibilia*: the merely possible objects we met, briefly, while talking of identity criteria in our Chapter 3 on the standard view. Wittgenstein died childless, but he could have had a daughter. Michelangelo could have shaped the marble out of which the David was made into an eight-legged dog, but he didn't. So we have Wittgenstein's merely possible daughter and Michelangelo's merely possible eight-legged sculpture: they only exist in unrealized situations or circumstances, not in reality. This makes them look very much like non-existents. Just as to be possibly but not actually red is not to be red, so to be possibly but not actually existent is not to be existent.

Yet other candidates for non-existence are things that *currently* lack existence. We have reasons to believe that Thomas Jefferson does not exist anymore (give and take certain beliefs on the immortality of the soul). However, we can still successfully refer to him today, using his name (we just did), or via definite descriptions like 'the third president of the United States'. Despite his current lack of existence, Jefferson can still bear lots of properties: he has, today, the feature of having been US president, the one of being self-identical (he is, after all, Thomas Jefferson), and the one of being still remembered by many patriots.

More controversially, we seem to be able to refer to, and make true claims on, future currently non-existent objects. Tomorrow's dawn was mentioned above. We can also speak of the first new-born of the twenty-second century (see Kaplan 1973). Or, closer to home, take some stuff we have here: wooden planks, nails, all that's needed to build an Ikea bookshelf. We can, of course, refer to the bookshelf (we just did), and pin a name on it – say, 'Georgina' – despite its current non-existence. Georgina will start to exist, say, tomorrow, when we are done assembling it. What if we never manage to build Georgina – either tomorrow or later – for whatever reason? Then rather than being a future object, it looks like Georgina is to remain an unrealized *possibile*. So much the better for our view, Meinongians may say: here's further evidence that we can refer to non-existent *possibilia*.

We thus have different kinds of things making for candidate non-existents. The key claim of Meinongianism, that some things are non-existent, commits Meinongians to the non-existence of none of these specifically. A Meinongian may accept that (purely) fictional objects like Sherlock Holmes are non-existent, for instance, but reject that *past* existents like Jefferson, Dante or Virgil should be seriously taken as non-existent objects at the present time. This triggers a common distinction in the metaphysics of time: the one between *eternalism* and *presentism*. Roughly: according to presentists, merely past and merely future objects not currently existing simply do not exist. For an ontologist who sticks to the standard-Quinean view of existence, of course, this means: there just are no such things *now* – and for presentists, there's no time like now: what really exists is what presently exists. According to eternalists, certainly merely past and, perhaps, also merely future objects exist and are as real as currently existing objects. Eternalism usually comes with a strong analogy between space and time: just as to exist and to be spatially located in Aberdeen entails to exist, so to exist and to be temporally located in the seventeenth century entails to exist. Time is, in a sense, as real as space, not just the content of our imagination or memory (for an introduction to the metaphysics of time, see Markosian 2008).

4 What is existence, then?

Anyone claiming that some things are non-existent is committed to an answer to the question making for the title of this section. If metaontology is (partly) about the meaning of being or existence, then the Meinongians' view is, as should be clear by now, metaontologically strongly opposed to the standard one: they disagree with Quineans on the very content of the notion of being or existence. By denying the Quinean claim that the notion of existence is captured by the quantifier, Meinongians also take a stance against a venerable tradition: against Kant, Frege, Russell and many others, they reject the slogan 'Existence is not a (real) predicate.' However, supporters of the mainstream view of existence can have their own existence predicate too. They can swiftly define it via their (perforce existentially loaded) quantifier: $E!x =_{df} \exists y(y = x)$. To exist is to be (identical with) something. In fact, this characterization poked its nose both in our exposition of Quine's Thesis Two in Chapter 2, and in the *contradictio in terminis* imputed to Meinong above. Such a predicate does not cut any ice, in the following sense: since everything is (identical with) something, everything exists. But the definition gives to Quineans a straightforward reply to the question making for the title of this section: to exist, or to be, is to be the value of a (bound) variable, of a variable of quantification.

Meinongians cannot go down this path. Existence does cut a lot of ice for them: it is not a trivial feature possessed by anything whatsoever, but a real, discriminating property splitting the world (or, the world at a time) into things having it and things lacking it. As we saw two sections ago, Meinongians define the existentially loaded quantifier using the existence predicate. They cannot in turn define the existence predicate using the existentially loaded quantifier. Their reply to that question is going to be more convoluted.

An initial option consists in claiming that existence has to do with the having of causal features – with taking part in causal relations, or at least, with the disposition towards taking part in them (this may or may not entail having a physical, spatio-temporal location, depending on one's favourite account of causation). As Alexander's motto has it: 'To be is to have causal powers' (Alexander 1920: 8). But the idea can be found already in Plato:

> Whatever has a native power, whether of affecting anything else, or of being affected in ever so slight a degree by the most insignificant agents, even on one solitary occasion, is a real being. In short, I offer it as the definition of *beings* that they are *potency*, and nothing else. (*Sophist* 247d-e)

This looks more like a gloss to existence than like a philosophical analysis or reduction of the concept: it is not the specification of a necessary and sufficient condition *C*, such that an object exists if and only if it satisfies *C*. Peter Geach similarly called 'actuality-sense' of existence the conception of it as a nontrivial property of individuals. After glossing it in ways similar to Plato, he suggested that a theorist is not to blame for leaving it undefined, for one just cannot do better:

> A provisional explanation of actuality may be given thus: *x* is actual if and only if either *x* acts, or undergoes change, or both; and here I count as 'acting' both the inner activities of mind, like thinking and planning, and the initiation of changes in things. ... I do not think this explanation or criterion can be developed into a definition. For it is not yet clear what counts as a thing's undergoing a change; when Plato counts being thought of as a change undergone by the object of thought, most of us will feel that he is playing a trick, whether or not he also deceived himself. (Geach 1968: 7–8)

Such a gloss agrees with some intuitions about what exists and what does not. Laymen can take as non-existent such things as Pegasus, Santa Claus, a golden mountain, Thomas Jefferson or one hundred imaginary dollars. These all seem to share the following feature: we cannot kiss Santa but we can kiss Brad Pitt; we can give to Varenne some fodder, but we cannot do it with Pegasus; we can stumble upon Obama, but we cannot stumble upon Jefferson; we can climb the Everest, but no golden mountain; with one hundred existing dollars we can go shopping, pay and get our change; nothing of the sort could be done with one hundred merely imaginary dollars. Existence does seem to make a difference: we cannot causally interact with things lacking it.

This triggers the following objection. People take as existent, not only concrete things like mountains and people, but also things we would label as abstract. People don't just claim that Obama exists, or that horses exist, but also that integers exist. Mathematicians speak about existence or existence-and-uniqueness proofs; they talk about the existence of functions such that..., etc. But integers and functions cannot have causal powers, not to speak about their being physically located. An account of existence in terms of causation is either partial or refuted by how such people as mathematicians talk.

Meinongianism has been developed in different ways to take this objection into account. One option is to introduce two modes of existence, one for *abstracta* and one for *concreta*. It was probably Meinong's own view, although this may not be terminologically accurate as a way to phrase his ontology. He spoke about *real* and *ideal* objects, the latter including numbers and geometrical figures. This may be approximately mapped to the current distinction between concrete and abstract things. For Meinong, there are two modes of being: existence properly so called (*Existenz*) and subsistence (*Bestand*). Things like Jefferson, Holmes or Obama may (concretely) exist or not, whereas things like sets and functions may (exist in the sense of) subsist or not. Existence for *concreta* is something like the having of causal powers and/or physical location. Existence-as-subsistence is something like consistency, or coherence of the relevant notion. In this sense, mathematicians claim that the set of natural numbers and the operation of division by seven exist, whereas the paradoxical set of all non-self-membered sets at the core of Russell's set-theoretic paradox, or division by zero, do not exist. Taking existence as the having of causal powers (and/or physical location), then, makes for an incomplete gloss: that is to *concretely* exist.

Is *being*'s being not univocal a theoretical minus? It certainly is a disadvantage in terms of theoretical simplicity. It cannot be a minus, though, in the sense of having to deal with van Inwagen's argument for the univocity of being that we met in Chapter 3. If a Quinean wants to stick to Aristotle and Ryle's view that being is not univocal, then she must rebut the van Inwagen argument. We already saw that ontological pluralists like Turner and McDaniel propose rebuttals. But the argument simply does not concern such non-Quinean conceptions of existence as the Meinongian's. If existence statements are just like number statements, and number words are univocal, 'exists' may be univocal, too, if van Inwagen is right. Then again, existence just has nothing to do with quantifying and numbering for Meinongians: we can count things that do not exist (how many are the Fantastic Four? Aren't they as many as the Fab Four?). Number words may be univocal, but this does not affect the Meinongian existences.

Another option for the Meinongian is to stick to the idea that being-or-existence *is* univocal. One then claims that, just like Santa or Holmes, abstract objects do not exist and have no mode of being-or-existence whatsoever. The gloss of existence as the having of causal powers (and/or physical location) is now stoutly taken as exhaustive: abstract objects just are non-existents.

This form of Meinongianism has been developed, under the label of *noneism*, especially by Routley 1980 and Priest 2005. Here a pro of the theory is uniformity or theoretical simplicity. Univocal Meinongianism *à la* Routley-Priest supplies a simple and uniform ontological outlook. Only some concrete objects actually exist: those with causal powers, or rather (in Routley's version), those with causal powers *now*. All the rest – fictional objects, past and future objects, mere *possibilia* and abstract objects of any kind – just does not exist.

One drawback of the position that it takes us back to linguistic revisionism: we need to paraphrase the mathematician's existentially loaded talk. Meinongianism was initially advertised as having the advantage of taking at face value ordinary language statements the Quinean had to paraphrase away. Now the noneist or univocist Meinongian has to explain away talk of existence-and-uniqueness proofs, etc. Is she thereby going to waste one presumed theoretical advantage of taking existence as a genuine property of individuals, namely rigorous descriptive ontology's adherence to ordinary talk and the intuitions that come with it?

Another issue for the univocist Meinongian or noneist is how to recapture the intuitive distinction between *abstracta* and *concreta*. Holmes and division by seven are things of quite different kinds. They are alike in being non-existent though. How do they differ? (For a sophisticated reply, see Priest 2005: Ch. 7).

Another popular objection, due to Lewis 1990, has it that Meinongianism collapses under translation into a prodigal form of (metaontologically Quinean) realism. Take a Meinongian who accepts objects of kind *F* in her ontology, in the sense that she allows them to be included in her domain of quantification. To a Quinean she may look very similar to a realist on *F*s meaning the one who claims that such things exist (in the *Quinean* sense) and accepts them in her ontology. Speaking Quinean, quantification counts as existentially loaded. On the other hand, a Meinongian asserting that an object exists in *her* sense, that is it has causal powers and/or physical address, will appear to a Quinean very similar to one who asserts that that thing is *concrete* (and, of course, exists). When the Quinean metaontologist translates Meinongian talk back into her own vocabulary, '*x* exists' turns into '*x* is concrete', and '*x* is an object' turns into '*x* exists'. So the Meinongian theorist is just one who phrases ontological views in a weird language.

One common reply by Meinongians is that there being a translation schema by itself is neither here nor there. To privilege one direction over the other is question-begging, pending independent arguments in favour of either. It might be said that, more than Meinongianism being reducible to realism (in the aforementioned sense), it is realism that is reducible to Meinongianism (Meinongians often rebut the charge of talking weird by stressing that they, not the Quineans, are those who speak ordinary people's English: see Berto 2012: Ch. 9). Furthermore, according to Priest 2005: 153–4, that Lewisian translation schema is not even good, as it fails to capture various versions of the Meinongian view.

5 The principle of comprehension and its troubles

Any Meinongian theory has to provide some 'principle of comprehension' for its objects. By this we mean a principle explaining what (non-existent) objects there are, and which properties they can bear. In its naïve formulation (of which, to be sure, it is unclear whether it was ever accepted by Meinong himself), Meinongianism endorses what Terence Parsons 1980 called an 'Unrestricted Comprehension Principle' for objects. This can be formulated along the following lines:

(UCP) For any condition Ax with free variable x, some object satisfies Ax.

By 'condition *Ax*' we understand any condition on properties: any formula with (as many occurrences as we want of) a variable not bound by a quantifier, which can be taken as expressing a property, or a bunch of features. Take such features as *x is a detective, x lives in Victorian London at 221b Baker Street, x is Moriarty's arch-enemy, x has amazing powers of observation and deduction, x always wears a deerstalker...* , etc. If *Ax* stands for the conjunction of the relevant predicates, then according to the (UCP) an object is characterized by *Ax*. Call it 'Sherlock Holmes', *h*. Then Holmes really has the relevant properties, *Ah*.

The twofold idea behind the naïve Principle is the following: (a) whatever properties we take into account, they characterize some object; (b) the object in some sense really has the properties it is characterized as having. Otherwise – so the intuition goes – how could we know what we are thinking and talking about when we refer to it? We can in principle causally interact with ordinary, concrete, existent objects, thus being perceptually acquainted with many of their features. But when the thing does not exist, we need something like a Comprehension Principle.

The combination of (a) and (b), however, is fatal to the theory. Russell raised two crucial objections to naïve Meinongianism, in *On Denoting* and in two reviews of works by Meinong and his students. The first one we can call the Objection from Inconsistency. Since *Ax* can stand for any condition on properties, we can take inconsistent conditions: if *Ax* = '*x* is a square and *x* is not a square', then by the (UCP) some object actually has this feature. Call it Non-square. Then Non-square is and is not a square. But this violates the Law of Non-Contradiction – a principle of minimal logic.

Russell's second objection can be called the Objection from Triviality. It aims to show that a Meinongian theory including the (UCP) allows one to prove the existence of anything whatsoever. The (UCP) has no restriction on the conditions, or packages of properties, which can deliver objects. In particular, existence for the Meinongian is, as we know, an ordinary property of things. It can, therefore, be embedded in characterizing conditions. So let *Ax* = '*x* is made of gold and *x* is a mountain and *x* exists'. The (UCP) allows *a priori* an object actually having the features of being a golden mountain and existing; so there actually exists a golden mountain. This will not do. Not only, as far as we know, there exists no golden mountains; but it is above all preposterous that we can make one exist *a priori* (as Kant remarked: if an existence predicate could legitimately enter into definitions or characterizations, we could define things into existence).

Worse, as pointed out by Graham Priest 2005: 83, via the (UCP) one can prove not only the existence of anything, but anything whatsoever. If *Ax* is '*x* = *x* and *B*', with *B* holding place for any sentence, then by the (UCP), for some object, say *b*, it is actually true that *b* = *b* and *B*, from which *B* follows by Conjunction Elimination, another rule of minimal logic allowing us to infer either conjunct from a conjunction. But *B* was arbitrary. So Naïve Meinongianism is trivial in the strict logical sense: it proves anything. One reason why the Meinongian theories currently on the market are often named with the prefix, 'neo-', is that neo-Meinongians try to improve on naïve Meinongianism's disaster.

6 Neo-Meinongianisms of various kinds

All the neo-Meinongian theories impose some restriction or qualification to the (UCP). The idea is to have a modified comprehension principle, strong enough to deliver as many objects as possible without lapsing into inconsistency or triviality. Different theories diverge on how the restriction is to be phrased. We saw that the combination of features (a) and (b) mentioned above ((a) *any* property, or bunch thereof, characterizes an object, which (b) *really* has the property, or bunch thereof) makes the (UCP) go down in flames. Some neo-Meinongians prefer to impose a limitation on point (a), while some others favour intervening on point (b).

A first family of neo-Meinongian theories limits the range of properties that can figure in characterizing conditions. So-called *nuclear Meinongianism* (Parsons 1980; Routley 1980; Jacquette 1996) distinguishes between two families of properties, the *nuclear* and *extranuclear* ones. Only nuclear properties can constitute the *Sosein* of objects. The Nuclear Comprehension Principle goes as follows:

(NCP) For any nuclear condition Ax with free variable x, some object satisfies Ax.

A 'nuclear condition' is one that embeds only predicates standing for nuclear properties. It is crucial to the approach that existence be extranuclear. Now we cannot prove *a priori* the existence of golden mountains, for 'x is made of gold and x is a mountain and x exists' is not a nuclear condition. Also, as the negations of nuclear properties generally are not themselves nuclear, 'x is a square and x is not a square' is also not nuclear and fails to deliver an object.

Each neo-Meinongian theory also comes with its own identity criterion for objects. The aim of the criterion, in each case, is to reply to qualms on mere *possibilia*, non-existent objects, and other 'creatures of darkness' like possible fat and bald men in doorways, which, as you will recall from Chapter 3, according to Quine should not be included in a safe and sane ontological catalogue. Each theory resorts to its own basic theoretical notion in the formulation of its identity criterion. In the case of nuclear Meinongianism, the criterion states: x and y are the same object if and only if they exemplify the same *nuclear* properties. Together with the (NCP), this guarantees that each package of nuclear properties characterizes precisely one object.

The most serious challenge for the nuclear approach is to provide a principled criterion to tell which properties are nuclear and which are extranuclear. The distinction is usually taken as primitive by nuclear Meinongians, and we only get lists of examples of properties, or of the corresponding predicates. The following are from Parsons 1980: 22–3: 'is blue', 'is tall', 'kicked Socrates', 'was kicked by Socrates', 'kicked somebody', 'is golden' and 'is a mountain'. They are predicates standing for sample nuclear properties. We also get further examples of four kinds of extranuclear predicates there: *Ontological:* 'exists', 'is mythical', 'is fictional'; *Modal:* 'is possible', 'is impossible'; *Intentional:* 'is thought about by Meinong', 'is worshipped by someone'; *Technical*: 'is complete' and 'is consistent'. Now this makes the distinction look a bit *ad hoc*: envisaged just in order to solve the problems of naïve Meinongianism.

A second family of neo-Meinongian theories intervenes, not on point (a) above – the properties admitted to comprehension – but on point (b) – the way in which objects can have them. In this neo-Meinongianism of the second kind a distinction is made, we may say, not between two kinds of predicates, but between two kinds of predication. A brilliant pupil of Meinong, Ernst Mally, had the idea of postulating two ways in which an object can relate to its properties: an ordinary one and another, introduced *ex novo*. In the jargon of Ed Zalta 1983, 1988, whose theory is the best developed version of this approach, when we claim that *x is F*, we can mean that *x* exemplifies *F* (this corresponds to the usual sense of the copula), or we can mean that *x encodes F*. The Meinongian objects of Zalta's theory are non-existents that encode properties, that is, that are somehow determined by them, but without exemplifying them in the ordinary sense. Since the theory postulates an ambiguity in the copula 'is' of ordinary language, it has been labelled as 'dual copula' Meinongianism.

The distinction between exemplification and encoding is taken as primitive. Ordinary, concrete, existent objects exemplify properties but encode none. Any object encoding some property or other is labelled by Zalta as *abstract*, meaning that it is neither a mental representation nor a spatiotemporally located thing. Abstract objects encoding properties do not exist (literally: they exemplify the property of being non-existent). And we have a Dual Copula Comprehension Principle:

(DCCP) For any condition *Ax* with free variable *x*, some abstract object encodes *Ax*.

The dual copula theory has its identity criterion to reply to Quinean worries on identity conditions. Again, the basic notion of the theory is embedded in it: *x* and *y* are the same (abstract) object if and only if they encode exactly the same properties. Taken together, (DCCP) and the identity criterion guarantee that to each bunch of properties corresponds a unique abstract object encoding precisely them.

The theory nicely deals with the two Russellian objections. As for the Objection from Inconsistency: the Non-square delivered by *Ax* = '*x* is a square and *x* is not a square' now is, at most, an abstract non-existent that only *encodes* inconsistent properties. That object *is* not a square that is not a square, in the sense of the usual copula 'is'. One can call 'impossible' the abstract objects which encode packages of properties that cannot be all co-exemplified, that is such that in no possible circumstance does some object exemplify them all. But this does not mean that such non-existents exemplify these inconsistent packs, thereby violating the Law of Non-Contradiction.

The problem due to the naïve Comprehension Principle's allowing to prove the existence of anything is solved analogously, by relying on the fact that non-existent objects can encode properties they fail to exemplify. According to the dual copula view, the properties of existing, being a mountain and being made of gold, determine an abstract object that does not exemplify them. The existent golden mountain is the object encoding the properties of being a mountain, being made of gold and existing. But the existent golden mountain does not exemplify those properties – it *is* not a mountain, made of gold, or existent, in the usual sense of 'is'. The (DCCP), then, does not entail the real world existence of golden mountains.

Perhaps the main problem with dual copula neo-Meinongianism is the basic insight of the theory: the double copula itself. How come no one has ever noticed a basic ambiguity of the predicative copula, making for a difference between 'is' ascribing a property to something that exemplifies it, and 'is' ascribing a property to something that encodes it? This looks like an *ad hoc* move: maybe the only aim Mally had in postulating such an ambiguity was that of having non-existents related somehow to properties without exemplifying them, in order to circumvent the inconsistencies of naïve Meinongianism. As Saul Kripke once said, one had better not postulate ambiguities just in order to avoid troubles, for any trouble can avoided that way.

A third kind of neo-Meinongian theory can be found in the aforementioned Priest 2005, and Berto 2012 texts. The view is relatively new and relies on a different conception of characterization as involving reference to other possible worlds (and even to *im*possible worlds!) – hence the name *modal Meinongianism* for it (see Berto 2011). We will not deal with the details of this third neo-Meinongian brand here, save for saying that, according to its supporters, it allows to extend characterization to properties of any kind without resorting to any form of non-standard predication.

Further Reading

Part II of Berto 2012 is an introduction to Meinongianism and the various kinds of neo-Meinongian theories, on which this chapter draws. Reicher 2010 is another nice introduction to various theories of non-existent objects. Grossmann 1974 is a classic guide to Meinong's thought, on which see also Lambert 1983. Chapter 3 of Sainsbury 2010 is a critical assessment of Meinongian accounts of fictional objects.

8

The Grounding Approach

Chapter Outline

In this chapter we introduce the approach of *grounding* theorists: a recent, non-standard metaontological view according to which the Quinean understanding of ontological questions as quantificational questions limits the explanatory power of ontological theories. In Section 1, we motivate intuitively the grounding theorist's key idea that ontology should not look just at what there is, but rather at what is *fundamental:* at what underpins and explains the existence of what, and at the things, if there are any, that underpin and explain the existence of anything else. Section 2 introduces the notion of *ground*, used in this approach to account for the idea of ontological fundamentality, and investigates its plausible formal properties. Section 3 examines what happens to the methodology of ontology if we accept the grounding view, and Section 4 looks at some open issues.

1 The fundamental question of ontology

Quine's metaontological Thesis One from Chapter 2 can be taken as the claim that the fundamental ontological question is: 'What is there?'. One may think that objecting to this would make little sense. If Quine wants to call 'ontology' the attempt to reply to the question of what there is, why should we have a problem with that? Nevertheless, *grounding theorists* think that Quine's approach to ontological inquiry is too restrictive. They don't think that one just cannot understand ontological debates in Quinean terms; but they object that, so interpreted, ontological debates are not as interesting as they could be. To conceive ontology in the mainstream way is to make it a bad service. According to grounding theorists, there is an alternative view of ontological debates, which makes of ontology a more stimulating project.

Let us start by helping ourselves with a metaphor. We are familiar with the notion of *status symbol*. A status symbol marks somebody's position in some social hierarchy: it identifies 'people who are someone'. It is intrinsic to the idea of status symbol that not everyone can be someone. If everybody were somebody, there would be no point in distinguishing between people who are someone and people who are not. When we say that Bill Gates is somebody, we don't mean to state the logical triviality that he is identical with someone, namely himself. Rather, we are stressing that he is somebody important, somebody who counts or matters.

For grounding theorists, the most interesting ontological question is not about what there is, but about what is more fundamental, or also, about what is *absolutely* fundamental – if anything is. Think about our Chapter 3 discussion of Aristotle, a philosopher whose ontology explicitly inspires some grounding theorists, Schaffer 2009, for example. Recall that, for Aristotle, being is spoken of in many ways, but not all ways are on a par. Some kinds of entities are more important than others. In particular, substances make for the fundamental ontological kind, that on which any other kind depends: colours, weights, relations, locations, etc., depend on there being substances which are coloured, have weights, are related, located, etc. Also, because of their ontological fundamentality, substances have explanatory or conceptual primacy in some sense: we need to better understand substances in order to better understand further ways of being. Grounding theorists may not agree with Aristotle on taking (whatever he meant by) substance as the fundamental kind, but they take fundamentality as the target of ontology and as having explanatory value. By calling something fundamental we want to stress its ontological status symbol: its place in the ontological hierarchy. As ontologists we want to know, given entities of some kind, whether they are grounded in more fundamental entities, to which we should resort while in the business of understanding and explaining the former. We also want to know if there are absolutely fundamental entities which, in a way similar to Aristotelian substances, ground and explain everything else without being themselves grounded in anything else – and if so, what are they. If there are such things, they shall be at the bottom of reality's structure. They shall be in the 'who's who' of ontology.

2 The features of grounding

The notion of grounding has been recently studied by various ontologists as a way to capture the idea of fundamentality or explanatory priority (a clear and concise introduction to grounding theories is Clark and Liggins 2012, on which we rely in the following). Schaffer 2009 and Rosen 2010 introduce the concept via examples such as these:

1 The brittleness of the cup results from the way its constituent atoms are arranged.
2 The truth-value of a proposition is determined by how the world is.
3 Actions have their moral properties in virtue of their non-moral properties.
4 Non-empty sets depend for their existence on their members.
5 A mental state is grounded in the brain state which realizes it.

Pointing at an instance of grounding is supposed to illuminate us on what is grounded: the grounded entity (a truth-value, a moral or physical property, a set, etc.) is somehow explained by what grounds it (an atomic structure, a property of a different kind, etc.). It is commonly agreed that grounding should be a relation of non-causal ontological underpinning: the grounding claims above are not very plausible if understood as expressing causal dependence. So the kind of explanation afforded by grounding is not causal explanation. Also, grounding does not seem to be a merely modal or intensional notion like *necessarily*, unrestrictedly understood as meaning something like 'In all possible situations or circumstances' (we will speak again of necessity, intensional notions, and possible circumstances in the third part of this book, mainly in the chapter on possible worlds). One compelling example, generalized in (4), is due to Kit Fine: Socrates' singleton, that is, {Socrates} – the set whose only member or element is Socrates – is arguably grounded in Socrates: we point at Socrates in order to explain the existence of {Socrates}. But it seems to be a necessary truth that Socrates exists if and only if {Socrates} does. Given such modal inseparability, the modal notion of necessity cannot capture the kind of ontological and explanatory dependence we aim at.

One popular approach takes grounding as what is usually called a *multigrade* relation: a relation between one grounded entity, x, and one, or two, or …, or n entities grounding x – say: $y_1, \dots, y_n$ (an alternative approach, pursued by Kit Fine, Fabrice Correia and others, takes grounding as a non-truth-functional operation, linguistically expressed by something like 'because' or 'in virtue of', which supposedly captures the explanatory but non-causal nature of the notion; we will not deal with this version of grounding here).

This immediately raises a number of questions. One is: what are the formal properties of such a relation? The majority view is that grounding should be, to begin with, irreflexive: nothing grounds itself; if you are grounded, you are grounded in something other than yourself. Also, grounding should be asymmetric: if x is grounded in y, y cannot be grounded in x in its turn. Also, the relation should be transitive: if x is grounded in y and y is grounded in z, then x is grounded in z. These features capture the intuitive idea that to be grounded is to exist in virtue of something else, which is, in some sense, more fundamental than you. Your ground may be further grounded in something else, which, being even more fundamental, grounds you too. More complex features sometimes ascribed to grounding include *non-monotonicity*. This means, roughly, that it can be the case that x is grounded in y, without being grounded in y plus something else – an additional z: Socrates' singleton is grounded in Socrates, but not in Socrates and Plato (that's what the set {Socrates, Plato} is grounded in).

An additional question is, which kinds of entities can stand in grounding relations? Some philosophers, like Rosen 2010, believe grounding to be a relation between facts (if so, then grounding needs an account of the metaphysics of *facts*). Other authors, like Schaffer 2009, have a more pluralistic approach in which different kinds of things can ground and be grounded, e.g., abstract objects like {Socrates} can be grounded in concrete objects like Socrates.

Yet another question, perhaps the ontologically most interesting one, is whether all grounding chains must sooner or later come to an end. If this is so, and if grounding accounts for fundamentality and/or explanatory priority, then not only are some things more fundamental than others, but some things are just absolutely fundamental and *ungrounded*, or such that pointing at them can they provide ultimate explanations. They don't depend on anything, while everything else depends on them. They make for the basic layer of reality: that without which, as Aristotle claimed of substances, nothing would exist.

While the picture looks attractively Aristotelian, discussions such as that in Schaffer 2003 should lead us to avoid taking for granted that grounding chains must come to an end, that is there is something like a fundamental layer. Hence our provisos above: for grounding theorists, ontology should investigate what is fundamental – *if* anything is; but it may come to establish that, while some things ground others and are, in this sense, more fundamental or such that they have explanatory priority, there is no ultimate grounding level in the world. Let us now look at how this grounding picture impacts on the methodology of ontology.

3 The metaontology of grounding

For a grounding theorist ontology ought to deal, more than with what there is, with 'what grounds what' (to quote Schaffer 2009). Understood in Quine's way, that is as quantificational debates, ontological disputes are either too easy to solve or of little explanatory value or both. Are there properties? Of course there are: Matteo and Francesco share the property of having co-authored a companion to ontology; therefore, there is a property that Matteo and Francesco share; therefore, there are properties. Are there numbers? Well, given that seven is a number, there are numbers, e.g., seven. It is as simple as that. Grounding theorists, however, disagree for example with neo-Carnapians insofar as they don't think that ontological questions are perforce either trivial or meaningless. They may be of modest explanatory value when understood the Quinean way. They can be genuinely interesting, though, once we move beyond quantificational questions. When we ask, as grounding ontologists, whether there *really* are numbers, we are not asking if there is at least one number (there are infinitely many!). We want to know to what extent they are part of reality's fundamental structure, to what extent we may or should resort to other entities in order to understand and explain their existence. This can now be cashed in terms of grounding: are numbers grounded in other stuff (and, if so, what stuff), or are they not?

Various other debates in metaphysics and ontology can be rephrased in terms of the metaontology of grounding. For instance, suppose we are atomists: we believe that reality's fundamental layer is made of atoms spinning in the void. This should not be construed as the claim that there is nothing else but atoms in the universe: no bananas, no tables, no human beings, no numbers, etc. There are, of course, tables; but they are ultimately grounded in something else, namely atoms. Interesting properties of tables can also be grounded in properties of atoms, for instance, their spatial disposition, the kinds of atoms they are composed of, etc.

For grounding theorists, therefore, there's a change with respect to the standard Quinean picture in what it means to be ontologically profligate, rather than restrained. One cannot be blamed for being ontologically profligate when it's about answers to questions on what there is. What matters when we wonder whether an ontologist is really being profligate is the basis (or the more basic), the fundamental (or more fundamental) entities: the ones that explain the existence of what is grounded in them. One can admit that there are lots of (kinds of) entities, and still be restrained, if one grounds them in a sparse basis of more fundamental stuff.

Perhaps the author who has most thoroughly explored what happens to the methodology of ontology in this framework is Kit Fine 2001, 2009. In Fine's picture, grounding theorists can make a distinction between a *thin* and a *thick* ontological commitment. We can, of course, keep claiming that we have 'ontological commitment' to whatever we quantify over. But insofar as what we quantify over is grounded, or (provided there is an ultimate level) not an ultimate constituent of reality, such commitment is cheap enough. It is only when we quantify over the important, grounding or basic stuff that our commitment is ontologically thick, or serious. The latter stuff makes for a sub-collection of the collection of all there is (in the thin sense).

As a consequence, thick ontological commitment is better expressed by a restrictor of (thin) quantification to fundamental entities. Fine proposes to express the restriction via a reality predicate, with 'is real' standing for the feature of being a genuine, fundamental or irreducible constituent of the world (Fine 2009: 171–2 also introduces a reality *operator* on sentences, to be read as 'It is constitutive of reality that'; we will not get into the details of this).

This notion of reality, according to Fine, should not be defined; in particular, it should not be reduced to the quantifier, as it happens with existence in the Quinean conception. It should be taken, instead, as primitive. This does not detract from its utility if we have, as Fine maintains, an intuitive working grasp of the concept of reality.

In this framework, we have something like the following division of labour between philosophers, specifically ontologists on the one hand, and scientists on the other. It is the job of mathematicians, not ontologists, to tell us whether there are numbers or functions of such-and-such kind; and it is the job of physicists to tell us whether there are quarks with such-and-such colours. The ontologist's task is to tell us which among the things we quantify over (in the thin sense), in science and mathematics as well as in ordinary talk, are grounded in other things, and which are the real or fundamental entities, that is those which ground and explain everything else – if there are any. Scientists tell us what exists, ontologists tell us in virtue of what it exists.

4 The problems of grounding

Grounding theories make for a promising alternative to mainstream Quinean metaontology. They have already found their critics, though. We quickly list here a couple of recent objections. One is to the effect that the notion of grounding is very obscure. The proponents of grounding usually refrain from defining it (they may or may not go for the explicit claim that it's primitive and intuitive, as Fine does with his notion of reality). Grounding is usually characterized in either or both of the two ways we looked at above: (a) by listing its intuitive formal features, and (b) by giving examples.

But as for (a), critics object, such merely formal features may be too coarse-grained to achieve individuation for a relation. Even if we agree on the intuitive formal features of grounding listed above, there are just too many relations out there which are irreflexive, asymmetric, transitive and non-monotonic: when a relation is characterized just thus, it's not clear that we have *grounding*, rather than something else.

As for (b), philosophers like Hofweber 2009 argue that there isn't much ontological work for grounding by stressing that all the examples usually proposed by grounding theorists are in fact examples of a bunch of disparate relations, none of which deserves to be called 'grounding' – unless we just mean by this a heavily disjunctive, gerrymandered notion. One may say, for instance, that a conjunction is grounded in its conjuncts taken together; but this just means that it is logically entailed by them taken together. Or, one may say that density is grounded in mass and volume, but this just means that the concept of density can be characterized or defined via those of mass and volume. Such a divide-and-conquer strategy may, however, be countered by seemingly irreducible grounding claims, and again, the Finean example of the dependence of {Socrates} on Socrates appears to be hardly reducible to other familiar relations.

Further Reading

Clark and Liggins 2012 is a useful survey of recent work on grounding, on which we relied in this chapter. A collection of cutting-edge papers on the topic is Correia and Schnieder 2012. For applications of the grounding approach to ontology, see Schaffer 2009 and Fine 2009. For scepticism about grounding, see Hofweber 2009; Daly 2012 and Wilson (forthcoming).

Part III

Ontology

9

Abstract Objects I: Numbers & Co.

Chapter Outline

The topic of this and the following chapter is the one of *abstract objects*. Examples include mathematical entities like the number seventeen, or Fermat's last theorem, but also things like the game of chess. Abstract objects seem to be very different from entities like a chair or a proton, even though it can be hard to define what makes an object abstract rather than concrete – as we are going to see in Section 1. Still, there is room for ontological debates about paradigmatic cases of abstract objects. We can ask whether mathematical objects like numbers, sets, functions or graphs, really exist. *Platonists* say yes, while *nominalists* say no. In Sections 2 to 5 we focus on the platonism vs. nominalism debate in the philosophy of mathematics: we discuss why someone may be attracted by either position (Sections 2–3), and how one could defend either from classical objections (Sections 4–5). Finally, in Section 6 we draw some general methodological morals from the platonism vs. nominalism debate.

1 Abstract vs. concrete entities

Platonism is the doctrine that there are abstract objects. Nominalism is the doctrine that there are no abstract objects (Field 1980). But what exactly is an abstract object? We could also ask what makes a concrete object concrete, given that being abstract means not being concrete and vice versa. As we already mentioned in the first part of our book, there seems to be general agreement on abstractness and concreteness being exclusive, exhaustive and, in some sense, intrinsic features of things. Also, it is easy to give examples of objects from both categories: puddings, donkeys and protons should fall on the concrete side of reality, whereas numbers, sets, and moral values should fall on the abstract one.

Trying to characterize a concept by just citing examples may be unsatisfactory. Lewis (1986: Ch. 1 (followed by Rosen 2012)), describes various 'ways' to characterize the abstract/concrete distinction. The most popular one is probably what Lewis calls the 'way of negation'. Abstract objects are denied features that (paradigmatic) concrete objects possess, but do not themselves get a positive characterization: to be an abstract object is to lack a spatiotemporal address and to have no causal powers, whereas a concrete object should enjoy these features. Francesco's cell phone is concrete: throughout its existence, it always has a unique location in space (it even has an app keeping track of this). It has a date of birth and will plausibly have one of extinction. It has a mass, an electric charge and many other features that confer causal powers upon it. A mobile phone can make things happen: it can cause you harm by hitting you, and it can generate heat and some kind of electromagnetic field. Things can be done to it, for example, you can break it. More importantly: you can *know* a lot about it by looking at it or touching it. Numbers, sets, functions and other mathematical objects are denied all these features. Nobody has ever seen or touched the number 17, and trying to assign it a date of birth or an address sounds weird.

Plausible as it seems, the way of negation is not without problems. One is that abstract objects seem to sometimes have causal powers (see again Rosen 2012). A mainstream view about causation is that causal relations hold first of all between events, that is, things that happen (we will speak of events in our final chapter), and not between objects. It's one's hitting the ball with a tennis racket that causes the ball's hitting of your face, which in turn causes your feeling of pain. One may say that the ball caused your pain in a derivative sense: it is one of the objects that compose or are somehow part of the event of one's hitting *the ball* (along with the person who hits, her racket and others things yet). If events are the primary terms of causal relations, then the only sense in which an object can be the cause of something is by being part of an event that causes something.

Now, consider the event of your passing the first mathematics exam in your life. Your having understood Pythagoras' theorem, say, is one of the causes of your passing the exam. Arguably Pythagoras' theorem is one of the objects that are part of the event of your understanding Pythagoras' theorem. This just means that Pythagoras' theorem has causal powers after all, at least in a derivative sense.

Or consider your weighing 80 kilos. This seems to be one of the causes of your having troubles in running up a hill. But your weighing 80 kilos can be understood as your bearing the having-mass-in-kilos relation with the number 80. Doesn't this show that the number 80, contributing to one of the causes of your having trouble in running uphill, has causal powers after all?

Also the claim that abstract objects lack spatiotemporal address can be disputed. Consider the set of all the copies of our book (this is often called an impure abstract object: a set whose members are concrete objects). Why shouldn't this set have a location? Lewis 1986 himself proposed that a set like this may be located exactly where its members are, that is, wherever there is one book copy: on a library shelf here, under the leg of a table there. If this makes the set look a bit scattered, consider that familiar objects like a bikini or an encyclopaedia in twelve volumes are plausibly located wherever a part of them is located, and these can end up quite far from each other.

Despite its problems, the way of negation is going to be our working characterization of the notion of abstract object. Even in the absence of a precise and spotless definition, one can focus on the discussion whether *some* paradigmatic and uncontroversial case of abstract object exists. In the following we are going to do just this, introducing the disputed issue of the existence of numbers, sets and other mathematical objects. This issue is known as the platonism vs. nominalism debate in the philosophy of mathematics: platonists believe in abstract mathematical objects, nominalists do not. It's now time to see why one may want to choose either position, and how one could defend it from objections coming from its rival.

2 Mathematical objects: Why 'No'

In super-rough words: because nobody has ever seen or touched or had any real contact with numbers. Where are you going to look for information about them? How can you even know that there are numbers if you never had any causal interactions with them?

It is true that nobody ever saw an electron either or any other subatomic particle. One can still see the traces of their actions, though. Electrons make things happen in the real, concrete world, and this is why we can spot the vestiges of their passage. But numbers leave no traces. They are disconnected from concrete reality, therefore they are undetectable. The abstractness of mathematical objects tells them apart from any citizen of the concrete world. This seems to preclude any account of how it is possible for flesh-and-blood mathematicians to gain *knowledge* of them. So this kind of challenge goes under the label of the 'epistemological objection to platonism'. It was famously put forward by Benacerraf 1973, a very influential paper. The original Benacerraf objection had the following form (see Liggins 2006, 2010a):

(P1) In order to have knowledge about the *F*s, we need to be in causal contact with the *F*s.
(P2) We are not in causal contact with mathematical objects.

Therefore:

(C) We lack knowledge of mathematical objects.

The problem with this way of phrasing the challenge is that premise (P1), taken as summing up the so-called *causal theory of knowledge*, is highly controversial, and generally discredited nowadays. It seems that we can know a lot about future events, or events happening in galaxies outside our light cone, without being in causal contact with them.

The core intuition behind the challenge, nonetheless, can survive this problem. A refurbished version of the epistemological challenge, which does not rely on controversial assumptions about knowledge, has been put forward by Hartry Field 1988, 1989. Field illustrates his point with an example. Imagine a remote Nepalese village you have no contact with whatsoever. Not only do you not live there, but also you don't get any report from people who live there, nor any image through satellite nor anything of the sort. Nonetheless, you happen to have accurate beliefs about the daily happenings of the village: if you believe that the sun is shining there, the sun is indeed shining there. If you believe it is raining, it is raining. And so on. A systematic correlation makes your beliefs about the Nepalese village reliable: whenever you believe something about it, what you believe is the case.

This looks hard to believe. The accuracy of your beliefs about the Nepalese village cries out for *some* explanation (see Field 1989: 26). But your being disconnected from it seems to preclude the possibility of any explanation. Now, Field goes on, if platonism were correct, something as strange as the Nepalese scenario would indeed happen. platonists think that mathematicians' beliefs about numbers are reliable. At the same time, they think that mathematical entities, being abstract objects, are no less disconnected from mathematicians than the imagined village is from you. This makes it very hard for platonists to explain the reliability of mathematicians' beliefs.

The point Field presses is that platonists face a *challenge*. They cannot provide a causal explanation of the reliability of mathematicians' beliefs, due to the causal inefficacy of abstract mathematical objects. And it's very hard, Field says, to see what form a non-causal explanation of such reliability could take. This does not mean that a non-causal account of mathematicians' reliability is ruled out. But the burden of proof is on the platonist.

We see how this challenge does not rely on controversial assumptions about the nature of knowledge. When talking about reliability, all Field means is a systematic correlation between mathematicians' beliefs and mathematical truths. The following Reliability Schema looks generally acceptable, and we should account for this:

(RS) If most mathematicians believe that *P*, then it is true that *P*.

Field's is just a request for explanation, which presupposes no special assumption about the form a theory of knowledge should take. In particular, (RS) and Field's challenge do not presuppose a *reliabilist* conception of knowledge: the view that a true belief counts as knowledge if and only if it is formed via a reliable process.

Another problem, which also goes back to a paper by Benacerraf (1965), is that if there were abstract mathematical objects, it would sometimes be very difficult to settle questions about their identity. We have clear identity criteria for sets, as we know from Chapter 3: *a* and *b* are the same set when they have exactly the same members. Now the notion of set is a key one for mathematics, because one can characterize basic mathematical notions in terms of it (e.g. one can define functions as sets of a certain kind). In fact, the natural numbers themselves (0, 1, 2, 3...) can be characterized in terms of sets. This had a lot of importance for programs in the foundations of mathematics of the late nineteenth century and early twentieth century, but we need not enter into the details. What matters for us is that the natural numbers can be mapped to equally good set-theoretic structures which are, however, distinct from each other.

There are, for instance, at least two reductions of the naturals to sets that seem to serve the purposes of pure and applied mathematics equally well. The sequence of natural numbers can be defined, as Ernst Zermelo did, by letting the *empty set* play the role of zero, and by defining $n + 1$ as $\{n\}$, the set whose only member is number n. The empty set, usually denoted as '$\varnothing$' or '$\{\}$', is the set with no members whatsoever; and there is only one such set: any set with no members has exactly the same members as $\varnothing$, namely none; given the identity criterion for sets, any such set just is $\varnothing$. So the sequence will look like this:

$$\varnothing, \{\varnothing\}, \{\{\varnothing\}\}, \{\{\{\varnothing\}\}\}, \ldots$$

One could also choose the characterization due to John Von Neumann: one still starts by letting $\varnothing$ play the zero, but defines n as the set of numbers that precede n in the sequence:

$$\varnothing, \{\varnothing\}, \{\varnothing, \{\varnothing\}\}, \{\varnothing, \{\varnothing\}, \{\varnothing, \{\varnothing\}\}\}, \ldots .$$

Now which of the two reductions is correct? Is 2 the same as $\{\{\varnothing\}\}$? Or is 2 the same as $\{\varnothing, \{\varnothing\}\}$? (notice that $\{\{\varnothing\}\}$ is different from $\{\varnothing, \{\varnothing\}\}$: the former has only one member, namely $\{\varnothing\}$; the latter has as members both the empty set and $\{\varnothing\}$; so you cannot answer 'Yes' to both questions). For the purposes of mathematics, the answer does not change much, in the precise sense that both structures make all the relevant mathematical theorems true. For a trivial example, '$2 + 2 = 4$' is true independently of which set you choose as the number two: in both the Zermelo and von Neumann series, the object that you find if you start from the object occupying the second position in the natural number sequence and move two steps forward is the object occupying the fourth position in the natural number sequence.

If such mathematical objects as numbers and sets existed, it seems that we would have to answer embarrassing questions about their identity. The situation radically changes, though, if we think that numbers and sets are not real entities, but something like fictional characters. There is no answer, in the Harry Potter fiction, to the question whether the fifth person encountered by Harry on his second day at Hogwarts is the same as the seventh person he met on his tenth day at the school. If mathematics worked like a fiction, something similar would be the case with the identity of the number two. This is another reason to think that numbers are just as unreal as wizards. Or at least, this is how muggles like to think, the platonists may reply.

3 Mathematical objects: Why 'Yes'

Here is a list of claims we shall return to various times in this chapter:

(1) $7 + 5 = 12$.
(2) There are infinitely many prime numbers. (Euclid's theorem)
(3) π is irrational.
(4) Ackermann's theorem: There are recursive functions that grow more rapidly than any primitive recursive function. (See Rosen 2006)
(5) The class of whales is included in the class of mammals.
(6) The number of cats is different from the number of dogs. (See Goodman and Quine 1947)
(7) The length in km of Manhattan's diameter is 11. (See Quine 1960: 245)
(8) $F = g\, M_a M_b / d^2$. (See Putnam 1971: 37)
(9) Königsberg's graph is not Eulerian. (See Lyon 2012)
(10) Some solutions to the field equations of general relativity contain closed time-like curves. (See Burgess and Rosen 2005)

A plain argument for platonism in mathematics (on which, see Linnebo 2013) starts from the apparent truth of claims like (1)–(10) and adds: it is difficult to see how these claims could be true if there were no mathematical objects. From such premises, it reaches the conclusion that there are mathematical objects. That is:

(P1) Claims (1)–(10) are true.
(P2) If claims (1)–(10) are true, then there are abstract mathematical objects.

Therefore:

(C) There are abstract mathematical objects.

The master argument for platonism is clearly valid (it's a simple *modus ponens*, an instance of an argument form of minimal logic): were all its premises true, the conclusion could not but be true. Thus nominalists must reject either (P1) or (P2). But (P1) enjoys conspicuous plausibility. (P2) can be motivated by noticing that claims like (1)–(10), on the face of it, quantify over and refer to abstract objects like numbers, functions and sets. According to standard Quinean metaontology (but also to various non-standard ones, e.g. neo-Fregeanism, or ontological pluralism, etc.), if this is correct and such reference and/or quantification cannot be dispensed with, then (1)–(10) commit us to the existence of mathematical objects.

Now it seems that the nominalist has the burden of proof: show that (1)–(10) are either (against (P1)) only apparently true, or (against (P2)) only apparently committed to mathematical objects.

4 Ways to be a nominalist

4.1 Denying (P1): Good without being true

One may insist, against (P1), that our asserting things like (1)–(10) in scientific or ordinary contexts does not force us to admit their truth. In the chapter on fictionalism, in the first part of our book, we encountered the idea that some fictions can be good without being true and that mathematics is one of these fictions. Then (1)–(10), the fictionalist nominalist will claim, may only be true within that fiction, rather than *simpliciter*. The 'good without being true' conception of the status of mathematical claims comes with a story on our attitude towards these claims: we can accept them without believing or asserting them. The principal task for this brand of nominalism, championed by Hartry Field 1980, 1989, is to explain how mathematics can be *good* without being true.

In the chapter on fictionalism we hinted at how Field 1980 maintains that mathematics works as an instrument, a 'theoretical juice extractor' (see Hempel 1945: 391) that allows one to infer new information on the empirical world from a set of data. An instrument and the operations we perform with it are not things that can properly be called true or false. An abacus, for instance, is just an instrument: it can work properly or not, but it is not true or false (this is an old chestnut by Goodman and Quine 1947 to illustrate how mathematics works for some nominalists). We can make true or false claims, have true or false beliefs, but the operations we perform with an instrument are things we just *do*: they can be effective or not, permissible or not, etc. Focusing for the moment only on examples (1)–(4) above, the basic point of Field's 1980 strategy is that they should be considered similar to operations performed with an abacus and therefore not properly true. Otherwise, if one wishes (see Field 1989: Introduction), to assert one of them actually is like saying that it is true according to the fiction of mathematics; this 'otherwise' marks the distinction between instrumental fictionalism and meta-fictionalism, which we saw in Chapter 6.

To get an idea of how mathematics can be taken as an instrument for empirical science, consider the case of arithmetic. According to the story told by Field 1980: Ch. 2, basic arithmetical claims like (1) can help us to quickly extract information about the empirical world. First of all, some claims that seem to be about the number of things of a certain kind can be construed in such a way that there is in them no mention of numbers at all. One may think that the following is about the number of bananas on my table:

(B) There are two bananas on my table.

The number word 'two' shows up in (B): isn't this a name for the number two? Well, we can translate (B) as follows:

(B*) There is an x and there is a y such that x and y are bananas on my table, and x is different from y, and any z which is a banana on my table is either x or y.

Now this doesn't commit us to numbers by Quine's criterion of ontological commitment. We translate into canonical notation, and note that we are quantifying only over bananas:

(B**) $\exists x$(x is a banana on my table) & $\exists y$(y is a banana on my table) & $x \neq y$ & $\forall z$ (if z is a banana on my table, then either $z = x$ or $z = y$).

What we did to the number word 'two' can also be done to 'three', 'four', etc. One just needs to add variables. Using the arrow, '$\rightarrow$', to express the conditional, 'if-then', and the symbol '$\vee$' to express disjunction, 'or', we get the following sequence of numerical quantifiers:

$$\exists_0 xFx =_{df} \sim\exists xFx$$
$$\exists_1 xFx =_{df} \exists x(Fx \,\&\, \forall y(Fy \rightarrow y = x))$$
$$\exists_2 xFx =_{df} \exists x\exists y(Fx \,\&\, Fy \,\&\, y \neq x \,\&\, \forall z(Fz \rightarrow z = x \vee z = y))$$
$$\exists_3 xFx =_{df} \exists x\exists y\exists z(Fx \,\&\, Fy \,\&\, Fz \,\&\, y \neq x \,\&\, x \neq z \,\&\, y \neq z \,\&\, \forall w(Fw \rightarrow w = x \vee z = y \vee w = z))$$

...

There are zero Fs if and only if it is not the case that something is F. There is exactly one F if and only if there is an x which is F and nothing else is F. And so on. Call a sentence committed only to nominalistically acceptable entities *nominalistically acceptable*, or *nominalistically kosher*. Now consider the following argument, which intuitively says that, given that we owe five cats and seven dogs and that nothing is both a cat and a dog, we owe twelve pets (cats or dogs):

(P1) $\exists_5 x$(x is a cat and we owe x).
(P2) $\exists_7 x$(x is a dog and we owe x).
(P3) $\exists_0 x$(x is a cat and x is a dog).

Therefore:

(C) $\exists_{12} x$(either x is a cat and we owe x, or x is a dog and we owe x).

The premises and the conclusion of the argument are nominalistically kosher sentences. Moreover, the argument looks valid. Indeed, we can prove in elementary logic that the conclusion follows from the premises. Still, it would be far simpler to prove the *following* argument correct:

(P1*) The number of cats we owe = 5.
(P2*) The number of dogs we owe = 7.
(P3*) The number of things that are both dogs and cats = 0.

Therefore:

(C*) The number of pets (cats or dogs) we owe = 12.

For one can prove in standard mathematics that the number of things that are either *F* or *G* is the number of things that are *F*, plus the number of things that are *G*, minus the number of things that are both *F* and *G*. Moreover, (P1), (P2), (P3) and (C) can be proved equivalent to (P1*), (P2*), (P3*) and (C*) respectively. It is obviously very easy to show that $7 + 5 - 0 = 12$. So it is very easy to prove – within standard mathematics – that (C*) follows from (P1*)–(P3*) and thus, given the equivalences just mentioned, that (C) follows from (P1)–(P3). Still, any statement of the form of (C) can be inferred by premises of the form of (P1)–(P3) using only elementary logic.

Let us put ourselves in the shoes of a nominalist who wants to derive (C) from (P1)–(P3). Call a proof nominalistically acceptable, or kosher, if it involves only nominalistically acceptable-kosher sentences. Now we know that, firstly, if there is a standard mathematical proof of (C), then there is a nominalistically acceptable proof of (C). Secondly, the proof employing just standard mathematics is going to be much simpler than the nominalistically kosher one.

Elementary logic, in which numerical quantifiers can be defined in the way explained before, can give us a nominalistically kosher theory, say, *N*, expressed in a nominalistically kosher language. Standard mathematics, on the other hand, is a platonistic/mathematical theory, say, *M*, expressed in a platonistic language involving reference to abstract mathematical objects. We can now state in an informal way a property of M relative to N. $N + M$ (the theory obtained by joining M and N together) is a *conservative extension* of N, which means that:

(Cons) Let $A_1, \ldots, A_{n-1}$ and A_n be sentences in the language of N. If it is possible to derive A_n from $A_1, \ldots, A_{n-1}$ in $N + M$, then it is possible to derive A_n from $A_1, \ldots, A_{n-1}$ in N alone.

According to Field, (Cons) is the key to understand how mathematics can be good without being true. Standard mathematics is not part of the content of claims of the form of (P1)–(P3) and (C). It's just a tool we can use to pass from a group of empirical sentences (e.g., sentences about cats and dogs) to other empirical sentences. Working with (P1*)–(P3*) to derive (C*) in M is easier than giving a nominalistically kosher proof of (C) from (P1)–(P3) in N. But, given (Cons), we know that this is *nothing but* a detour to simplify our life.

Conservativeness is, however, just one ingredient of Field's strategy. Even granting that we can account for the utility of *pure* mathematical statements by explaining how they can be useful in speeding up deductions, there is still the possibility for mathematics to be useful also in a different way.

Claims like (5)–(10) from our list above come from *applied* mathematics. They are used to express facts about the physical world, although in mathematical language. There seems to be no simple way to express the contents of such claims in a nominalistically kosher language. The charge for nominalism is that of being guilty of imposing an impoverished language, inadequate to the needs of science.

Field's reply consists in providing nominalistic reformulations of actual scientific theories, thus showing that a platonistic mathematical language is not essential to represent and explain facts about the physical world. The title of Field 1980 is *Science without Numbers*, and science without numbers is for him a nominalistically kosher science. We cannot illustrate Field's strategy in full detail here, but we can get some sense of how it works by looking at David Hilbert's reformulation of Euclidean geometry, which Field took as a model for his reformulation of Newton's theory of space.

Distance seems to be a physical concept at root. Still, in analytic geometry, such as the Cartesian geometry studied at school, distance is represented via a function mapping physical entities onto real numbers. The function $d(x, y)$ measures the distance between x and y. This means that it assigns a unique number to the pair x, y. Which number it assigns will depend upon the choice of a unit of measure. Say that we choose meters and $d(a, b) = 1$. Had we chosen feet to measure the same distance, we would have a different function, say d^*: this time $d^*(a, b) = 3.2808399$. So there is no unique distance function. But there is a conversion rate between meters and feet: 1 meter = 3.2808399 feet, which means that $d^*(a, b) = d(a, b)$ multiplied by 3.2808399.

The same can go for other notions such as mass, temperature and so forth. Analytic quantitative theories represent such physical quantities by relating concrete objects to abstract ones via the choice of a scale of measure. The function $d(x, y)$, say, maps a pair of points x, y onto a number, which measures the distance between x and y relative to a scale of measure. One example of this is our claim (7) from the list above: 'The length in kilometres of Manhattan's diameter is 11'. The diameter of Manhattan – a concrete object – is mapped onto the number 11 by the *length-in-kilometre* function.

In the case of geometry, an alternative to analytic-quantitative geometry was provided by Hilbert 1971. Hilbert's version of geometry is synthetic and qualitative, in that it only involves points, segments and comparative relations between them. It is a *number-free* geometry. The key qualitative relations are that of *betweenness*, which we can take here as expressed, say, by the predicate '*Bet*', and *congruence*, expressed by the predicate '*Cong*'. Read '$Bet(x, y, z)$' as saying that point x lies between points y and z, and '$Cong(x, y, z, w)$' as saying that the segment xy (the segment whose extremes are x and y) is congruent with the segment zw (that whose extremes are z and w). Taking a and b to be the two extremes of the standard meter ab (which is a physical object: a bar kept in Paris), we can express the claim that the distance between points c and d is two meters without mentioning numbers. We just say that:

- **a** There is a point x that lies between c and d: $\exists x Bet(x, c, d)$.
- **b** x is in the middle of c and d, that is, cx and xd are congruent: $Cong(c, x, x, d)$.
- **c** The segment cx (half of cd) is congruent with the standard meter: $Cong(c, x, a, b)$.

The same method of paraphrase allows one to say in a nominalistically kosher way that the distance between two given points x and y is three, or four, … or 11,000 times that of the two extremes of the standard meter, which is equivalent to saying that the distance between x and y is one, two, … or 11,000 meters. So one can paraphrase (7), dispensing with reference to numbers.

An interesting fact about the relationship between the synthetic and analytic versions of geometry is that in standard mathematics, which includes both theories, one can prove a representation theorem stating some important properties about the distance function. In every model of the platonistic version of geometry obtained by expanding the nominalistic version via the addition of a function, say d, representing distance, we have that:

- **i** $d(x, y) = d(z, w)$ if and only $Cong(x, y, z, w)$.
- **ii** $d(x, y) + d(y, z) = d(x, z)$ if and only if $Bet(y, x, z)$.
- **iii** In technical terms: d is unique up to a multiplicative constant (the unit measure).

Now we are in the position to appreciate that Field's project consists essentially of two tasks: (a) Nominalize science: find nominalistic reformulations of applied mathematical claims; (b) account for the utility of pure mathematics.

Representation theorems help with both tasks. They help with (a) because they map platonistic claims into nominalistically kosher ones. They help with (b) because they explain that within a platonistic theory one can translate quantitative platonistic claims into qualitative, nominalistically kosher ones. This is, for Field, the key to see how the detour into mathematics can be used to reach nominalistic conclusions. Combined with the conservativeness of mathematics with respect to nominalistic theories, which guarantees that the nominalistic conclusions we reach in enriched platonistic theories are nominalistically acceptable, representation theorems account for the utility of mathematics as a deductive instrument.

Field's nominalization of science just described has not been developed in full generality. He limits himself to providing a nominalistic treatment of classical physics: replacements of Newton's theory of gravitation (alluded to by our claim (8) above), indications about how to apply the strategy to thermodynamics and hints on how to deal with theories of curved space-time. There is some scepticism (see Urquhart 1990) about the possibility for Field's strategy of dealing with contemporary physics, in particular with relativity theory (as per statement (10) above) and quantum mechanics (see Malament 1982). Limited as it may be, the strategy is much more systematic than early nominalistic attempts like those provided by Goodman and Quine 1947, which we are going to discuss more in detail below.

Field's way to nominalism has been called by Colyvan 2010 'hard-road nominalism': Field attempts to specify the content of science acceptable by nominalists, that is the nominalistic content of our scientific theories, through nominalistic paraphrases of applied mathematical sentences, and this is indeed a hard task. But some philosophers think that there can be an easier route to the nominalistic content. Yablo 2012 presents a way of getting it by just subtracting from our scientific theories the assumption that there are mathematical objects. The idea is that the content of science is correct as far as the concrete world is concerned, but it is not correct about the existence of mathematical objects. The nominalistic content of a scientific theory is just its ordinary content, minus the claim that there are mathematical objects. Joseph Melia 2000 has defended a similar approach to nominalistic content under the label of weaseling, which we mentioned in our chapter on fictional metaontology, arguing that it is indeed an ordinary linguistic practice.

Colyvan 2010 points out that this plain subtraction procedure does not always make sense. Try to imagine *The Lord of the Rings* without the Hobbits, or try to subtract from the claim that this rose is scarlet the claim that this rose is red (Yablo 2012). Colyvan thinks that 'mathematics without numbers' is a bit like Tolkien's world without Hobbits, or a scarlet rose that is not red. Weaseling away the existence of mathematical objects from the content of our mathematical assertions would make such content obscure. He asks, for instance, what would be the content of a claim like: 'There is a function that maps spacetime points onto real numbers, but there are no mathematical objects.' In the absence of a *paraphrase* elucidating the meaning of such a claim, it is hard to see how to interpret it, except as a contradictory claim. Only hard-road nominalism ventures into into offering such a paraphrase. Then easy-road nominalist strategies such as weaseling are actually parasitic on hard road ones. However, one could sympathize with Colyvan on the need for a criterion separating cases where weaseling is permissible and cases where it is not, while at the same disagreeing with him on the idea that weaseling is permissible only in the presence of a nominalistic paraphrase.

Another strategy pursued by Yablo in early papers was to consider mathematical language as a kind of figurative language. This is the figuralist strategy we met in our chapter on fictionalism. Metaphorical language can be a very effective representative aid, even though metaphorical statements put forward in a fictional spirit are not literally true. This is witnessed by the famous example from Walton we already discussed in that chapter, 'Crotone is at the arch of the Italian boot'. Also, for Yablo 1998, 2005 metaphors are sometimes *essential*, in that there just is no way to convey their content via a literally true statement. Colyvan 2010 objects to this strategy, too, this time on the ground that metaphors can be essential for representing something but they cannot have explanatory power, whereas mathematical statements play an explanatory role in scientific theorizing. Easy-road nominalism has been the subject of a lively debate, as witnessed by a recent symposium hosted in the journal *Mind* (issue 121 (484)).

4.2 Denying (P2): Truth without objects

Another possibility to resist the master argument for platonism is to argue that one can accept mathematical theorems as literally true, thus keeping its first premise (P1) above, while at the same time rejecting mathematical ontology.

Some proposals have been put forward on how to reinterpret mathematical claims in such a way that their content does not involve the existence of abstract mathematical objects, even when they are literally true. This brand of nominalism usually goes under the label of 'paraphrase nominalism' (we know from our Chapter 3 on standard metaontology that, within this framework, paraphrases can be understood in at least two different spirits, the hermeneutic and the revolutionary one; but the choice of either shall not bother us here).

One way to reinterpret mathematical claims would be to just prefix, e.g. every pure arithmetical claim with the clause: 'If the axioms of arithmetic are true, then' (this is a cartoon version of what is usually called *deductivism*, Shapiro 2000: 150). (1) and (2) from our list of statements above would then become:

(1*) If the axioms of arithmetic are true, then $7 + 5 = 12$ (but: there is no number twelve).

(2*) If the axioms of arithmetic are true, then there are infinitely many prime numbers (but: there are no numbers).

Another proposal, due to Hellman 1989 and known as *modal structuralism*, appeals to the idea that there can be various systems of objects sharing a common structure. For instance, all of the following are sequences of objects (called 'omega sequences') that share the structure of the natural numbers:

$\varnothing, \{\varnothing\}, \{\{\varnothing\}\}, \{\{\{\varnothing\}\}\}, \ldots$
$\varnothing, \{\varnothing\}, \{\varnothing, \{\varnothing\}\}, \{\varnothing, \{\varnothing\}, \{\varnothing, \{\varnothing\}\}\}, \ldots$
1, 2, 3, 4, …
Genius, meta-genius, meta-meta-genius, meta-meta-meta-genius, … (see Hofstadter 1979)

Now the claim that $7 + 5 = 12$, in Hellman's proposal, means something like this:

(H) In all possible omega-sequences, the object occupying the twelfth place is identical with the object that one gets by adding the object that occupies the seventh position and the one that occupies the fifth position.

Modal structuralism is only committed to the possibility of there being omega-sequences, not to their actual existence. The key reference to the notion of possibility in (H) gets to Hellman's position the name of *modal* structuralism (see Hellman 2005 for a survey of modal structuralism and some rival accounts).

Yet another way to challenge premise (P2) in the master argument for platonism takes issue with the view that numerals are really referential expressions (see for instance Hofweber 2005b). We have already stressed at various times that not all meaningful words are used to pick up and denote an object. Names work thus, but other expressions (adverbs, connectives, articles) do not. In particular, quantifiers seem not to be referential expressions in the same way in which names are. Quantifiers serve to indicate how many things of a certain kind we are talking about. We are familiar with the existential and universal quantifier, but there are lots of others: 'many', 'most', 'almost all'. Why not add also 'one', 'two', etc., to the list? Sometimes number words do seem to behave like quantifiers: we have seen with our 'bananas' example above that saying that there are two *F*s is like saying that there is some *x* that is *F*, some *y* different from *x* that is also *F* and that whatever is *F* is either *x* or *y*. And we have seen how to generalize the suggestion and define numerical quantifiers of the form '$\exists_n x$', 'there are *n* things such that…'.

Now once this reading of number words is in place, it is also possible to reinterpret the content of basic arithmetical claims, like simple identities. To say that $7 + 5 = 12$, according to this view, is not to affirm the identity between the object denoted by '12' and the object described as 'the sum of 7 and 12'. The real content of '7 + 5 = 12' would be expressed as something like (taking '*F*' and '*G*' as schematic placeholders for any predicate you may like):

$$(1^{**})\quad \exists_5 xFx \,\&\, \exists_7 xGx \,\&\, {\sim}\exists x(Fx \,\&\, Gx) \rightarrow \exists_{12} x(Fx \vee Gx).$$

This reads: 'If there are five things of kind *F*, and there are seven of kind G, and the two kinds don't overlap, then there are twelve things overall'. All instances of (1**) are logical truths.

It may not be easy to extend this strategy to mathematical claims with a more complex structure, like our theorem (2) from the list: 'There are infinitely many prime numbers'. This is linked with another problem: quantification over numbers seems to be possible because numerals sometimes behave more like names than like quantifiers. Numerals figure in identity statements like the one made famous by Frege: 'The number of Jupiter's moons = four'.

To elaborate: 'The sum of seven and five is twelve' grammatically looks just like 'The father of John and Mary is James.' The latter is true if and only if the individual denoted by the name 'James' is the same as the individual picked out by the definite description 'the father of John and Mary'. Similarly, one is tempted to think, it is true that 7 + 5 = 12 because the object denoted by '12' is the same as that which is picked out by the description '7 + 5'. Then there must be numbers denoted by such numerals for '7 + 5 = 12' to be true, just as there must be persons denoted by names in order for 'The father of John and Mary is James' to be true.

Or, to cite the example by Benacerraf 1973: 663, consider the two sentences:

(B1) There are at least three large cities older than New York.
(B2) There are at least three perfect numbers greater than 17.

(B1) and (B2) share the same grammatical form – something like:

(B3) There are at least three *F*s that bear *R* to *a*.

But, Benacerraf goes on, sentences with the same grammatical form should have structurally similar truth conditions. Now (B1) is true if and only if there are three things of the relevant kind *F* (large cities) that are in the relevant relation *R* (being older than) with the thing *a* (New York). Then also (B2) is true if and only if there are at least three things of the relevant kind (perfect numbers) that stand in the relevant relation (being greater than) with the relevant object (the number 17). But then, there must be numbers for (B2) to be true. The language of mathematics is just part of our ordinary language. Then it is plausible that the semantics of mathematical sentences of a certain form be similar to the one of sentences of other parts of our language with the same form.

Hart 1996: 2–3 illustrates the problem of providing a uniform account of truth with this example. It seems obvious that a sentence of the form '*P* & *Q*' (i.e. the conjunction of sentences *P* and *Q*) be true if and only if *P* is true and *Q* is true, regardless of whether *P* and *Q* are mathematical sentences or not. But how could this be the case if truth for mathematical sentences were a radically different property from truth for non-mathematical sentences?

Keep in mind that, just like fictionalist nominalists *à la* Field, so paraphrase nominalists should account for applied mathematics. Pure mathematical claims like (1)–(4) may be thought of as asserting only modal truths ('It is possible/necessary that …'), or conditional ones ('If the axioms are true, then …'), but applied mathematical claims are about the actual world. This is why the crude version of deductivism we presented at the beginning of this section is unlikely to provide a satisfactory account of the applications of mathematics. It is an important question how nominalist accounts that resort to modal notions, like that of Hellman, can be extended to the case of applied mathematics (see on this Burgess and Rosen 1997: 196–9 and 201–2).

Now this is connected with the problem of how to harmonize the semantics of mathematical language with that of the rest of our language. Sentences like (5)–(10) mix mathematical and non-mathematical vocabulary and it is not obvious how the different accounts of the meaning of the quantifiers are to interact. Nominalists have answers to this challenge, too. Some accounts, like Hellman 1989, are pretty complex. Others are simpler. According to Hofweber 2005a, the problem of offering a uniform semantics is not fatal. Recall from our chapter on neo-Carnapians that in Hofweber's account the quantifier has a double reading (inferential and referential) already in our ordinary, non-mathematical language. In mathematical language the quantifiers take one of these two readings, the inferential one, which does not carry ontological implications. If this is correct, then the semantics Hofweber is offering *is* uniform, after all: 'there are' always means *there are*. It's just that the English phrase 'there are' is itself ambiguous between an internal-inferential and an external-referential reading. But if Hofweber is right, this is no more a problem for mathematical English than it is for English at large.

In fact, according to the approach of Hofweber and of another prominent nominalist, Jody Azzouni 2004 (reviewed by Hofweber 2007), there is at least one sense in which it is true that there are numbers. According to Hofweber, on the internal reading of the existential quantifier, it is trivial that there are numbers. This just means: There is a way to obtain a true statement filling in the dots in the phrase: '… is a number'. This is clearly the case: 'One is a number', 'Two is a number'.

A similar conclusion seems to be forced on paraphrase nominalists. They too should say that there is at least one reading of the claim 'There are numbers', such that it turns out to be true on that reading. Hellman interprets the theorem that there are infinitely many prime numbers as meaning roughly that in all possible omega sequences there are infinitely many prime numbers. But then, for the sake of uniformity, Hellman should interpret the claim 'There are numbers' as meaning that no omega sequence is empty. On Hellman's reading of mathematical claims, then, the claim that there are numbers turns out to be true. Therefore, he shouldn't reject it. But if he accepts that there are numbers, why should Hellman call himself a nominalist? (See Burgess and Rosen 1997: 234–5 for a version of this objection).

A solution to this tension seems to be provided by the metaontological framework laid down by Hofweber's double quantifier reading: one formulation of nominalism, in this context, wouldn't be the thesis that there are no numbers (which would be false, on the internal reading), but the thesis that number words are not referential. Another formulation would be to claim that, on the *external* reading of the existential quantifier, there are no numbers.

5 Ways to be a platonist

The epistemological challenge to platonism is to show how we can know things about a domain of abstract objects we have no causal contact with. The replies can be divided into two groups. The first group connects our knowledge of numbers to our knowledge of theoretical entities of physics, like black holes or electrons. One accounts for mathematical knowledge by arguing that mathematics is part of our best theories of the world, such as physics, and that the scientific confirmation of these theories is inherited by their mathematical parts. By knowing that the atomic weight of beryllium is 9.012182 we also know that there is something like the number 9.012182 (see Burgess and Rosen 1997).

Another group of replies sees mathematical knowledge as akin to logical knowledge combined with knowledge of definitions. Knowing that 7 + 5 = 12, according to this view, is similar to knowing that there cannot be a deck of cards containing 53 cards – something we know by reflecting on the definition of 'deck of cards' and using a little logic. Both kinds of reply also aim to support premises (P1) and (P2) of the master argument for platonism: by showing how we know that 7 + 5 = 12, they aim to provide evidence for our knowing that the claim is just true. They also aim to account for how the truth of mathematical statements should convince us that there are mathematical objects. We will examine the two kinds of reply in the following two Sections.

5.1 Of numbers and electrons

Physicists believe in black holes even though they have never seen one. The same is true of atoms, electrons, or any other subatomic particle: these so-called theoretical entities or posits of physics are unobservable. Why believe that they exist? Because postulating them has great explanatory power. In the first part of our book we mentioned what philosophers call 'inference to the best explanation'.

Roughly, it consists of something like this: we observe some phenomena and we compare possible accounts of why these phenomena happen. If there is one explanation that strikes us as clearly superior to the others, we believe that explanation. This happens in ordinary life. If you suddenly stop talking to us, we try to figure out why: we come up with various hypotheses and, if one strikes us as clearly the best one, we believe it.

Sometimes we can directly check whether our explanation was correct. Suppose we believe that there is a fire in our house because this is the most plausible explanation of our seeing smoke coming out of a window. We can go in and check. But sometimes, as in the case of subatomic particles, this is not possible. There is no direct way to perceive them. Still, if the hypothesis that there are particles of a certain kind yields the best account available so far of a variety of phenomena and successful predictions about future events, inference to the best explanation gives us reason to believe that there are such particles. If a theory's explanations and predictions are systematically correct, the theory must have got something right and this gives us reason to believe in the unobservable entities it posits: otherwise, the success of the theory would be a miracle (this is the gist of the so-called 'no-miracles argument', due to Putnam 1975: 73, for realism on the theoretical entities of science; for critical discussion see Chakravartty 2013: Section 2.1). Our best explanation of a variety of physical, chemical, electromagnetic phenomena does involve reference to unobservables like molecules, atoms, protons, field forces, etc. This gives us reason to believe that there are such things.

Now according to a tradition stemming from Quine and Putnam, the reason for believing in the existence of abstract mathematical objects is the same that leads us to believe in the existence of electrons and other subatomic particles. Sometimes the very same theoretical explanations that mention electrons also mention numbers, functions, sets, etc. A reason to believe in the existence of electrons is that these explanations are the best we have, and they involve electrons. But they also involve numbers; so this is a reason to believe in the existence of numbers as well. The following is a nice example by Field:

> There is a bilinear differentiable function, the electromagnetic field function, that assigns a number to each triple consisting of a space-time point and two vectors located at that point, and it obeys Maxwell's equations and the Lorentz force law. (Field 1989: 16–17)

We should believe this claim: it part of our best scientific theories. Thus we should take on board its ontological commitments.

The platonist's appeal to the role of mathematics in the empirical sciences is a defensive move. Confronted with the epistemological challenge, she replies that our belief in mathematical entities is justified by the fact that mathematics is part of our best scientific theories, which are confirmed by their impressive empirical success.

This means, as Quine stressed, that we have *empirical* reasons to believe in the existence of numbers. We have empirical reasons to believe claims like (5)–(10) from our famous list above, and translating them into canonical notation we see that they are ontologically committed to numbers, functions and other mathematical entities.

A positive argument for platonism in the same vein has also been presented, though. This is usually referred to as the 'Quine-Putnam indispensability argument'. There are different versions of it but, following Colyvan 2011, we can phrase it thus:

(P1) We ought to have ontological commitment to all and only the entities that are indispensable to our best scientific theories/explanations.

(P2) Mathematical entities are indispensable to our best scientific theories/explanations.

Therefore:

(C) We ought to have ontological commitment to mathematical entities.

Notice a little shift here. Platonism's defensive strategy (of the kind we are exploring now) pointed out that mathematics is part of our best scientific theories and should inherit their epistemic respectability. Now this argument, as its name suggests, adds that mathematics is an indispensable part of our scientific theories. One could wonder what would happen if, against premise (P2), this were not the case, that is if mathematics were dispensable. If Field's project described above in Section 4.1 were to succeed, a full-fledged nominalistic version of physics would be available, and this may pull in the direction of dispensability for standard mathematics.

However, it is not obvious that this would be sufficient to dismiss platonism. A nominalistic version of physics would be very different from our current physics. It may not be a *superior* version. Burgess and Rosen 1997, 2005 have stressed that ontological parsimony is just one virtue of scientific theories; others are familiarity of principles, naturalness, fruitfulness of consequences and simplicity. Nominalized science would score better on the side of ontological parsimony, but platonist science may well score better on the other sides. Burgess and Rosen also propose a challenge for nominalists: submit a version of their theories to a scientific journal and see whether it gets accepted. This would be a way to decide whether nominalistic physics really is the best theory from a scientific viewpoint. In such argumentative contexts, the real question seems not to be whether nominalistic reformulations of science are possible, rather whether they are better than the current platonist versions.

Setting indispensability considerations aside, there are various problems, highlighted in the literature, with the idea that the success of scientific theories confirms the truth of the mathematics employed therein. One is that basic mathematical truths like that $2 + 2 = 4$ strike us as obvious (see Parsons 1979). Do we really need to wait for the result of CERN experiments to be reassured that two and two is four? Should this be counted as one offspring of the research? Another problem is that crucial scientific experiments usually are contrastive tests: we test a hypothesis against rival ones. Scientific theories have mathematics as their common background. This suggests that what really gets confirmed in a crucial experiment is the *empirical* rather than the mathematical part of a theory.

Moreover, the indispensability argument as presented above relies on an epistemologically 'holistic' view of theory confirmation, according to which when a theory gets confirmed, all of its parts are confirmed. But confirmation holism is controversial nowadays: we have mentioned some reason to be dissatisfied with it in the foregoing paragraph and there are others as well (Sober 1993).

5.2 Of numbers and directions

Let us now turn to a second group of answers to the epistemic challenge. These are more 'traditionally philosophical' than the appeal to empirical sciences and the indispensability of mathematics for them. The idea is, to put it a bit emphatically, that we know about numbers by virtue of pure reason.

We already considered *neo-Fregeanism* as a metaontological view in Chapter 4. Neo-Fregeanism in the philosophy of mathematics can be seen as the combination of two theses, the first ontological, the second epistemological:

(NF1) *Platonism*: Numbers are objects.
(NF2) *Logicism*: Mathematical knowledge is *logical* knowledge.

We will soon see what 'logical knowledge' means in (NF2). We already saw in Chapter 4 that (NF1) follows, according to the Neo-Fregeans, from two facts: (a) Numerals and other singular terms purport to refer to numbers; the truth of arithmetical claims like '7 + 5 = 12' entails that the numerals in them refer to numbers, and therefore numbers exist (they are objects: to be an object is to be the potential referent of a singular term). (b) Arithmetical claims like that *are* indeed true. Now (a) and (b) can be seen as way to spell out the two premises of our master argument for platonism above.

In that chapter, we discussed Frege's idea of introducing the concept of direction by laying down the direction principle as an implicit definition (a kind of abstraction principle):

(DIR) $dir(a) = dir(b)$ if and only if $a//b$.

(DIR) tells you that the direction of line a is identical with the direction of line b just in case a is parallel to b. Now the neo-Fregean defence of (b) is based on making a series of purely logical steps starting from the definition of the concept of number, given by another abstraction principle which we also met: Hume's Principle.

To better understand this, it is now time to get into what *being 1-1 related* is. Pretend that monogamy holds everywhere in the world. Then even if you don't know how many husbands and wives there are, you still know that the number of husbands is the same as the number of wives, given that each husband is married with just one wife, and each wife is married with just one husband. Similarly for the number of your right and left shoes: it's the same number, regardless of how many pairs of shoes you have, given that in each pair the left shoe is matched with its right mate. These are examples of 1-1 mappings or relations.

It seems to be a conceptual truth that the number of *F*s equals the numbers of *G*s if and only if there is a relation, *R*, between the *F*s and the *G*s, such that:

(1-) For every x that is an F, there is just one y that is a G such that x bears R to y.
(-1) Every y that is a G is such that just one x that is an F bears R to y.

Call a relation *R* that satisfies both (1-) and (-1) a one-to-one (1-1) relation. Now the definition of *number* is provided, according to neo-Fregeans, by that particular abstraction principle which is Hume's Principle:

(HP) The number of *F*s = the number of *G*s if and only if the *F*s and *G*s are 1-1 related.

Or, in a more compact notation, reading '#' as 'the number of' and '*1-1*' as '1-1 related' (and again, '↔' as the biconditional 'if and only if'):

(HP) $\#(F) = \#(G) \leftrightarrow 1\text{-}1(F, G)$.

Now whatever kind of things the *F*s are, they can be 1-1 related with the things that are *F*: just match each *F* with itself. This seems to be a piece of logical knowledge:

(L1) $1\text{-}1(F, F)$.

From (L1) and the right-to-left direction of the (HP) equivalence (taking $F = G$), it follows by *modus ponens* that:

(HP + L1) $\#(F) = \#(F)$.

That is, the number of the *F*s is identical with itself. From (HP + L1), by the logical rule of introduction of the existential quantifier, we get the conclusion:

(C) $\exists x(x = \#(F))$.

... That is, there is the number of the *F*s. Thus, as the neo-Fregean story goes, we have proved the existence of numbers by just relying on (i) the definition of the concept of number, as given by (HP) *qua* abstraction principle, and (ii) purely logical reasoning (*modus ponens*, quantifier introduction, etc.).

And this is just the beginning. Neo-Fregeans employ a logical framework called *second order logic* (we will see what this is below, in Section 6), within which one can derive from (HP) the basic axioms of arithmetic, known as the *Peano* (or *Dedekind-Peano*) *axioms* (these are principles which express basic features of the natural number series, e.g. its starting with zero and its being such that each natural number has an immediate successor in the series). And from such axioms one can derive basic arithmetical identities like (1) from our list, '$7 + 5 = 12$', and more complex arithmetical theorems like the claim (2) that there are infinitely many primes. This result is known as *Frege's theorem,* and the version of arithmetic in second order logic that takes as its one non-logical axiom (HP) is known as *Frege's arithmetic.*

Overall, if the following assumptions are true then our arithmetical knowledge is just logical knowledge, plus knowledge of definitions:

(A1) Second order logic is logic.
(A2) (HP) is a legitimate definition of the concept of number.
(A3) Frege's arithmetic accounts for how we get arithmetical knowledge.

These can be, and have been, challenged. Let us just focus on the first two. (A1) was already heavily criticized by Quine, who thought that second order logic is 'set theory in sheep's clothing' (see Section 6 on the details of this). Set theory is just mathematics. If second order logical principles were disguised set-theoretical principles, there would be no big gain in deriving arithmetical knowledge from knowledge of principles of second order logic (plus definitions): we would just get some mathematical knowledge (the arithmetical bit) out of some other mathematical knowledge (the set-theoretical bit). This would be pretty unimpressive. So it is vital for a successful defence of the logicist claim (NF2) above to show that second order logic is indeed logic. Remarkably, in this respect the interests of neo-Fregeans overlap with those of some of their nominalist foes: those who want to make use of second order logic to expand what would be called, in Quinean terms, their *ideology* (see again Section 6 below on what this means).

A problem with (A2) is that abstraction principles are not always as innocent as they may look, and this casts doubts on the idea that it is always legitimate to use them to define a concept. To see why abstraction principles are not always innocent, we will introduce a very famous set-theoretic paradox: *Russell's paradox.* But before coming to Russell's *paradox,* we introduce the so-called Russell-Cantor *theorem,* which says that, for any relation R you might choose, the following holds: there is nothing that bears R with all and only all the things that do not bear relation R with themselves. In logical symbols:

(RC) $\sim\exists y \forall x(R(x, y) \leftrightarrow \sim R(x, x))$.

The proof is a simple *reductio.* Suppose there were a thing bearing R to all and only the things that do not bear R to themselves. Then you would have that:

$$\forall x(R(x, y) \leftrightarrow \sim R(x, x)).$$

By elimination of the universal quantifier, we get:

$R(y, y) \leftrightarrow {\sim}R(y, y)$.

... This is contradictory: it says that something (*y*'s being *R*-related to itself) is the case if and only if it is not the case (or at least, it is contradictory in that it entails a contradiction in *classical* logic: in some non-classical logics, as in Field 2008, the situation is different, since from a biconditional of the form $P \leftrightarrow {\sim}P$ one cannot generally infer an explicit contradiction of the form $P \,\&\, {\sim}P$).

So we must reject the assumption that there is a thing that bears *R* to all and only the things that do not bear *R* to themselves, which is what (RC) says. Some concrete instances of this abstract (RC): there is no (Russellian) barber who shaves all and only those who do not shave themselves; no teacher who teaches to all and only those who do not teach to themselves; no lover who loves all and only those who do not love themselves; etc.

So far we have a theorem, but no paradox. A paradox is typically characterized as the derivation of an apparently unacceptable conclusion, via apparently unproblematic reasoning steps, from a group of apparently acceptable premises. That there is no Russellian barber shaving all and only those who do not shave themselves is hardly an unacceptable conclusion: we can do without this troublesome barber. We get the Russell paradox by noticing that theorem (RC) shows that a *highly intuitive* principle leads to a contradiction – a paradigmatically unacceptable conclusion. The highly intuitive principle is the so-called *Naïve Comprehension Principle* of set theory.

It seems intuitive that, given any concept or property or condition *F*, *x* is a member of the class of the *F*s if and only if *x* is an *F*: after all, being *F* just is being one of the things which are *F*. So for any *F* whatsoever, it would appear, there must be a class whose members are exactly the *F*s. Intuitively, it would seem that for any *F* there are just two kinds of things in the world: those that are *F* and those that aren't (there might be concerns involving vagueness and fuzziness, but we need not bother with this here). And the class of *F*s is nothing but what groups together all the things of the first kind (see Boolos 1971). The Naïve Comprehension Principle encodes this intuition by saying that, no matter what *F* is, there exists a set of all and only the things *x* which are *F*. In logical symbols (using the notation '$x \in y$' to mean that *x* is a member of – or an element of, or belongs to – class *y*):

(NCP) $\exists y \forall x(x \in y \leftrightarrow Fx)$.

Consider now the notion *is not a member of itself*. This also seems to divide the world into two kinds of things. On one side, you have what we can call 'normal' things: things like a banana, which is not a class and thus is not a member of itself; and classes like the class of all bananas, which is not itself a banana, and thus it is also not a member of itself. On the other side, you have more peculiar classes, like the class of all abstract objects: this is a member of itself, given that it is itself an abstract object. Now according to (NCP) there is a class corresponding to *x is not a member of itself* (let us abbreviate this as '$x \notin x$'). Taking '$x \notin x$' as the relevant *Fx* in (NCP), we get:

$$\exists y \forall x (x \in y \leftrightarrow x \notin x).$$

So there is some class whose members are those things which are not members of themselves – and, by the extensionality of sets, there is just one such class: *the* class of all normal things. Call it 'R', the Russellian class. We thus get:

(R1) $\forall x (x \in \mathrm{R} \leftrightarrow x \notin x)$.

But that's incompatible with the Russell-Cantor theorem (RC). There cannot be a Russellian class containing all and only the things that do not belong to themselves, for the same reason for which there cannot be a Russellian barber who shaves all and only those that do not shave themselves. It's just an application to this special case of the general proof of (RC). (R1) entails the following contradictory claim:

(R2) $\mathrm{R} \in \mathrm{R} \leftrightarrow \mathrm{R} \notin \mathrm{R}$.

So (NCP), despite its intuitive attractiveness, leads to an unacceptable conclusion. It clashes with (RC), which is a logical theorem. (NCP) has to go. But (NCP) is on the same footing as one very (in-)famous abstraction principle, namely Frege's *Basic Law V*. This is (reading '*e*' as 'the extension of'):

(V) $e(F) = e(G) \leftrightarrow \forall x (Fx \leftrightarrow Gx)$.

The extension of a concept *F* can be thought of as the collection, or, in modern terminology, as the class, of things that are *F*. (V) says that the extension of *F* is the same as the extension of *G* if and only if whatever is *F* is also *G* and vice versa. This also looks intuitive. It seems part of the notion of extension that the extensions of two concepts are the same if and only if the two concepts apply to (or are true of, etc.) exactly the same objects. However, it can be shown that (V) entails the (UCP), and it is therefore contradictory: given the logical truth $\forall x (Fx \leftrightarrow Fx)$, it follows from (V) that for any concept *F*, $e(F) = e(F)$, which in turn entails that every concept *F* has an extension. And by defining the membership relation in an appropriate way, it can be shown that *x* is a member of $e(F)$ if and only if *Fx*.

Of course, this only proves that some abstraction principles, like (V), are inconsistent. It does not show that all abstractions principles are in trouble. Indeed, there are good reasons to think that (HP) is not contradictory: see Hale and Wright 2001. But then, a natural problem arises: how to tell the bad abstraction principles like (V) apart from the good ones like (HP). This is known as the *bad company objection*; the name seems indeed appropriate (on the bad company objection see Hale and Wright 2001: Introduction, Hale and Wright 2005, and the special issue no. 170 (3) of the journal *Synthèse*).

The tenability of the *logicist* approach of neo-Fregeans hinges upon the possibility of defending (A1)–(A3) from objections of these kinds, whereas the tenability of its *platonism* depends much on the possibility of finding a good reply to the Caesar Objection we met in Chapter 4 (on which, see Hale and Wright 2001: Introduction, Hale and Wright 2005, and the special issue no. 59 (2) of the journal *Dialectica*)· Overall, the success of the neo-Fregean philosophy of mathematics depends on the possibility of combining the defences of logicism and platonism in a coherent way.

6 Ontology and ideology

In Quine 1951b, Quine called *ideology* the stock of primitive predicates and logical operators that a theory makes use of, whereas, as we know well, a theory's *ontology* is given by the domain of its quantified variables. The terminology is now handy, for it allows us to give a compact formulation of the following rough trade-off principle: ontological economy often calls for ideological prodigality. The evaluation of the trade-off between ontology and ideology permeates various ontological debates. As you are going to learn in the chapter on possible worlds, for instance, David Lewis tried to dispense with the ideology of modal notions by reducing them to quantification over possible worlds, thereby offering 'an improvement in what Quine calls ideology, paid for in the coin of ontology' (Lewis 1986: 4; we say 'tried to': it is controversial whether he succeeded).

The platonism vs. nominalism debate offers a good standpoint to observe this trade-off. The choice between a version of modal nominalism like that of Hellman, and platonism, for instance, is, in Quine's light, a choice between simplicity in ontology and simplicity in ideology. And Quine clearly refused to trade off ontology for ideology in this ballpark:

> Long ago, Goodman and I got what we could in the way of mathematics … on the basis of a nominalist ontology and without assuming an infinite universe. We could not get enough to satisfy us. But we would not for a moment have considered enlisting the aid of modalities. The cure would have been far worse than the disease. (Quine 1986b: 397)

Note a difference in this respect between Field and such nominalists as Hellman above: no use of modal notions is involved in Field's strategy. Field is playing the ontological match on Quine's playground (while Charles Chihara is another prominent nominalist who adopts a modal strategy: for an overview, see Chihara 2005 and references therein).

But there are many other linguistic resources beyond modal idioms that the nominalist can make use of, to enrich Quine's very economical choice of sticking with the language of elementary classical logic. We have mentioned second order logic above. The language of elementary logic, which is also called 'first order logic' because of this, only allows you to bind via quantifiers individual variables (variables that can occupy the same syntactic places as names in formulas). You get a 'second order' logical language when you add variables for predicates (variables that can occupy the same position as predicate letters), and quantifiers to bind them. To get an idea of what this means, note that in elementary or first order logic you can easily express an argument like the following:

(P) John is good and John is pretty too.

Therefore:

(C) There is someone who is both good and pretty.

This becomes (with 'j' standing for 'John', 'G' standing for 'is good', 'P' for 'is pretty'):

(P) $Gj \,\&\, Pj$.

Therefore:

(C) $\exists x(Gx \,\&\, Px)$.

The variable x takes the position of name j, called nominal position. Now you might also be interested in a language that allows us to express an inference of this kind:

(P*) John is good and Paul is good too.

Therefore:

(C*) There is something that both John and Paul are.

However, you cannot express this in first order language. You need variables that occupy predicate positions different from the nominal position. This is what you get in the language of second order logic. We can use capital letters as variables for this purpose: X, Y, Z, W.... The previous piece of reasoning then becomes ('p' standing for 'Paul'):

(P*) $Gj \,\&\, Gp$.

Therefore:

(C*) $\exists X(Xj \,\&\, Xp)$.

We mentioned above Quine's belief that second order logic is just a notational variant of (first order) set theory. To say that $\exists X(Xj \,\&\, Xp)$, according to him, was just to say that there is a class, x, to which both j and p belong: $\exists x(j \in x \,\&\, p \in x)$. Then second order existential quantification, '$\exists X(\ldots X \ldots)$', just is first order quantification over sets. Given his own criterion of ontological commitment, second order logic is ontologically committed to sets. Quine took this to be enough to conclude that second order 'logic' is not really *logic*: logic should not bear such existential commitments as the commitment to mathematical entities like sets.

Still, there is at least one way to read second order quantification that is different from that of Quine. George Boolos (1984, 1985) has proposed to read '$\exists X\, Xa$' as: 'There are some things such that *a* is one of them.' The idea is to read second order quantification as *plural quantification* (notice the difference between 'There *are* some *F*s' – plural – and 'There *is* a set of the *F*s' – singular). One can approach the idea of plural quantification by reflecting on plural reference. A proper name like 'Fido' refers to just one dog, and here we have a case of singular reference. But it is natural to think that a term like 'dogs' is not a proper name: it does not refer to one individual dog, but to all the dogs that there are, which are many. Note that this is not like saying that 'dogs' refers to the *set* of all dogs, which would be one single object. Analogously, the values of second order variables are just many individuals, not a set that contains them.

Now Boolos made a case for the plural reading of second order quantification considering a sentence like:

(GK) Some critics admire only one another.

There is no way to translate (GK) into first order languages, whereas there is a natural way to render it in the language of second order logic (say that '$A(x, y)$' stands for '*x* admires *y*' and that, to simplify things, we restrict first order variables to critics):

(GK²) $\exists X(\exists x Xx \,\&\, \forall y(Xy \rightarrow \forall z(A(y, z) \rightarrow z \neq y \,\&\, Xz)))$.

The plural reading of (GK²) Is that there are some critics such that someone is one of them, and every one of them is such that if she admires someone, then this latter person is one of those critics as well. (GK) seems not to be about sets at all: it seems to be just about critics. The plural reading of (GK²) vindicates this intuition, which has been seen as a case for adopting it.

The debate about the ontological innocence of second order logic is still lively. An irony of the situation is, as we hinted at above, that both nominalists interested in second order quantification, like Rayo and Yablo 2001, and neo-Fregean platonists like Hale and Wright, defend the ontological neutrality of second order logic (on the relation between second order logic and the neo-Fregean program, see MacBride 2001; for Boolos' defence of second order logic, see Boolos 1984, 1985; for a nominalistic treatment of second order logic, see Rayo and Yablo 2001).

Another interesting possibility for a nominalist who wants to enrich his or her language is to consider the possibility of expressing in it infinite conjunctions and disjunctions. Take for instance claim (6) of our initial list:

(6) The number of cats is different from the number of dogs.

One way to interpret (6) is as follows. We have already seen above how to characterize numerically defined quantifiers of the form '$\exists_n x$', to be read as 'there are exactly n x such that'. Now (6) is *false* if and only if one of the following holds: either there are neither dogs nor cats, or there is one dog and one cat, or there are two dogs and two cats, or there are three dogs and three cats, or … . So it will be true if none of these cases hold. In symbols:

(6*) $\sim(\exists_0 xCx \ \& \ \exists_0 xDx) \ \& \sim(\exists_1 xCx \ \& \ \exists_1 xDx) \ \& \sim(\exists_2 xCx \ \& \ \exists_2 xDx) \ \&$
$\sim(\exists_3 xCx \ \& \ \exists_3 xDx) \ \& \ \ldots$

One way for the nominalist to express the content of (6) is to take seriously what we just wrote – especially the dots. One can adopt a language offering (formal counterparts of) the dots, thus allowing the construction of sentences expressing the content of an infinite conjunction or disjunction in a finite shape. There are other ways too: adopting what is known as 'infinitary logic' (another way to handle infinite conjunctions/disjunctions) or substitutional quantification, for instance: see Field 1984 and Burgess and Rosen 1997.

Once this possibility is open, the nominalist can also render in her enriched language claims of pure arithmetic. One interprets existential quantification as an infinite disjunction. '$\exists nPn$' gets translated into: '$P(1) \vee P(2) \vee \ldots$'. If you combine this with the method sketched in Section 4.2 to render arithmetical identities of the form '$n + m = q$' by using numerical quantifiers, you see a way to reinterpret arithmetic in this framework. Indeed, you get much more than this. Burgess 2008b reviews in fascinating detail how much mathematics nominalists can recover in such a language, and concludes that one actually gets enough to reinterpret all the mathematics that is needed in the applications of empirical sciences.

It is interesting to compare this strategy to render (6) in a nominalistically acceptable way with that adopted by Goodman and Quine 1947, which was based on the use of mereological concepts like those of *part*, *overlap* and *fusion* (mereology is the formal theory of the notion of parthood: we will come back to it in our chapter on material objects below). Putting these concepts to work, we can find an alternative nominalistic paraphrase for (6). This time, we are going to say that there are more cats than dogs (which seems to be the most likely alternative). Introduce into your ideology a predicate for the mereological relation *part of*, and the following predicates: 'x is bigger than y', with its obvious meaning, and 'x is a bit of y', meaning that x is a part of y and it is as big as the smallest animal that is either a cat or a dog.

Now the classical mereological principle called 'Unrestricted Mereological Composition' claims that, given objects $x_1, \ldots, x_n$, there is an object y whose parts are exactly $x_1, \ldots, x_n$ (their 'mereological sum' or 'mereological fusion'). In particular, there is an object which is obtained by taking a bit from each cat and one that is obtained by taking a bit of each dog. Now (6) can be rendered as:

(6**) Every individual that overlaps with a bit of every cat is bigger than an individual that overlaps with a bit of every dog.

The choice between (6*) and (6**) illustrates the choice between trading platonistic ontology for ideology and trading platonistic ontology for mereological ontology.

Further Reading

Shapiro 2000 is an excellent introduction to the philosophy of mathematics. Part IV of the book covers many issues related to the ontological status of mathematical entities. See also Colyvan 2012, in particular, Chapters 1, 3, 4. Linnebo 2013 provides a beautiful overview of arguments for and against platonism in mathematics. On the epistemological objection to platonism, see Liggins 2010a. On the indispensability argument, see Colyvan 2011 and Panza and Sereni 2013: Chapters 6–7. For an overview of nominalistic accounts of mathematics, see Bueno 2014. The classical reference for this debate is still Burgess and Rosen 1997. See also Burgess and Rosen 2005. On Field's program, see MacBride 1999. On easy road to nominalism, see Colyvan 2012: Chapter 3, Colyvan 2010, and the symposium hosted in the journal *Mind*, issue 121 (484). On Neo-Logicism, see MacBride 2003 and the introduction to Hale and Wright 2001.

10

Abstract Objects II: Linguistic Types, Propositions and Values

Chapter Outline

The mathematical objects encountered in the previous chapter make for the most classical kind of abstract objects, but they are not the only one. Language seems to provide other interesting cases. What are letters, words, sentences, theories, literary works, etc.? Strange as it may sound at first, there are reasons to consider them abstract rather than concrete objects (Section 1). Moreover, the contents of the sentences we utter, which many philosophers call *propositions*, have been considered as another kind of abstract object we should add to the list of what there is (Section 2). After reviewing arguments pro (Section 2.1) and contra (2.2) the existence of propositions, we look at how the adoption of some non-standard metaontological standpoint may help in dealing with them (2.3), and discuss the issue of their metaphysical status (2.4). Finally, we briefly consider the problem of the ontological pedigree of entities like *values* or *responsibilities*, whose existence seems to be presupposed by our moral discourse (Section 3).

1 Types vs. tokens

Consider this claim:

(B) Charles Chihara, a prominent nominalist, has written four books.

Now Chihara has indeed written four books. But is a book a concrete or an abstract object? If you are tempted to think of a book as a concrete material object, made of paper and ink, you probably identify the copies of a book with the book itself. There seems to be a difference between the copies of Chihara's books and the books that he wrote: the number of copies of *A Structural Account of Mathematics* is alone much bigger than four, which, given (B), means that there are many more copies of Chihara's books than there are books written by Chihara. So it seems that (B), on its intended reading, is not about the material copies of Chihara's books.

The point generalizes. Books can be seen as sequences of words and words are themselves concatenations of symbols. The heart of the matter is that symbols can be conceived in two ways: after Peirce, it is common to distinguish between abstract *types* and concrete *tokens*. A type is an abstract model (a proto-type, we may say) which can have various concrete instantiations: the tokens. In the following line, which we are going to refer to as 'Line *a*', you see four tokens of the same type:

aaaa

If one says that one can *see* four letters on Line *a*, then one is conceiving letters as *concrete* tokens: distinct inscriptions made out of matter (ink, chalk, pixels or whatever) that can share a common shape. On the other hand, we are conceiving the letter '*a*' as a type when we say that in Line *a* there is just one letter that appears four times. Similarly, we are thinking of the book you are reading as a type when we say: even if all the copies of this book disappeared, it would still be true that Matteo and Francesco wrote a book together.

We saw in the previous chapter that the distinction between types and tokens is important to evaluate the prospects of nominalistic accounts of mathematics. Numerals and other symbols of formal languages, for instance, need to be conceived as tokens, concrete inscriptions made of ink or chalk, in order to be acceptable entities for ontologists who reject abstract objects. The same goes for syntactic objects: formulas are just concatenations of symbols, proofs are sequences of formulas of a certain kind, and theories can be seen in a formal way as made of all the formulas provable from the principles or axioms one started with.

One reason to conceive of numerals, formulas, proofs, etc., as types is that there are too many for them to be concrete. It is true that the words of a natural language like English are only finitely many, so that you could identify an English word with a concrete token (at least until the last English dictionary in the world will be destroyed). But numerals ('1', '2', '3', …) are infinitely many and the same goes for formulas, theorems and so on. There would not be enough ink or chalk in the world to associate each numeral with a concrete inscription of it, even on a liberal understanding of inscriptions. Goodman and Quine 1947, for instance, submit that every configuration of ink or chalk with an appropriate shape counts as an inscription. According to them, then, there are inscriptions of numerals that nobody has actually written down. Still, assuming the finiteness of the empirical world, some numerals or theorems would be just too long to be written down, even implicitly, in the world.

The type-token distinction involves some subtleties. One needs to distinguish, for instance, between *tokens* and *occurrences* of a type. The distinction can be appreciated by noticing that Line *a* can itself be conceived as a type, of which you see four concrete tokens here:

aaaa
aaaa
aaaa
aaaa

The letter *a* (as a type) occurs four times on Line *a* (as a type). So there are four occurrences of the letter-*a*-type in the line-*a*-type. But these occurrences cannot be concrete tokens, given that they are part of an abstract type. So a distinction should be drawn between tokens and occurrences of types.

The type/token distinction is not important only for the study of language. We say that Beethoven wrote nine symphonies, or that we ate the same pizza or that all men share the same chromosome (see Wetzel 2011). Moreover, as we are going to see in our final chapter, the distinction between types and tokens is also important to evaluate disputes about the existence of universals: if linguistic types are themselves universal forms, those who want to get rid of universals must also get rid of linguistic types.

2 Propositions

So far we have been looking at linguistic entities, so to speak, from the typographer's point of view. We have conceived of sentences and the words that compose them as strings of symbols and asked whether a symbol is better thought of as a concrete token or as an abstract type. But sentences are not mere sequences of signs. Sentences have meanings and they are used to make claims, which have content. That there is a distinction between the sentences we utter and the content we convey by uttering them can be understood by reflecting on simple examples. Suppose Matteo and Francesco utter the following:

Matteo: 'Batman loves Robin'.
Francesco: 'Robin is loved by Batman'.

There is a sense in which Francesco and Matteo said the same thing with different words. So a distinction should be drawn between the sentences they used, (which are different: Matteo's is in active form, Francesco's in passive form, for instance) and the content they conveyed by uttering those sentences, which is the same. Next, suppose Matteo and Francesco believed what they said. It is tempting to claim that the content of Matteo and Francesco's statements is also a content of the respective belief boxes. Of course, one can not only assert or believe that Batman loves Robin, but also hope, desire or suppose that this is the case (Robin, for instance, may desire that Batman loves him). These things, the contents of beliefs, assertions, etc., are what philosophers call *propositions*. It is essential for propositions to be sharable, in the sense that I can believe, assert, etc., the same thing you believe, assert, etc.

Propositions are also often taken to be the meanings of sentences: when we claimed that there is a sense in which Matteo and Francesco said the same thing via the sentences above, that could be understood as the claim that those two sentences express the same proposition. It is not clear that things of the same kind can play both roles, working as the contents of beliefs, etc., and also as the meanings of sentences (see Lewis 1980, 1986: 54 for qualms on this). Still, we won't discuss this problem here. Guided by our ontological scruples, in what follows, we will take as our primary question the one whether there are propositions at all.

2.1 Friends of propositions

One often-cited motivation for believing that there are propositions is that quantifying over them is very useful to account for the intuitive validity of a number of inferences (Davidson 1991; Schiffer 2003: 12–13). Consider the following argument:

(P1) Matteo believes everything that Francesco believes.
(P2) Francesco believes that Quine is wise.

Therefore:

(C) Matteo believes that Quine is wise.

We can represent the premises and the conclusion of this inference in the elementary notation in a natural way as follows (read '$B(x, y)$' as 'x believes y', and let 'm', 'f' and 'q' stand for 'Matteo', 'Francesco' and 'that Quine is wise' respectively):

(P1*) $\forall x(B(f, x) \rightarrow B(m, x))$
(P2*) $B(f, q)$.

Therefore:

(C*) $B(m, q)$.

Formalized in this way, the inference can easily be proved valid in elementary logic. And the variable of quantification in (P1*) ranges over propositions.

This way of arguing that there are propositions rests on a certain way of understanding phrases of the form 'x believes that P', 'x claims that P', 'x hopes that P', etc. These are called *attitude ascriptions* because we use phrases of this form to ascribe mental attitudes to subjects. The analysis of these expressions usually adopted by advocates of propositions is the so-called *relational* analysis, according to which 'x believes that P' is true if and only if x stands in the relation of believing with a certain object, the proposition that P (and similarly, 'x hopes that P' is true if and only if x stands in the relation of hoping with the proposition that P, etc.). It is a common remark that propositions are introduced in discourse by 'that-clauses' (e.g. Francesco believes *that* Quine is wise; the sentence 'Quine is wise' expresses the proposition *that* Quine is wise). In the relational analysis, that-clauses work like singular terms referring to propositions: 'that Quine is wise' denotes the proposition that Quine is wise.

One understands the advantages of this analysis by wondering how to do without it. Suppose one understood 'Francesco believes that Quine is wise', as just ascribing a property to Francesco, that is, as something like 'Francesco has the property of believing-that-Quine-is-wise'. This ought to be formalized as a plain atomic formula, Bf, where 'B' expresses the property of believing-that-Quine-is-wise. If one adopts this analysis, one can quantify in the position occupied by the name f, and represent claims like 'Everyone believes that Quine is wise', that is, 'Everyone has the property of believing-that-Quine-is-wise': $\forall xBx$. One can also render such sentences as 'Everyone who believes that Quine is wise also believes that Quine is a great logician'. If 'G' expresses the property of believing-that-Quine-is-a-great-logician, we have: $\forall x(Bx \rightarrow Gx)$.

However, on this analysis, it is difficult to represent a claim such as (P1) that Matteo believes everything Francesco believes. Something similar happens for an inference like:

(P1**) Francesco believes that Quine is wise.
(P2**) Matteo believes that Quine is wise.

Therefore:

(C**) There is something both Matteo and Francesco believe.

The relational analysis offers a straightforward account of the validity of this inference as well. From *B*(*f*, *q*) (formalizing (P1**) in the relational reading) and *B*(*m*, *q*) (formalizing (P2**)), it follows by logic that $\exists x(B(f, x) \ \& \ B(m, x))$, which is just (C**). It is not easy to see which alternative analysis could account for this.

In spite of all this, some philosophers are reluctant to accept the existence of propositions.

2.2 Foes of propositions

Propositions are usually taken to be abstract entities. One who is dissatisfied with abstract entities in general will then be sceptical about propositions. The epistemological challenge to platonism and the identification problem presented in the previous chapter may then be applied equally well to propositions as they are to numbers. The case of the epistemological problem is pretty clear: as we said, it arises for *all* abstract objects. Also the identification problem we discussed in relation to numbers seems to arise with equal force in the case of propositions. Just as the number two can be identified equally well both with the set {∅, {∅}} and with the set {{∅}}, so the proposition that snow is white can be identified with different set-like entities or set-theoretic constructions (see Moore 1999, on this).

There is a more specific reason to resist the argument for propositions presented in the previous section. One can think that there must be something wrong with it precisely because it relies on the relational analysis of attitude ascriptions, and there are reasons to be dissatisfied with that analysis. One problem with the relational analysis goes under the label of 'substitution effect' (Moltmann 2003). The relational analysis comes with the view that that-clauses work like terms denoting propositions. So 'that it will rain' is a singular term, and denotes the same object as 'the proposition that it will rain'. But if the two expressions 'that it will rain' and 'the proposition that it will rain' are co-referential, they should be interchangeable – which seems not to be the case. There seems to be a difference between these two:

(A) I hope that it will rain.
(A*) I hope the proposition that it will rain.

(A*) looks ungrammatical for 'hope' is not a transitive verb. But even considering verbs that can be transitive, like 'fear' (I can fear you, besides fearing that you will come), there still seems to be a difference between the content of the following sentences:

(B) I fear that it will rain.
(B*) I fear the proposition that it will rain.

The relational analysis seems to have what has been called (Moltmann 2003: 87) an 'objectivization effect': the effect of obliterating the difference between (B) and

(B*), forcing us to read the former as an equivalent to the latter. The point is not only that (B*) sounds weird, but that is the only reading permitted by the relational analysis.

Another reason for discontent with propositions could be the lack of clear identity criteria. It should be no surprise that Quine, who pushed the 'No entity without identity' veto, often pressed this worry. Quine came to accept some abstract objects, namely mathematical objects, as we saw in the previous chapter. His discontent with propositions did not have to be with their abstractness. Recalling the view of propositions as those things which are the meanings of sentences, we can appreciate the following Quinean quote:

> Hypostasis of meanings is a red herring. I keep urging that we could happily hypostasize meanings if we could admit synonymy. We could simply identify meanings with the classes of synonyms. ... The point ... is that the *prior* assumption of an *unexplained* domain of objects called meanings is no way to explain synonymy or anything else. Synonymy, not hypostasis, is the rub. Given synonymy, a domain of meanings is trivially forthcoming for whatever good it would do. (Quine 1986a: 73)

In his mature phase Quine was happy to accept the platonic ontology of sets or classes. Once these are available, one could try to reconstruct propositions as classes of a certain kind. The natural suggestion is to identify propositions with classes of synonymous sentences: the proposition expressed by the sentence 'Snow is white' would then be the class of all the translations of that sentence. But Quine was not satisfied with this suggestion, for he thought there to be no criterion to determine whether two sentences are synonymous. Quine 1951a famously argued that all attempts to define synonymy run into circles. If you try to use synonymy to explain what is for two sentences to share the same meaning, you cannot go on saying that two sentences are synonymous if they have the same meaning. That would be circular. We see, then, how the problem for Quine was not that propositions are abstract entities. Propositions for Quine lack identity criteria. This just gives yet another example of the importance Quine attached to the slogan 'No entity without identity'.

2.3 Metaontology to the rescue?

While quantification over propositions seems very useful to account for the intuitive validity of some inferential patterns, the relational analysis, which treats propositions as the referents of that-clauses, seems to run into the substitution problem and the objectification effect. However, some metaontological positions we encountered in earlier chapters seem to be well equipped to solve this kind of problem: if correct, they would allow you to have your cake and eat it too, in this context. Hofweber's theory of the double reading of the quantifier, which we met in Chapter 5, is designed to accommodate quantification over propositions (see in particular Hofweber 2006, 2009). It allows one to quantify over propositions without treating them as objects. In order to do so one only needs to adopt the inferential/internal reading of the quantifier.

Call 'internalism about propositions' the view that the internal/inferential reading of the quantifiers is appropriate when dealing with quantification over propositions. On this view, the claim that there is something that both Matteo and Francesco believe is just a reminder that there is a way to fill in the dots in the following, which yields a true statement:

Matteo believes that … and Francesco believes that … .

According to internalism about propositions, existential quantification over propositions amounts to a shorthand for an infinite disjunction like: 'Either Matteo believes that Quine is wise and Francesco believes that Quine is wise, or Matteo believes that snow is white and Francesco believes that snow is white, or. ...'

It is interesting that Hofweber also raises a potential *problem* for internalism about propositions. In order for quantification over propositions to be equivalent to a disjunction of possible sentences, every proposition must be expressible by some sentence of our language, and it is not obvious that this is indeed the case. Other languages seem incapable to express some propositions that are expressible in English and, if this were the case, it would sound preposterous to think that our language does not suffer from this limitation, too, with respect to other propositions. To cite Hofweber's example: it is not obvious that the proposition that Coke tastes better than Pepsi is expressible in ancient Greek, which simply lacks the singular terms 'Pepsi' and 'Coke'. Hofweber thinks that this difficulty can in the end be overcome, but how to do so is a matter of some delicacy. To give you a glimpse of the reasoning: the proposition that Coke tastes better than Pepsi is expressible in ancient Greek once one is allowed to use expressions whose referent is determined in part by the content. Of course, one can say even in ancient Greek that *this* liquid (pointing to a sample of Coke) tastes better than *that* (pointing to a sample of Pepsi). We mention this issue just to give an idea of how the dispute between internalism and externalism should be carried on according to Hofweber.

Other non-mainstream metaontological positions may also allow one to have all the expressive benefits of quantification over propositions without their ontological costs. Meinongians may claim that it is perfectly possible to maintain that propositions do not exist, but for some propositions, such as *P*, both Matteo and Francesco believe *P*. Fictionalists will claim that pretending that there are propositions is useful to enhance our expressive powers. Neo-Carnapians may argue that, once the framework of propositions is adopted, to say within it that the proposition that snow is white is true just is to say that snow is white (see Rayo 2013).

2.4 The nature of propositions

We saw since our Introduction that one way of understanding the relationship between ontology and metaphysics is that ontology is about what there is, while metaphysics is about the nature, structure and fundamental features of what there is. The case of propositions offers a nice example of the interaction between metaphysical and ontological issues, so understood (other examples are possible, of course: sets are usually taken as abstract by those who admit them in their ontology, but Maddy 1990 departs from this piece of conventional wisdom; and we will see in the chapter on possible worlds that ontological realists on worlds disagree on their nature: some – Lewis – take them as largely concrete entities, while others – nearly all the others – take them as abstract entities of some kind).

Our case in point is this: whether there are propositions is an ontological issue. Whether propositions are abstract is a metaphysical one. The connection is this: as McGrath 2012: Section 7.1 notes, some philosophers reject propositions because they think that propositions share the typical problems of abstract objects. This is a way of arguing for the ontological conclusion that there are no propositions, which rests on the metaphysical assumption that propositions are abstract.

It is customary to assume that propositions are abstract and mind-independent, irreducible to our mental activities and representations, for this seems to be forced by plain considerations. Take the content of the statement '2 + 2 = 4'. That content being the proposition that 2 + 2 = 4 (let us designate it with '<2 + 2 = 4>'), it would be true even if there were neither minds nor any concrete object. Doesn't this show that <2 + 2 = 4> would exist also in the absence of any mind or concrete object and is therefore no concrete or mind-dependent object?

This conclusion can be resisted, however. Let us resort to possible worlds idiom, and let us say that a proposition is true *at* a world when the proposition correctly describes it; a proposition is true *in* a world when it exists in that world (see Adams 1981 for this distinction). Now *conceptualism* on propositions – the view on the metaphysics of propositions according to which they are products of our mental activity of conceptualizing the world – is not ruled out by the simple considerations just described (see for instance Iacona 2003). To say that <2 + 2 = 4> correctly represents a certain possible situation or world, that is, it is true at a world, does not mean that <2 + 2 = 4> is true *in* it, that is it is part of that situation or world, or exists there.

Yet another option comes from the view that propositions are *pleonastic* entities (see Schiffer 2003), in the sense that there is a very short story to be told about the nature of propositions:

(E) The proposition that *P* is true if and only if *P*.

This is the key axiom about the 'propositions framework', to use the Carnapian terminology we encountered in Chapter 5: (E) tells you all there is to know about propositions and their features. Consequently, the only way to know about propositions is via our knowledge of the conceptual truth (E), plus some additional information. One can still claim that propositions are abstract objects: after all, <2 + 2 = 4> has no space-time location or causal powers. And one can still say that <2 + 2 = 4> would be true even if there were no human minds: this is just to say that, whether there are humans or not, two plus two always makes four. So claims about the abstractness of propositions are not denied by this approach. Their importance, though, is clearly reduced. To say that propositions are abstract objects is not to say they are the kind of objects we get in contact with via some weird intellectual faculty like a kind of super-sensorial perception. This would raise epistemological worries like those reviewed in the previous chapter (compare Schiffer's position about propositions with that of neo-Fregeans about numbers: see Sections 2 and 5.2 of the previous chapter). We get to know about propositions just in virtue of our mastery of the concept of proposition, plus some additional information, that is by knowledge of an ordinary, mundane kind.

3 Ethics with ontology?

In the preface of their classic monograph on nominalism, Burgess and Rosen 1997 acknowledge their 'intellectual debts' and make a joke about the fact that nominalism is refuted by the existence of such intellectual debts, which presumably are abstract entities. One who takes seriously the problems raised by abstract objects in general, like the epistemological challenges they raise, may not be light-hearted about this point.

Intellectual debts, if they exist, are presumably entities with a moral connotation. Since Mackie 1977, the ontological commitments of our discourse about responsibilities, values, and so on, have started to be carefully scrutinized. The analogy between the mathematical and the moral case may in fact be remarkable: Liggins 2010a and particularly Enoch 2012 stress that the epistemological challenge for platonism advanced by Field 1989 can be extended to the case of moral values. One can argue that moral entities are as queer as abstract objects – at least in the eye of the nominalist. As Mackie puts it:

> If there were objective values, then they would be entities or qualities or relations of a very strange sort, utterly different from everything else in the universe. (Mackie 1977: 38)

For a discussion of Mackie's views, see Joyce 2009. So-called *error theorists* (see Daly and Liggins 2010) about moral discourse think that everyday claims like that there is an obligation not to kill children, or a responsibility to keep our promises, are ontologically committed to queer entities like values and obligations. In general, an error theorist about a region of discourse thinks that claims belonging to that discourse are ontologically committed to *F*s, and *F*s do not exist. Error theorists on moral discourse are the counterparts for the moral case of those nominalists we met in our previous chapter, who deny that claims from mathematical discourse, taken literally, are non-vacuously true. An analogy may be helpful here. Discourse about phlogiston is committed to the existence of phlogiston. But there is nothing like phlogiston. So claims belonging to phlogiston-discourse cannot be but untrue or vacuously true. In the eye of an error theorist about mathematical or moral discourse, these kinds of discourses are analogous to discourse about phlogiston. Given that there are no things like numbers or values, and that mathematical/moral claims presuppose their existence, mathematical/moral claims just cannot be non-vacuously true.

As in the mathematical case, one way to tamper with the impression that error theories are outrageous is to combine an error-theoretic position with a fictionalist attitude towards a certain region of discourse. This can be done in the moral case (Joyce 2001) as well as in the mathematical case (Yablo 1998, 2002, 2005, discussed in Chapter 6). If one goes for this strategy, the possibility is open to distinguish the literal content of our moral claims, which is untrue or vacuously true, from their real content, which might be true in many cases. And, again as in the mathematical case, one could defend the thesis that there are values by appealing to an inference to the best explanation (Majors 2007).

One possible moral (!) of all this is that *ontological* problems can be of more general interest than it might appear at first sight. If you are tempted to dismiss the debate about the existence of abstract objects as devoid of any practical interest, you should remember that radical nominalists may challenge you to justify things you take for granted throughout your whole practical and intellectual life, including that you have an obligation to keep your promises – because there may be no such things as obligations.

Further Reading

On the ontology of types, see Wetzel 2011. For a connection with the philosophy of mathematics, see Linnebo 2012a. On propositions, see McGrath 2012 and Iacona 2002, 2003. On error theories in general, see Daly and Liggins 2010. For more on moral error, see the supplement *Moral Error Theory* to Joyce 2009.

11

Possible Worlds

Chapter Outline

In this chapter we speak of the ontology and metaphysics of *possible worlds:* one of the most useful, but also most controversial notions of contemporary philosophy. In Section 1 we introduce possible worlds intuitively and list some of their uses. The twofold ontological and metaphysical question in this area is: do possible worlds really exist and, if so, what are they? In Section 2 we examine *realist* replies: the answers of those philosophers who, within a broadly Quinean metaontological framework, accept ontological commitment to such entities: Section 2.1 introduces David Lewis' (*genuine*) *modal realism* on worlds, according to which possible worlds are largely concrete things just like our surroundings, but causally and spatiotemporally isolated from us and from each other. Section 2.2 explores various versions of *actualist realism*, according to which, on the contrary, possible worlds are abstract objects and belong to actuality. Section 3 looks at non-Quinean perspectives on worlds by focusing on two cases. Section 3.1 describes the approach of *modal fictionalism*: a fictionalist interpretation of possible worlds talk. Section 3.2 speaks of the Meinongian view, which takes worlds other than the actual one as non-existent objects.

1 A philosopher's paradise

When philosophers and logicians talk of our actual world, as opposed to other (merely) possible worlds, by the former they don't just mean the Earth, or the solar system or our current times. Even the most distant galaxies belong to the actual world. Ancient Greeks and men of the future belong to it as well. The actual world can be initially understood as the most general and comprehensive way in which things are. In the actual world, the Nazis lost World War II, Barack Obama won the 2012 US elections and the sky that one of us sees from his office in Amsterdam is cloudy.

We can, however, easily imagine that things might have been otherwise: the sun may be shining on Amsterdam, the Nazis may have won and Obama may have lost. What we are imagining – no doubt, not in all detail – are different possible situations, or ways in which the world may be or may have been. These things we call 'possible worlds'.

Possible words resemble in some aspects the actual world: a world where Obama loses the US elections still is a world where there are US elections and Obama is a candidate. Some possible worlds embed minimal changes with respect to actuality: think of a world just like the actual one, save that you are one centimetre shorter. Some other worlds can be extremely different: think of a world where the laws of physics and biology are turned upside down, so that one can be born twice, or be wholly present in two distant places simultaneously.

Talk of possible worlds is ubiquitous in contemporary philosophy, and we ourselves resorted to it various times in this book before reaching this chapter. The notion plays serviceable roles in several branches of the discipline – to begin with, modal logic: the logic of such expressions as 'necessarily', 'possibly', 'it is contingent that', 'it may be the case that', etc. A first use of such expressions consists in qualifying the truth of a sentence (or of the expressed proposition, if we are into propositions):

(1) It is necessary that $2 \cdot 2 = 4$.
(2) It is possible that Obama loses the US elections.
(3) Necessarily, Socrates is human.

Modalities of this kind are called *de dicto*, for expressions like 'necessarily' and 'it is possible that' are attached to *dicta*, that is to sentences or pieces of language, in order to let us know about the way in which the sentence, or the proposition expressed by the sentence, bears its truth-value. According to (1), that two times two is four is a necessary truth; according to (2), that Obama loses the US elections is a possible truth.

Modal expressions can also qualify the features of objects – their having such and such properties, their standing in such and such relations:

(1a) 2 is necessarily an even number.
(2a) Obama might lose the US elections
(3a) Socrates is such that he is necessarily human.

Modalities of this kind are called *de re*, for what is qualified by the modal modifiers is a feature of a *res*, a thing: (1a) says that the number two has the property of being even in a necessary way; (3a) says that Socrates has that of being human in the same way, while (2a) says that Obama has the feature of being an election loser in a possible way.

Contemporary modal logicians and philosophers rely on Leibniz's insight that what is necessary is what holds or obtains at *all* possible worlds, that is no matter how things turn out; while what is possible is what holds or obtains at *some* possible world (and what is contingent is what obtains at some worlds, but not at others, etc.). Necessity and possibility, thus, are interpreted as quantifications over worlds, that is given our intuitive characterization above, over ways things can be. Each of the two notions can be characterized by means of the other: that it is necessarily the case that *P* means that it is not possible that not-*P*. Vice versa, that is it possible that *P* means that it is not necessary that not-*P*. One can thus define one via the other, plus negation (in technical terms, the two are the 'dual' of each other).

On the other hand, modal notions are highly ambiguous. It is common to distinguish between logical necessity (e.g., that if sentence *P* is true, then sentence *P* is true), mathematical necessity (e.g., that $2 \cdot 2 = 4$), and metaphysical necessity (e.g., that water is H_2O). Some of these kinds of necessity are more controversial than others, but many philosophers take the three of them as unrestricted, that is, as holding at *all* possible worlds, none excluded: there just is no way at all for $2 \cdot 2$ to fail to be 4; there just is no possible situation where *P* is true but at the same time fails to be true.

Other modal notions are more naturally understood as restricted forms of necessity or possibility. We often speak of things being impossible, but only in a relative sense or from a certain viewpoint. If you are stuck in a traffic jam in Paris at 2 p.m., and your flight is leaving from De Gaulle airport at 2:15 p.m., you may moan: 'There is no way that I can make it to the airport in time'. What you mean is that, given the timing, the means of transport available and the laws of physics of our world, it is impossible for you to reach the airport in time. It is not unrestrictedly, absolutely impossible: if you had *Star Trek*'s transporter, you could do it. But a *Star Trek* world in which you can be instantaneously disassembled into atoms, and be re-assembled exactly with the same atomic structure in a different place, is a world quite different from ours. Some may doubt that such a world is physically possible.

This hints at the idea of physical possibility or necessity as restricted possibility or necessity – restricted from the standpoint of a given world: to be physically possible or necessary with respect to our world is to hold in some or, respectively, all of the possible worlds that are compatible with the laws of physics holding at our world. A *Star Trek* world, on the face of it, looks like a possible world, taking 'possible' in an unrestricted sense. It may fail to be physically possible, that is compatible with the actual laws of physics. Similarly, we can speak of what is biologically possible as what is compatible with the actual laws of biology, that is as what obtains at some possible world where those laws hold (necessities of this kind, the physical and biological, are often called *nomological*, as they are understood in terms of scientific *nómoi*, the Greek for 'laws').

Many other notions can be captured in terms of possible worlds. The concept of *knowledge* has been analysed by Hintikka and others by claiming that cognitive agent x knows that P if and only if P is true at all possible worlds compatible with x's evidence. All of these notions (logical or mathematical necessity, nomological necessity, knowledge) share the feature of being *factive*. Factivity can be expressed by saying that the actual world must always be one of the possible ones, with respect to the relevant kind of possibility. If x knows that P, P must, as a matter of fact, be true (this marks the difference between knowing and believing: x can believe that P and be wrong; P can, as a matter of fact, be false). And as '$2 \cdot 2 = 4$' expresses a mathematical necessity, it has to be, as a matter of fact, true – that is, true at the actual world.

Possible worlds have also been used to capture important notions from other branches of philosophy. For instance, propositions, taken as the meanings of sentences (we spoke of them in the previous chapter) have been identified by authors like Montague and Stalnaker with sets of worlds. The informative job of a sentence like 'Snow is white' is to split the totality of possible situations, or ways things may be, into two sub-collections: those where the sentence is true (the worlds where snow is white), and those where it's false (the worlds where snow is not white). And it has been proposed that the proposition that snow is white, expressed by that sentence, should be identified with the first sub-collection.

Other venerable notions of traditional metaphysics have been phrased in terms of worlds, for instance, the concept of *essence*. In one sense, essences can be taken as packages of properties: those which an object has at all possible worlds where it exists. When we say that Socrates is essentially a human being (while, say, only accidentally hirsute), we claim that the property of being human is part of Socrates' essence. This can be understood as the claim that Socrates has the property of being human at all possible worlds where he exists. This is not the case for Socrates' being hirsute: he could be bald, that is, there are possible worlds where (he exists and) is not hirsute.

Yet another notion often understood in terms of possible worlds, and popular in metaphysics and the philosophy of mind, is the one of *supervenience*. Some reductionist philosophers of mind claim that mental properties (M-properties), features of our mind, 'supervene on' physical properties (P-properties), such as features of our brain. By this they want to stress that the realm of the mental does not float freely from the physical, but is in some important sense reducible to it, or completely determined by it: there could not be a difference in your mental states without some difference in the underlying states of your brain. This can, again, be captured in terms of worlds: M-properties supervene of P-properties in that there is no possible world with M-differences without P-differences, or in that, at each world, things which are indiscernible with respect to their P-properties are indiscernible with respect to their M-properties (there are, in fact, different ways of appealing to possible worlds when expressing such dependences, originating supervenience claims of different strengths: we need not enter into the details of this).

2 Ontological realism on worlds

So far, so good: possible worlds make for an extremely useful philosophical tool. The twofold question for us is: Should we include possible worlds in our ontological catalogue? And if so, what kind of entities are they? Very different replies are triggered, to begin with, depending on one's underlying metaontological convictions. In this section we will examine a range of answers proposed by philosophers who work within a Quinean ontological methodology.

The point of talk on possible worlds, as we have seen, is that sentences like the examples above are understood as involving quantification over worlds. For instance, (1) and (2a) can be rendered as:

(1w) At all possible worlds, $2 \cdot 2 = 4$.
(2aw) There is a possible world at which Obama loses the US elections.

These paraphrases generate ontological and metaphysical issues. Here's one: for Obama to lose the US elections at some possible world, one would think that he must exist at that world. But how can Obama, the election winner of our world, be the same as the Obama of that world – Obama the loser? This is generally (and, a bit generically) called the problem of *trans-world identity*: can one and the same individual, Obama, exist and be endowed with different properties at different possible worlds? We will come back to this in a moment. For now, the most immediate issue raised by sentences like (1w) and (2aw) has to do with the ontological commitment that they bring to a mainstream, Quinean metaontologist. Given Quine's criterion of ontological commitment, if we accept (1w) and (2aw) as literally true, we are committed to there being worlds: we quantify over them in our serious talk, and if what we claim is true, these things have to exist.

Some paraphrase strategy may be available. Maybe talk of possible worlds can be dispensed with, like talk of holes in pieces of cheese in Chapter 3, if we are systematic enough and can find the right adverbs. However, many philosophers believe that no systematic paraphrase strategy can preserve all the benefits of philosophical analyses in terms of explicit talk of, and quantification over, possible worlds. They believe that the ontological cost of admitting worlds in the catalogue is compensated by a theoretical gain: the one provided by the explanatory utility of worlds in lots of philosophical applications. Philosophers who have added worlds to their ontological catalogue have then faced the second key question mentioned above: what are worlds?

2.1 (Genuine) modal realism

According to David Lewis 1986, possible worlds are things just like this actual world surrounding us. They differ from our world only in terms of what goes on in them, not in kind. This may be understood as the claim that worlds are, for Lewis, concrete things just like our surroundings: they are composed of (other-worldly) trees, mountains and chairs – to be sure, when such things exist at them (worlds need not be made only of concrete things, if one believes in abstract objects like sets and numbers; but the distinctive feature of Lewisian worlds resides in their concreteness, broadly understood). This position has become famous with the label of *modal realism*. Since other philosophers believe that possible worlds really exist (and, in this sense, are 'modal realists'), but disagree with Lewis on their nature, John Divers 2002 has appropriately relabelled Lewis' stance as 'genuine modal realism', and we will stick to Divers' terminology.

Lewisian worlds differing from the actual one can include things which belong to kinds or species uninstantiated in the actual world. It seems intuitive that there could be talking donkeys (even though, as a matter of fact, there are none). The standard rendering of this claim in terms of possible worlds is: There are possible worlds such that, in them, there are talking donkeys. For Lewis, this should be taken at face value: some concrete possible worlds are inhabited by very real talking donkeys. Thus, there really are talking donkeys – only, they do not inhabit our world. So Lewis' ontology has room for concrete *possibilia* in the following sense: it admits the existence of non-actual objects, things that exist only at other worlds, such as talking donkeys, but which are as real and existent as ourselves. How does this match with that other intuitively true claim, that there are *no* talking donkeys (even though there could be)? For Lewis, we can truly claim 'There are no talking donkeys' insofar as the 'there are' in it expresses a *restricted* quantification: talking only about, that is, quantifying only over, things of the actual world, there are no talking donkeys. But we can extend our quantifiers to range also over other-worldly things, including talking donkeys.

The actual world has no ontological privilege in this framework. For Lewis, 'actual' works like an indexical expression. Indexical expressions like 'I', 'here' and 'now', can refer to different things in different contexts of utterance. For instance, 'I', when uttered by Francesco, refers to Francesco, but when it is uttered by Matteo, it refers to Matteo. Similarly, 'here' refers to the place of utterance, and 'now' to the time of utterance, whatever they may be. For Lewis, 'actually' is a world-indexical term: when uttered at world w, it refers to w. From the standpoint of each world, that very world is actual and the others are non-actual. What is actual for us is what is part of our world, but this brings no ontological advantage to ourselves. From the viewpoint of those other-worldly chatty donkeys, they are the actual folks; we are non-actual *possibilia*.

What makes a non-actual world a different world from ours, rather than yet another part of actuality? According to Lewis, worlds are causally and spatiotemporally isolated from each other. It doesn't make sense to claim that event e_1, taking place at world w_1, occurs before, or after, or simultaneously with, event e_2, taking place at a different world, w_2. Also, nothing happening at one world can causally influence anything at any other world. In particular, do not expect trans-world journeys to be possible: one cannot move between causally disconnected spacetimes. In fact, Lewis has a ready solution also to the problem of trans-world identity mentioned above: there is no such thing. In Lewis' ontology, individuals are world-bound (things are, in fact, slightly more complicated: because Lewis accepts a principle of unrestricted mereological fusion, given two entities x and y which are part of different worlds, there is their mereological fusion $x + y$, which is a trans-world object; still, no individual can be *entirely* part of more than one world).

How do we account, then, for the claim (2a) that Obama might lose the US elections? Lewis would not accept the paraphrase of (2a) as (2aw), *understood* as claiming that our world-mate Obama exists both at the actual world and at that other world. *De re* modal sentences like (2a) are understood by Lewis in terms of *counterparts*. A counterpart in world w_2 of a given individual, x_1, who is part of world w_1, is an individual, x_2, who is at least as similar to x_1 as anything else in w_2 in the relevant respects. Claim (2a) should be understood as:

(2al) There is a possible world with some Obama-counterpart who loses the US elections.

(Or, more pedantically: 'There is a possible world with a part which is a counterpart of Obama and who loses the US elections'). Lewisian worlds represent possibilities *directly*, by instantiation. That it is possible that there be talking donkeys is represented by there being real, concrete possible worlds of which very real and concrete talking donkeys are part. That it is possible for Obama to lose the US elections is represented by there being a very real Obama-counterpart at some world, who does lose the US elections (in a sense, then, Lewis *could* accept the claim that Obama exists both at the actual world and at other worlds, once this is appropriately understood as the claim that even though our Obama is part of our world only, he 'vicariously' exists at the worlds at which he has a counterpart).

Essentialist claims can be understood in terms of counterparts. That Socrates is essentially a human being can be analysed as the claim that all of Socrates' counterparts, that is, all individuals sufficiently similar to Socrates, at all worlds, are human beings. Counterparts work by similarity, and similarity is a vague and context-dependent notion. But Lewis claims that it is a virtue of his theory that it can model the vagueness and instability of our intuitions on what is possible and what is necessary for an individual. We could have, for instance, a stricter view on what is essential for Socrates, so that to be sufficiently similar to Socrates one has to be a male: all of Socrates' counterparts at all worlds will then have to be males, and Socrates will be essentially a male.

Lewis believes he can account for intensional notions (property, proposition, necessity, essence, etc.) in purely extensional terms. Genuine modal realism promises a reduction of modality to non-modal concepts – to speak Quinean: an improvement in modal ideology, paid for in the coin of ontological commitment to concrete worlds and *possibilia*. Lewis' ontology only includes material objects and sets, and the latter, as we know from the first part of our book, are purely extensional entities. Necessity and possibility claims are analysed as quantifications on worlds, and worlds are completely extensional objects in their turn. To be necessarily (possibly) true is to be true at all (some) worlds, that is at all (some) disconnected spacetimes; and disconnected spacetimes are extensional objects.

Or take, for instance, properties. Recall the Fregean example from Chapter 3: the property of being an animal with kidneys and that of being an animal with a heart are distinct. But the corresponding sets are one: sets are completely determined by their members, and anything (normally endowed) with a heart has kidneys and vice versa. But for Lewis the coincidence only obtains at the actual world. The difference between those two properties can be accounted for in purely set-theoretic terms. The property of having a heart is but the set of all things, this-(, or other-)worldly, with a heart; the property of having kidneys is but the set of all things, this-(, or other-)worldly, with kidneys. Now these two sets do not coincide. There could be things with kidneys but not a heart, or vice versa. For Lewis, this means: there really are (other-worldly) things with kidneys and not a heart, or vice versa. So some things belong to one set, but not the other. So, the two are distinct.

Genuine modal realism may look rather implausible, and many criticisms have been raised against it. On the other hand, Lewis has brilliantly responded to his critics, mainly in his *On the Plurality of Worlds*. We only list a few sample objections, together with (summaries of) Lewis' replies.

One epistemological objection from Skyrms 1976 is this: how can we be justified in believing that there are Lewisian possible worlds, that is (mostly) concrete entities, since by Lewis' own story we can have no causal contact with them, thus no empirical evidence of their existence? Perhaps there is good *a priori* evidence for the existence of abstract things like numbers or functions. But evidence for there being such concrete things as talking donkeys should be *a posteriori*, dependent on causal connectedness. We just cannot know that Lewis' story is true.

Lewis' 1986 reply is: what requires causal connectedness for knowledge is not the realm of the concrete, as opposed to the realm of the abstract. *Contingency*, as opposed to necessity, is what requires causal connectedness. Now the key ontological claims of genuine modal realism are not contingent, but necessary – either necessarily true, or necessarily false. An intuitive motivation for this may perhaps be pushed as follows: that there are many concrete worlds – the typical claim of Lewisian realism – cannot be contingent, for this would amount to there being many concrete worlds at some world, not at some other, which doesn't make much sense. When we say that there are many concrete worlds, the term 'there are' is not restricted to specific worlds. Claims of modal ontology, or claims that quantify unrestrictedly over everything there is – if such quantification is feasible – are either necessarily true or necessarily false.

A parenthetical remark: things are, in fact, not as simple as the intuitive motivation presents them. If we treat 'Is necessary that there are concrete possible worlds' via a standard translation in terms of possible worlds, it becomes: 'At each possible world, there are concrete possible worlds' – which doesn't make much sense either. As Divers 2002: Ch. 4 has pointed out, claims about the plurality of worlds itself cannot be contingently true or false in the radical sense that the modal modifiers 'necessarily' and 'possibly' just become *redundant* for them: if *P* is one such claim, *P* is true if and only if 'Possibly *P*' is true if and only if 'Necessarily *P*' is true. Contingency, in this context, is simply inconsistency.

Let us move on to another objection, found in Haack 1977. This claims that Lewis is committed to an extremely prodigal ontology. He has us accept the existence of an infinity of concrete worlds, inhabited by lots of non-actual *possibilia*: talking donkeys, flying horses, Wittgenstein's merely possible daughters, possible bald men in doorways, etc.

Lewis' reply is that prodigality in ontology should be measured by the number of ontological kinds one has to posit, rather than by the number of instances of each kind. What matters is how many general categories we list in the ontological catalogue, not how many things fall under each category. And from this viewpoint, Lewisian ontology is rather sparse: it only admits, as we said, concrete material objects and, among the abstract objects, sets. Everything else (properties, propositions, etc.) is claimed by Lewis to be reducible to constructions out of concrete individuals and sets. Of course, there will be lots of *possibilia* out there, which we may still be reluctant to accept: the various other-worldly chatty donkeys, etc.; but these will only be yet other instances of concreteness.

Another criticism, due to Saul Kripke 1972, targets Lewis' account of *de re* modality via counterparts. When we analyse the *de re* modal claim that Obama could lose the US elections by claiming that some other-worldly counterpart of

Obama loses the election, we seem to have changed the subject. We were interested in what *Obama* could and could not do, and now we end up talking about what someone else could or could not do. Obama does care about winning the US elections, but he could not care less about what may happen to other individuals in disconnected spacetimes.

The reply to Kripke is that, first, in (2al) we do not speak of what *could* happen to some Obama-counterpart, but of what *does* happen to him: there is no explicit modality in (2al). Second, it is not true that the *de re* rendering of claims like (2a) as (2al) is not about Obama. That Obama could lose the US elections is made true by there being a counterpart *of Obama*, that is someone sufficiently similar to *him*, who is an election loser. Sufficient similarity with Obama is needed to do the job, thus (2al) makes explicit reference to Obama.

2.2 Actualist realism

Few modal ontologists and metaphysicians have endorsed genuine modal realism. Perhaps the most resilient attitude towards the view is what Lewis labelled the 'incredulous stare': in spite of Lewis' intelligent defence, people remain unconvinced. The majority of philosophers working within a Quinean metaontological framework, who take quantification over possible worlds at face value and as existentially committing, pursue a more moderate form of realism, often called *actualist realism*.

What would the moderation consist in? According to actualist realists, unrestrictedly everything is part of actuality: there are no non-actual worlds, inhabited by non-actual *possibilia*. How can other possible worlds, which are supposed to be in some sense maximal (this is what makes of them *worlds*), be proper parts of the actual world, or completely included in it? There does not seem to be enough room in the realm of actuality! Actualist realists reply that possible worlds are indeed part of actuality, but as *abstract* entities, not as concrete things like Lewisian worlds. What about what we call 'the actual world' then? These surroundings of ours – chairs, mountains, people – seem to be very concrete. Actualists reply that, while all possible worlds are abstract, one is actual*ized*, that is realized by this actual, largely concrete reality surrounding us. We must distinguish between the actual world taken as that abstract object which, among the many abstract objects that are possible worlds, is actualized by actuality, and actuality itself.

The agreement between actualist realists ends more or less here. Positions diverge on what kind of abstract entities possible worlds are. Ironically, one of the best overviews of the various forms of actualist realism is provided by genuine realist Lewis in 1986 (Ch. 3). Lewis calls actualist realism *ersatzism*, from the German word *ersatz*, meaning 'substitute' or 'fake'; so actualist realists' worlds are sometimes called *ersatz worlds*.

A crucial question for actualist realists or ersatzists is how worlds represent possibilities. Lewisian worlds, as we know, represent by instantiation: the unactualized possibility of talking donkeys is represented by there being a concrete world different from the actual one, that is, from ours, and including non-actual but real donkeys that talk. This cannot be so for actualist realists, who cannot believe in the reality of Lewisian concrete *possibilia*: if worlds are abstract entities, they cannot include concrete things like talking donkeys as their part.

According to authors like Plantinga 1974 and van Inwagen 1986, worlds are particular states of affairs or ways for things to be: those states of affairs which are both possible and maximal. States of affairs are things which can, in an important sense, succeed or fail, or, perhaps more appropriately, obtain or fail to obtain. Think of the state of affairs consisting of Paris' being in France. This one obtains, for Paris happens to actually be in France. The state of affairs consisting of Paris' being in Italy, on the other hand, fails to obtain. Both are possible states of affairs, though, that is both may obtain or have obtained – unlike the state of affairs consisting of Paris' both being and not being in France, which cannot obtain, that is which is not possible.

It is also intuitive that states of affairs can be, in some sense, included in larger states of affairs. Given that the fifth arrondissement is part of Paris, the state of affairs consisting of the fifth arrondissement's being in France seems to be included in the state of affairs consisting of Paris' being in France. We can then get the idea of a possible state of affairs being maximal: a state of affairs s_1 is maximal when, for any state of affairs s_2, either s_1 includes s_2 (s_1's obtaining entails s_2's obtaining), or s_1 precludes s_2 (s_1's obtaining rules out s_2's obtaining). Possible, maximal states of affairs are the possible worlds. Of them, only one succeeds or obtains, and that is the actualized world. Its obtaining precludes the obtaining of any other possible world: all the others are merely possible.

This kind of actualist realism, sometimes called Plantingan realism (Divers 2002: 174), commits us to an ontology of states of affairs, and specifically, of maximal states of affairs, which some may find unpalatable for independent reasons. Lewis 1986: Section 3.4 has also objected to Plantingan realism that it is not clear how states of affairs are supposed to represent possibilities. Actualist realists of this kind tend to understand representation by worlds as a primitive, brute fact, which Lewis took as invoking a kind of 'magic'.

Another potential shortcoming of the view is the following: in order to make sense of the notion of possible and maximal state of affairs, we have to resort to a bunch of modal notions. We have to characterize possible worlds as things that *can* obtain, and we need to understand their maximality in terms of preclusion: when one world obtains, it is *impossible* for another world to obtain. But in Section 1 of this chapter, we introduced worlds in order to make sense of modal notions to begin with. So, on the one hand, we claim that possibility and necessity have to be understood as quantifications on possible worlds; but on the other hand, we understand worlds as things such that it is possible that they obtain, that it is impossible for two of them to co-obtain, etc. We seem to be caught in a circle of modal notions. We can, at most, explain some of them by means of others, but we can never reduce them to non-modal notions: we are doomed, in Lewis' words, to 'primitive modality'.

The reply of Plantingan realists to this charge has usually consisted in biting the bullet, but in claiming that no fully reductive account of modalities is feasible. The reduction of modality to non-modal notions promised by genuine modal realism may or may not succeed; but it comes with the ontological cost of Lewisian worlds, which is unbearable to actualists.

Another form of actualist realism, versions of which are due to Quine 1969 and Cresswell 1972, is often called 'combinatorialism'. The name is due to the fact that possible worlds are taken here as recombinations of actuality. The view can be made precise in different ways, one of which is the following: how things are at the actual world depends on a certain distribution of actual properties and relations among the actual objects. For instance, in the actual world Paris has the property of being in France, and it is to the north of Rome. But we can imagine things being arranged otherwise: Paris having the property of being in Italy, and being to the south of Rome. Worlds represent possibilities by being maximal rearrangements: redistributions of actual properties and relations among the actual objects. Arrangements and rearrangements, or combinations and recombinations, are abstract things, so worlds still count as abstract.

Combinatorialism is very much in the spirit of actualism: it only needs actual things (in the version briefly considered: objects, properties and relations) as the basic stuff out of which worlds are constructed. Hence, the view faces a limitation, often labelled as the 'problem of aliens'. It seems possible for there to be alien objects and/or alien properties and relations – roughly: objects such that they are not recombinations of (parts of) objects from the actual world; and properties and relations uninstantiated at the actual world, and which cannot be obtained as recombinations of actually instantiated properties, but which are instantiated at other worlds. No rearrangement of actuality can account for these possibilities. Within combinatorialism, one can, at most, tamper with actual objects and their parts, and with properties and relations which are actually instantiated. It seems that combinatorialism will not manage to represent all possibilities: there are possible worlds that cannot be delivered by the theory.

Another form of actualist realism may be called *linguistic* realism. In this view, worlds are collections of sentences or sentence-like entities: Carnap 1956 talked of state descriptions, and Jeffrey 1965 and Adams 1974 of world-stories or sets of propositions. The sentence-like entities at issue need not be those of any natural language: they can belong to some artificial or *ad hoc* 'world-making' language. Worlds represent possibilities linguistically (that is in whatever way sentences or propositions represent what they are or speak about), and are still abstract, for they are collections or sets of things.

But worlds are not just any old assemblage of sentences or propositions. Bracketing issues of expressive limitation, let us pretend that English is the world-making language and, for brevity, only talk in terms of sentences. The set {Snow is white, Grass is green} does not make for a world, for it is highly incomplete; the set {Snow is white, Snow is not white} does not represent a possibility for (besides being incomplete) it is inconsistent: its elements cannot all be true. Worlds must be *consistent* and *complete* collections of sentences: something like coherent and maximally detailed novels or stories. Of these maximal consistent sets, exactly one has as members all and only the sentences of the world-making language that happen to be true, and this one is the world that is actualized. All the other worlds are maximal consistent collections of sentences, at least one of which is false.

One problem for this view is that its explanatory power seems to be limited. We saw in Section 1 that worlds are invoked in the semantics of modal logics, and modal logics are about logical entailment in modal contexts: what follows logically from what, when expressions like 'necessarily' and 'possibly' are around. Now for a set of sentences to form a world, it must be closed under logical entailment: as *P* and *Q* taken together entail their conjunction, then a set of sentences which includes *P* and *Q* but not their conjunction is not a possible world. A world which represents that snow is white and represents that grass is green, but which fails to represent that snow is white and grass is green, fails to represent a logical possibility. But the machinery of possible worlds in modal logic was supposed to perform the task of capturing logical entailment; and now we find ourselves invoking logical entailment to capture the notion of possible world.

A connected issue for linguistic realism is, again, the one of primitive modality. We claimed that worlds are maximally detailed, *possible* stories, that is maximal sets of sentences which *can* be true all together. To select, among all the sets of sentences, those which are to count as worlds, we still seem to have to resort to modal notions. One option available to linguistic realists is to specify possibility (and maximality) purely syntactically, e.g., in terms of negation-consistency (and completeness) for the relevant sets of sentences: for each sentence *P* of the world-making language, either *P* or ~*P*, but not both, must be in the set. Lewis' 1986 retort is that this would deliver too narrow a conception of necessity and too broad a conception of possibility: worlds where something is a male vixen, or where water fails to be H_2O, would count as unrestrictedly possible by the syntactic criterion.

Another form of explanatory limitation awaits those like Adams 1974, who take worlds specifically as sets of propositions. As we also saw above, a popular account of propositions explains them as sets of worlds: the proposition expressed by a sentence the set of worlds where the sentence is true. But we cannot have this, if we want to explain worlds as sets of propositions in their turn.

Yet another form of actualist realism, mainly due to Robert Stalnaker 1976, takes seriously talk of worlds as 'ways things might be'. In general, properties are ways things might be: that snow is white means that being white is (part of) the way snow actually is, a property it actually has. But things might have been different, in that snow may have been green. That is it may have had the property of being green. So the property of being green is a way snow might be. Stalnaker proposes to take possible worlds as world-properties: *maximal* ways things might be, that is something like structured properties of actuality as a whole. Properties are abstract objects, and so are worlds. In particular, the actualized world is the unique world-property, or structural-maximal property, which is instantiated: it's the way reality as a whole is. All the other worlds are uninstantiated.

One accidental drawback of this form of actualist realism is that the view is metaphysically under-developed (see Divers 2002: 177–8). Also, the objection raised by Lewis against other forms of actualist realism seems to apply to Stalnakerian realism as well: it is committed to primitive modality. After all, what makes a maximal property a possibility, thus a possible world, is that it *can* be instantiated by reality as a whole.

3 Non-standard approaches

All the views we have inspected so far approach the ontology of possible worlds from a broadly Quinean metaontological viewpoint. We quantify over possible worlds in our best theories. Quantification is ontologically, that is existentially committing. So we are committed to the existence of possible worlds, and it is up to us to give a coherent ontological and metaphysical account of worlds. But after the development of the non-standard metaontological views we met in the first part of this book, some philosophers have explored alternative approaches to modal ontology. We briefly examine two of them: the fictionalist and the Meinongian.

3.1 Talk of worlds as fictional talk

We already hinted at the doctrine of modal fictionalism in Chapter 6 on fictionalist metaontology. This is in fact a recent application, to talk of possible worlds, of the general strategy of fictionalism. 'Modal fictionalism' is standard terminology (Nolan 2011), but we said in that chapter that it is a bit misleading, for modal fictionalists are not fictionalists about modality: they are fictionalists about worlds. Talk of/ quantification over possible worlds ought to be understood as literally false: it is only true within a 'possible worlds' fiction', which we make-believe because it delivers useful results in the explanation of modal notions. Modal fictionalism promises the theoretical benefits of modal realism, but aims to dispense with the ontological costs by treating the relevant ontological theory as a fiction. We should not include worlds (other than the actual) in our ontological catalogue, but talking as if there were other worlds is useful.

A major proponent of the view, Gideon Rosen 1990, has taken Lewisian genuine modal realism as the relevant fiction. We can formulate the view in a way which is neutral between Lewisian counterpart theory and (the standardly accepted by actualists) trans-world identity. We will soon see, though, that the issue of choosing which modal realist approach counts as the right fiction is not trivial for fictionalists.

A (genuine or actualist) realist about a modal sentence *P*, as we know, will paraphrase it into a sentence involving quantification over possible worlds, *P**. She will then assert instances of the realist's equivalence:

(R) *P* if and only if *P**.

A typical instance of (R) is:

(R1) There could be talking donkeys if and only if there is some world at which there are talking donkeys.

Modal realists will take such instances of (R) as literally true. Not so for the modal fictionalist: they involve quantification over worlds in their right-hand side; but according to fictionalists there are no such things (other than the actual world), so the right-hand side is literally false. But unreconstructed modal sentences like 'There could be talking donkeys' or 'Obama may have lost the US elections' can be strictly and literally true (modal fictionalists, if we recall, are not fictionalists about such modal claims). When the left-hand side is, as it appears with (R1), true, the biconditional will be false.

The fictionalist's alternative proposal is to use, again, a non-factive 'according to fiction F' operator. The right scheme is:

(A) *P* if and only if, according to fiction F: *P**.

Here, F is the relevant story about possible worlds. Now (A) will deliver true instances such as:

(A1) There could be talking donkeys if and only if, according to the possible worlds' fiction, there is some world at which there are talking donkeys.

As modal fictionalism is a relatively new view, so are criticisms of it. Here's one. Recall the issue of primitive modality: according to Lewis, only his own (genuine) modal realism can free us from it, whereas actualist realists are stuck with it. However, according-to-the-fiction operators seem to be intrinsically modal in their turn. Rosen did not interpret, of course, the relevant fictional operator as a quantifier on worlds for, as a modal fictionalist, he did not believe in such things. He took the operator as officially primitive. But 'According to fiction F: P^*' just seems to mean something like: 'If things were as fiction F represents them, then P^* would be true'. This is a subjunctive conditional (if the fictionalist is right, a counterfactual: the antecedent is false), that is, a modal conditional. Which marks a discrepancy between (R) and (A): a modal realist like Lewis, if his view is right, can deliver a purely extensional account of worlds. He has, via instances of (R), an extensional reduction of modality. Not so for (A), even if modal fictionalism is right: modal claims such as that there could be talking donkeys are reduced to other modal claims, according to which, if things were as told in the possible worlds fiction, then, etc.

A reply to this objection may be provided by relying on a distinction, which can be found in Rosen's paper, between *strong* and *timid* modal fictionalism. The former view aims at explaining the real metaphysical nature of modal notions via the possible worlds fiction. The latter view only takes instances of (A) as establishing enlightening correlations. Primitive modality may be a trouble for strong fictionalists, but not for timid fictionalists.

Another objection has been raised by Sainsbury (2010: Ch. 8). How do we choose the right fiction? That is: which of the many and radically different stories told by modal realists is to replace the 'F' in the fictionalist scheme (A)? We explained the view in a way that is neutral between Lewisian counterpart theory and trans-world identity. But according to Sainsbury, it is difficult for a modal fictionalist to justify taking the counterpart story told in *On the Plurality of Worlds*, rather than some realist actualist's account, as the right fiction. This is likely not to be so for other forms of fictionalism, like fictionalism on mathematical discourse. For here we have, as we saw in Chapter 9 while talking of Field's approach, a conservativeness constraint: only fictions which are conservative with respect to the results of standard mathematics are acceptable. Established mathematical facts provide, thus, the relevant constraints. But, if one can talk of 'established modal facts' at all, they are much less certain than mathematics.

3.2 Worlds as non-existents

Parsons 1980, and more recently Priest 2005, 2008, have proposed that all worlds other than the actual be taken as Meinongian non-existent objects. The proposal is rather sketchy and in need of development, but *prima facie* intuitive enough. One fast way to mark the difference between what is actual and what is merely possible, or an unrealized possibility, is to claim that what is actual is what really exists, while what is merely possible is what could exist but, as a matter of fact, does not. That something does not exist, for the Meinongian, does not perforce mean that there is no such thing, as we know: it may mean that the thing is a non-existent object. Just as Santa Claus or Holmes are non-existent objects, so merely possible worlds can be non-existent objects which are, in some sense, maximal.

Notice that various objections one could advance against non-existents in general – to the effect that they have no clear identity conditions, or that we cannot know them for they are devoid of causal powers and not located in the physical world, etc. – apply to more traditional forms of modal realism as well. If worlds are constructions out of propositions, or maximal property-like entities, then a Quinean may ask for an account of identity criteria for propositions and properties in general before accepting worlds as respectable entities in a safe and sane ontology. As we hinted in Chapter 3, Quine himself was sceptic about the possibility of such an account. If worlds are abstract existents, as any form of actualist realism has them, then they are devoid of causal powers and physical location. And even Lewisian worlds, which are (largely) concrete entities, are causally and physically inaccessible to us. So it is not clear that Meinongianism on worlds has a disadvantage over other accounts here.

Besides, Priest claims that modal facts can be known, in this framework, largely by stipulation and imaginative exercise, in the same way in which we know facts about fictional characters, which Meinongians take as paradigmatic non-existents. Doyle was free to stipulate that Holmes lived in Baker Street, not Oxford Street (Priest 2008: 31). Similarly, we can stipulate worlds that are such-and-such and so-and-so, for example, such that Obama loses the US elections at them. But this raises a problem. Just as we can stipulate and imagine Holmes as living in Baker Street, it seems that we can stipulate and imagine the Mad Mathematician as squaring the circle. But squaring the circle, as has been proven, is a mathematical impossibility. If mathematical necessity is unrestricted, the Mad Mathematician's squaring the circle does not count as a possible situation. So imaginative stipulation as such does not guarantee that what is represented via it is a *possibility*. We may postulate via imagination non-existent scenarios or situations which are not possible at all. Thus, we need some criterion to discriminate between non-existent worlds that are possible, and non-existent worlds that are impossible. Whether we can so discriminate without resorting to other modal notions, and therefore without being stuck with primitive modality, is an open problem for the Meinongian approach (the Meinongian may, of course, bite the bullet and accept primitive modality, as many actualist realists do).

Another potential problem for the view is that possible but unactualized – thus non-existent – worlds will have to include lots of existent things. Even when these things do not exist at the actual world (take Wittgenstein's merely possible oldest daughter), they should be existent at the non-existent worlds that represent them as existing (take a world where Wittgenstein gets married, has a daughter, etc.). It is not clear how a non-existent object, such as a world, can include, or host, or have as parts, existent things. This is no fatal objection as such, but calls for some precise account of what kind of inclusion, or hosting or parthood relation is in play here – or, more generally, for some precise account of how non-existent worlds can represent possible situations having existent things as their constituents.

Further Reading

Anyone should read Lewis 1986. The most detailed guide to the ontology and metaphysics of worlds is Divers 2002; see also Menzel 2013. On the problems of trans-world identity, see Mackie and Jago 2013. An excellent introduction to actualism in modal ontology and metaphysics is Menzel 2008; see also Menzel 1990 for a general defence of the view. Loux 1979 is a collection of classic essays on modal metaphysics. On modal fictionalism, see Nolan 2011.

12

Material Objects

Chapter Outline

In this chapter we deal with the objects that make up the physical world surrounding us. Ordinary material beings like cats and armchairs look familiar, but they raise difficult ontological puzzles. Section 1 introduces the topic, while Section 2 presents the basics of *mereology*, the doctrine of the notion of parthood, as a general framework to discuss about material objects. Section 3 introduces the *decomposition* problem: can such objects be decomposed into smaller and smaller parts *in infinitum*, or must their decomposition end with 'atoms', mereological simples? Section 4 discusses the *composition* problem: under which conditions do material objects compose a further object as its parts? Two opposite revisionary ontologies are introduced here: *mereological nihilism*, for which only mereological simples exist, and *mereological universalism*, for which composition is unrestricted. Section 5 addresses issues of synchronic identity and co-location. The central question here is: can two distinct material objects occupy exactly the same place at the same time? Finally, Section 6 deals with issues of diachronic identity. The central question here is: under which conditions does the same material object persist through different times (in particular, while it undergoes change)? *Three-dimensionalist, four-dimensionalist*, and *sequentialist* conceptions of material objects are examined.

1 What are material objects?

Of more or less any putative ontological kind (properties, propositions, sets, worlds, *possibilia*…), philosophers – especially, but not only, those working in the Quinean metaontological tradition – debate whether we should include it in our ontological catalogue. It would seem that few could question, at least, the existence of what Austin called 'moderate-sized specimens of dry goods': armchairs, cars, laptops and so on – but also, familiar living beings like cats, flowers and trees. These are sample *material objects*, and refusing to include them in our ontology may seem to amount to a radical scepticism on the very existence of an external world. However, 'the metaphysics of material objects has come to be recognized as one of the most difficult parts of philosophy' (van Inwagen 2001: 6). Various authors have proposed radically opposed views of such objects, and this area of inquiry, as we will see, makes stark the contrast between descriptive and prescriptive ontological methodologies.

Characterizing material objects in a precise way is not trivial. Their being material, that is, made of matter, points at their being concrete (as opposed to abstract): provided with causal powers, therefore, in principle accessible to sensory experience. Material objects are often characterized as *particulars* (as opposed to *universals*), to mark their occupying a single place at any instant of time. The property of being an armchair may have no spatiotemporal address at all, or may be multiply located: one could say that the property of being an armchair is wherever there's an armchair. But this particular armchair one of us is sitting on while doing armchair metaphysics has a unique and unrepeatable location in space and time.

However, as we have seen in Chapter 9, the very distinction between abstract and concrete is not easy to draw (recall the discussion on Lewis' 'way of negation'). Contemporary physics gives us a more and more abstract and mathematized conception of matter. It teaches us, for instance, that some subatomic particles may lack a definite spatiotemporal location, although this would probably not lead us to qualify them as abstract objects or universals. Also the accessibility of such particles to sensory experience is out of question, unless we stretch the meaning of 'sensory experience' beyond the limits of our human perceptual apparatus. Finally, invocation of 'causal powers' only helps that much, given that causation is itself a metaphysical conundrum.

We shall therefore content ourselves with a coarse and intuitive initial understanding of material objects as constituents of this physical world surrounding us. While few would dispute that there is such a physical world, exactly what it is composed of is a matter of debate. As we will see, some ontologists reject that Austin's ordinary objects are genuine constituents of reality; others admit such objects as cats and armchairs, but also include in their catalogue other material beings few laymen would ever think about. A nice general framework to discuss the ontology of material objects is provided by *mereology*: the theory of parthood relations (from the Greek *méros*, 'part'), to the basics of which we now turn.

2 Mereology

Mereologists often take the theory as a most general ontological framework, spelling out the principles governing the relations between parts, or between parts and their wholes, for things of any kind. While it makes sense to say that what comes after the '@' is part of the e-mail address, or that the antecedent is part of a conditional, parthood relations matter especially for material objects. That an armchair is located and extended in space intuitively means that it has spatial parts: the back, the arms, the legs, etc. Spatial parthood makes for a very intuitive case of parthood (whether material objects also have *temporal* parts is a matter of debate: we will address this issue later on in this chapter; for now, we just focus on the spatial composition of material objects).

Parthood can be naturally taken as a binary relation: *x is part of y*. Let *y* be an armchair, a human being or a bikini; then *x* can be the armchair's arm, the human being's arm or the bra of the bikini. Some principles governing the relation are fairly uncontroversial: Varzi 2009 claims that they just fix the lexical meaning of 'part'. First, everything should be part of itself (*reflexivity* of parthood, in technical terms). Second, if *x* is part of *y* and *y* is part of *x*, then *x* just *is y* (*antisymmetry*). Third, if *x* is part of *y* and *y* is part of *z*, then *x* is part of *z* (*transitivity*). In technical terms, these three principles make of parthood a *non-strict partial ordering*.

Some philosophers have doubted even the lexical principles for parthood. Against antisymmetry, Thomson 1998 claimed that if parthood accounts for material constitution, then an object and the matter it is constituted of can be part of each other, despite being numerically distinct: take a statue and the bunch of clay that it is made of. Some ontologists, however, take material constitution as a non-mereological relation, and this complicates the picture (see again Varzi 2009: Section 2.1). We will postpone a discussion of Thomson's point to include it in a more general setting in Section 5 below.

Parthood as a non-strict ordering admits 'improper' cases in which a thing can be part of itself. Sometimes people speaking of parts have in mind, rather, what is often called *proper* parthood, a parthood relation ruling out improper cases: the armchair is part of itself, but not a proper part; the armchair's arm is a proper part of the armchair. Proper parthood can, however, be defined from parthood: *x* is a proper part of *y* if and only if *x* is part of *y* but *y* is not part of *x* (technically, proper parthood is a *strict* partial ordering). Vice versa, one could start with proper parthood and define parthood out of it: *x* is part of *y* if and only if *x* is either a proper part of *y*, or identical with *y*.

More controversial mereological principles govern *composition* (the existence of wholes given the parts) and *decomposition* (the existence of parts given the wholes). We may wonder whether, as we take smaller and smaller parts of our armchair, we could in principle go on forever, or whether such decomposition must come to an end. We may also wonder whether, when we glue together two armchairs, we have thereby composed a new material object or not. It is with such questions that substantive ontological debates begin.

3 Decomposition

The issue whether the decomposition of matter can go on *in infinitum* has a venerable history in Western philosophy, ranging from ancient Greek atomists like Democritus, to Kant, who took the opposition between discrete and continuous views of reality as an antinomy of pure reason in the Transcendental Dialectic of his first *Critique*.

We can start with a definition of *atom*. In mereological terms, an atom is a mereological simple: something with no proper parts. Are there atoms? The view is debated in contemporary ontology (see van Inwagen 1990; Markosian 1998). Perhaps there are none, that is everything is divisible *in infinitum* or, as Lewis said, 'gunky'. In mereological terms, this amounts to accepting a 'gunk principle': Everything has proper parts. Or perhaps we should accept an opposite 'atomicity principle': everything ultimately has atoms as parts (this can ground a *digital ontology* where everything, from objects to space-time, is discrete and computationally tractable: see Berto and Tagliabue 2012). These two views are contraries: they cannot be true together, but they leave room for intermediate positions. For instance, perhaps space-time is continuous but the mereology of material objects is discrete. This may happen, if mereological simplicity is not tied to lack of spatial extension.

This debate becomes especially intriguing, on the one hand, when understood in the metaontological perspective of grounding theories, and on the other, when compared to the results of contemporary physics. Atomicity may be understood in a grounding-friendly framework as the idea that decomposition comes to an end when we reach a fundamental layer of physical reality: the atoms, in this sense, would be the ultimate grounding entities on which material objects ultimately depend. If, instead, the physical world is gunky, this may be expressed as a kind of non-well-foundedness for grounding: material things are grounded in smaller and smaller things, all the way down *in infinitum*. Schaffer 2003, for instance, has contested the very idea of an ultimate grounding level in this sense.

Also, one may wonder whether the notion of atomicity has any connection with the subatomic particles of contemporary physics: are the atoms just what microphysics talks about? Ladyman and Ross 2007 have argued that physical science offers no evidence that atomicity holds of the physical world, and that the very opposition between atomistic and gunky views of reality is misguided from the viewpoint of contemporary natural science.

4 Composition

Perhaps the most debated mereological issue in contemporary ontology is the one concerning the existence of *mereological sums* or *fusions*. In fact, we already hinted at the topic elsewhere in our book. Take material objects $x_1, \ldots, x_n$. Their mereological sum or fusion y is the smallest thing including $x_1, \ldots, x_n$ as parts, or, equivalently, the thing whose parts are whatever is part of $x_1, \ldots, x_n$ and nothing else.

Three provisos on fusions. First, one can think of mereological sums of things of different ontological kinds – say, the sum of Socrates and its singleton, the set {Socrates}. As our interest is now confined in material objects, we will disregard such (admittedly weird) fusions. Second, as we will see in Section 5 of this chapter, it is doubtful that we can always talk of *the* sum of a bunch of objects: according to some ontologists, numerically distinct things can sometimes be composed exactly of the same proper parts. In this section we can, however, disregard this complication as orthogonal to the debate on composition. Third, we speak of 'material objects $x_1, \ldots, x_n$', again, for the sake of simplicity: we don't want to thereby rule out the possibility of infinitary sums – sums of infinitely many *x*s.

The debate on sums has focused on what van Inwagen 1990 called the *Special Composition Question*, which was already mentioned in our chapter on Carnap and neo-Carnapianism. The very formulation of the question involves some subtleties, but for our purposes the following will do: Under which conditions do objects $x_1, \ldots, x_n$, have a mereological sum y? This is a way of asking in what circumstances a bunch of objects compose, add up to, or form an object – a whole of which the objects we started with are the parts.

Common-sense intuition suggests that, under some but not all conditions, a bunch of objects composes a sum. The bones, flesh, skin, internal organs, etc., of Tibbles the cat add up to Tibbles. But when we deal with scattered and seemingly unrelated things, like Queen Elizabeth's ear-rings, the Moon, and David Lewis' left shoe, there does not seem to be anything which is composed exactly of these things.

However, it is extremely difficult to pin down the conditions which have to be satisfied by objects $x_1, \ldots, x_n$, for them to compose a y. One may, for instance, take mereo-topological connection (having overlapping parts, sharing a boundary, etc.) as a necessary condition. This seems intuitively wrong, though, for we count as full-fledged things scattered material objects like bikinis, the Amsterdam University Library copy of the first edition of the *Handbook of Philosophical Logic* (which is composed of four volumes), or the United States of America (as a geographical entity composed of scattered parts, like Alaska and Hawaii).

Conversely, such connection does not even seem to be intuitively sufficient. Gluing together the two authors of this volume would lead few of us to accept that a new object, their mereological sum, has come into existence. Besides, whether some objects compose a whole seems to be an intuitively vague matter. Suppose we slowly and gradually increase the distance between the body parts composing Tibbles (say, the reciprocal distance between Tibbles' cells): at what point shall we claim that Tibbles has been disintegrated, that is, that those parts cease to compose a whole?

Given that our intuitions on mereological constitution produce such puzzles, some revisionary ontologists have given seemingly counterintuitive, but allegedly ontologically more perspicuous answers to the Special Composition Question. Revisionism takes two opposite directions here. According to authors like Rosen and Dorr 2002, under *no* condition whatsoever do the *x*s compose a *y*: there just is no mereological composite. In this view, often called *mereological nihilism*, parthood collapses into identity: the only way for *x* to be part of *y* is for *x* to *be y*. A similar view is embraced by van Inwagen 1990 himself. According to him, composition can take place, but only when the relevant *y* is a living organism: something such that the *x*s composing it form a life. This view is sometimes called mereological quasi-nihilism.

The nihilist or quasi-nihilist ontologist who embraces a Quinean metaontology has to reject the existence of most or all ordinary material objects: strictly speaking, there exist no armchairs, tables, mountains or Austin's mid-size specimens of dry goods (van Inwagen can spare Tibbles the cat as a living being, but armchairs, tables and mountains still have to go). The standard strategy here is to paraphrase away sentences referring to, or quantifying over, such commonsensical material objects, just as we saw Argle paraphrasing away quantification over holes in pieces of cheese in Chapter 3. We speak as if we were sitting on an armchair, thus, as if there were armchairs. There really are, though, only simples arranged armchair-wise ('armchair-wise' making for the relevant shape-characterizing adverb). These simples may be the subatomic particles physics talks about, or they may be something else, (still) unknown to physics. What matters is that they cannot be composing a material object, the armchair, to be included in our ontological catalogue as genuine (worldly) furniture. According to Rosen and Dorr, composition is, at most, a useful fiction: we talk as if there were armchairs (or cats, for that matter) for reasons of practicality, but there are no such things in reality.

Authors like Lewis 1986, Casati and Varzi 1999 and Sider 2001 are at the opposite side of the spectrum. Their reply to the Special Composition Question is that *any* old bunch of things has a mereological sum. We need not speak of conditions under which composition takes place. We must do nothing special to objects $x_1, \ldots, x_n$ for them to compose a *y*: they already do. This principle, called 'Unrestricted Mereological Composition' and to which we already hinted in our Chapter 9 on abstract objects, is embedded in classical formal presentations of mereology. The corresponding ontological position is often called *mereological universalism.*

In a standard, Quinean metaontological framework, universalism ontologically commits us to implausible things: scattered objects composed of disparate, unrelated things of different kinds, like the mereological sum of the right half of Lewis' left shoe plus the Moon plus the sum of all Her Majesty's ear-rings. While universalism is unacceptable to ontologists like van Inwagen himself or Simons 1987, Lewis has advanced a powerful argument in its favour.

Any putative restriction of composition, Lewis claims, if it respects our intuitions on when the *x*s compose a *y*, has to be vague, for such intuitions are themselves vague (and context-dependent), as we saw above. However, composition cannot be vague. We can ask the question in a perfectly crisp fragment of our language: given the *x*s, is there a *y* composed by them? Since for Quineans ontological, that is existential commitment is fully captured by the quantifier, the answer can be no more vague than existence can: either *y* exists or it does not. So any sensible restriction on composition, by having to be crisp, will be gratuitous: it will not fit the intuitive, vague motivations for restricting.

How do we reconcile the scattered and weird objects accepted by universalism with our common-sense picture of the world? Lewis' reply is: 'Restrict quantifiers, not composition' (Lewis 1986: 213). Given any old bunch of objects, there exists their mereological sum. However, some mereological sums are more cognitively salient and important for us than others. We tend to restrict our quantifiers to them in our everyday language: we tend not to talk about (and not to focus on) uninteresting, scattered and highly heterogeneous objects. Such a practical restriction of our quantifiers, however, has no ontological import:

> We are happy enough with mereological sums of things that contrast with their surroundings more than they do with one another; and that are adjacent, stick together, and act jointly. ... We have no name for the mereological sum of the right half of my left shoe plus the Moon plus the sum of all Her Majesty's ear-rings, except for the long and clumsy name I just gave it. ... It is very sensible to ignore such a thing in our everyday thought and language. But ignoring it won't make it go away. (Lewis 1986: 213)

Another Lewisian argument in defence of universalism has to do with the so-called 'ontological innocence' of mereology. Lewis 1991 proposed to take mereological composition (a many-one relation: the relation between the *x*s and the *y* they compose) as *somehow* like identity (the one-to-one relation each thing has only with itself). To the extent that *y*, the sum of the *x*s, just *is* (identical with, nothing over and above) the *xs*, then, once the *x*s are countenanced in our ontological catalogue, commitment to their sum, *y*, is not an additional ontological commitment. To the extent that composition is reducible to identity, the admission of mereological composites is ontologically innocent.

The Lewisian argument is very controversial. To begin with, it is controversial (hence that italicized 'somehow' above) whether mereological composition is only similar in various respects to identity (the so-called *weak* thesis of composition as identity), or it is a 'plural form' of identity (the *strong* thesis of composition as identity). The weak reading of composition as merely similar to identity, however plausible, seems incapable to vindicate the full innocence of ontological commitment to a whole once one is committed to the parts. The strong reading, on the other hand, by allowing identity to be a one-to-many relation requires us to admit that one thing (the sum, *y*) can be numerically identical with many things (the composing *x*s). Some ontologists, for example, van Inwagen 2001, find this simply unintelligible: how can *one* thing *be several* things?

5 Synchronic identity and co-location

Issues of identity are also triggered by the question we hinted at in Section 2 of this chapter: Are material objects with the same proper parts perforce always identical, or should we sometimes admit numerically distinct things with the same proper parts? Insofar as we stick to spatial parthood, this can be taken as an issue of 'synchronic identity' for material objects (we will move to the issue of temporal parthood in Section 6 below).

Intuitively, by having spatial parts a material object like Tibbles the cat occupies some region of space at a given time. Once (*pace* Rosen and Dorr) we have counted Tibbles in our ontological catalogue, do we need to count anything else occupying precisely that region of space at that same time? That is: is anything having exactly Tibbles' proper parts (at that time) identical with Tibbles? You may recall from Chapter 3 that Quine's reply was in the affirmative: according to Quine, a good criterion of identity for material objects has it that *a* and *b* are the same when they share their physical address. Other ontologists, however, disagree.

5.1 *Sortal theories* and pluralism

A widely though not universally accepted principle in this debate, often called Locke's Principle for having been formulated by John Locke his *Essay* (II-xxvii-1), claims that two material objects of the *same sort* cannot occupy the same place at the same time. The problem is what 'same sort' means. Some broadly neo-Aristotelian theories of material objects, called *sortal theories* (Lowe 1989; Wiggins 2001), make a lot of a distinction between ordinary and *sortal* predicates (also called 'individuative predicates', 'articulative predicates', 'substance names', 'shared names', etc.: See Strawson 1959: 168–9; Quine 1960: §19; Wiggins 2001: Ch. 3).

Unlike ordinary predicates such as 'red', 'round', or 'dirty', predicates like 'man', 'cat', 'armchair' or 'tree' can be employed within an answer to the question: What is it? – the question by means of which Aristotle characterized the category of substance, which, as we know from Chapter 3, was for him the fundamental kind of being. Suppose we ask, 'What is that?', pointing at a man – a plausible example of Aristotelian substance. If you answer, 'It's a man' or 'It's a human being', that may sound good. But if you answer 'It's pink', or 'It's wearing a kilt', we may protest that our question was, *what* the thing is, not what its colour is, or what it's wearing.

Sortal predicates get this name because they categorize the various objects of our world into sorts or kinds. Philosophers like Strawson claimed that the distinction between sortal predicates and ordinary predicates can be 'approximately' (Strawson 1959: 137) mapped to the linguistic distinction between nouns on the one side, and adjectives and verbs on the other. Nouns allow us to count objects, therefore to settle identities and differences, whereas adjectives and verbs can only describe the features and activities of things we have already identified.

In this neo-Aristotelian view, sortal notions are therefore relevant for issues of identity: the sortal kind something belongs to is taken as determining its identity and persistence conditions. In Lowe's words, things belonging to different sorts in general can 'have different criteria of identity associated with them, and … no individual of a sort *f* can intelligibly be said also to belong to a sort *y* if *f* and *y* have different criteria of identity' (Lowe 1989: 70). Things can satisfy different predicates at different times, but they cannot change the kind of being they are, which is essential to them. To be sure, 'boy' is also a sortal term and boys become men. But 'boy' is, in Wiggins' jargon, a *phased* sortal predicate. Now, 'a phased or restricted sortal predicate can always be supplanted *salva veritate* by a comprehensive unrestricted sortal predicate or (as I shall say) a substance predicate' (Wiggins 2001: 63). And any object has to satisfy its own substance predicate throughout its ontological career. In the following, we can take 'sortal predicate' just as a synonym of 'substance predicate' in Wiggins' sense.

The kind something belongs to fixes the further range of predicates the object can satisfy. By being an armchair, this thing one of us is sitting on while writing these lines can be meaningfully (albeit falsely) said to be yellow or round or dirty; but it does not make sense to claim that this armchair is left-handed, or short-sighted or primitive recursive.

Mainstream sortalism makes for a common-sense-friendly ontology, preserving many of our intuitions on ordinary material objects as found in our colloquial language and manners of speaking; not by chance, the view was advocated in Strawson's descriptive approach to metaontology. Also, most versions of sortalism (though not all) entail a form of ontological pluralism (not to be confused with pluralism in metaontology, as per Chapter 4 of our book), in the sense that distinct material objects can be in the same place and share exactly the same proper parts at a given time (see Wiggins 2001), provided they satisfy different sortal predicates (thus, without contravening to Locke's Principle).

How can this be? Arguments for the numerical distinctness of co-located objects, or of objects having exactly the same proper parts, typically rely on the Indiscernibility of Identicals. As you may recall from Chapter 3, this very plausible principle claims that, if *a* is identical with *b*, then any feature of *a* must be a feature of *b*, and vice versa. How could there be any feature or property making a difference? It's *one and the same* thing. Nothing can differ from itself. By contraposition (a law of minimal logic, allowing us to infer, from a conditional of the form 'If *P*, then *Q*', one of the form 'If not-*Q*, then not-*P*'), we can rephrase the Indiscernibility of Identicals as claiming: If there is some feature which *a* has but *b* lacks (or vice versa), that is which makes the difference, then *a* is not identical with *b*. Ontologists who allow for distinct co-located material objects, therefore, will look for some feature making the difference.

Typically, they look for modal or temporal differences. Take Tibbles the cat again, and the amount of feline tissue composing Tibbles – call this 'Tibs'. According to Wiggins, Tibbles and Tibs are distinct objects. Suppose Tibbles' tail is removed and destroyed. Tibbles can survive such an (admittedly stressful) episode. However, Tibs cannot: by definition, the amount of feline tissue composing Tibbles must be made exactly of *those* parts, tail included. As an instance of the (contraposed) Indiscernibility of Identicals, we have: Tibbles could survive the destruction of the tail; Tibs could not survive the destruction the tail; then, as they have incompatible modal features, Tibbles and Tibs are distinct.

One can run similar arguments involving temporal rather than modal features. The sheets of paper composing the concrete copy of the book you are plausibly holding in your hands (unless you got the e-book version!) existed before the book, for example, when the book was being printed by the publisher, but the pages hadn't been tied together yet. So there is a temporal feature that makes the difference: the aggregate of the pages composing the book existed at a certain time when the book did not exist yet. So, the two are distinct, despite being co-located.

The underlying intuition is that the mereological constitution of a material object need not exhaust its identity: Tibbles can be constituted by that amount of feline tissue, but Tibbles is not identical with (nothing over and above) that amount of feline tissue. Among the ontologists who subscribe to this view are Lowe 1989, Baker 1997 and Thomson 1998. Some authors go even further, and claim – this time, against Locke's Principle – that also things of the *same* sort can be spatially co-located, yet distinct: (see Kit Fine's 'double letter' example in Fine 2000. See also Spolaore 2012).

This view faces various objections. One, to be found, for example, in Varzi 2009, claims that the argument for pluralism on co-located objects can be reproduced *ad absurdum*. If Tibbles is distinct from the amount of feline tissue composing it, it is distinct from infinitely many co-located things: the thing composed of its upper and lower half, the thing composed of its left and right half, and, in general, the thing composed of any proper part of Tibbles plus its reminder. This may seem preposterous.

Another objection is tied to the so-called *modal supervenience* thesis. You may recall the rough characterization of supervenience we gave in our chapter on possible worlds: B-properties (properties of a certain kind) supervene on A-properties (of a different kind), if and only if there could be no difference in something's B-properties without there being a difference in its A-properties. Now modal supervenience is the view (shared by ontologists like Jubien 1993, and Sider 1999) that modal properties (roughly: properties whose specification involves reference to other worlds) supervene on actual properties: any difference in the modal features of an object must be rooted in some actual difference.

Now pluralist ontologists who take Tibbles and Tibs as distinct seem to allow, so to speak, for 'extensionally indiscernible' objects: things that are allegedly distinct, but indiscernible with respect to their non-modal features. And extensionally indiscernible objects are unacceptable for modal supervenientists. Tibbles and Tibs have the same size, shape, weight, physical constitution, location, etc. What could underpin the alleged modal differences between them, if modal properties supervene on actual properties? Generalizing: how could one resort to alleged modal differences to settle the issue whether objects *a* and *b* actually are the same? How can we meaningfully wonder how things *could* differ, that is differ at other worlds, before settling the issue whether they are the same at the actual world?

A retort proposed in Fine 2003 consists in finding differentiating predicates which are neither temporal nor modal. Fine's example refers to a statue and the alloy that makes it up: one could wonder whether the statue is *insured*, *admired*, *Romanesque* or *well made*. *Prima facie*, there is no modal element here. For Fine, such predicates can hardly be meaningfully asserted or denied of a piece of alloy – but we are about to see that other ontologists beg to differ on this too.

5.2 One object to one place

Ontologists like Lewis 1986, Noonan 1988 and Varzi 2000 reject such pluralism and stick to the Quinean, monistic view that there is (at most) one object in a certain place at a given time. For them, the pluralist's view that two things can be in the same place at the same time is 'a bad case of double vision' (Noonan 1988: 222). For our purposes, and leaving some subtleties aside, this can be understood as acceptance of the mereological principle that sameness of proper parts entails identity.

Sortalists generally claim that Tibbles could survive the loss of proper parts, while Tibs could not. But that what we refer to with the expression 'Tibbles' is the same as what we refer to with the expression 'Tibs' cannot be ruled out beforehand, on pain of begging the question against those who want to have only one object out there. The intuitive difference between Tibbles and Tibs, or between a dishpan and the amount of plastic it is made of, for example, for monists is to be explained as a difference between two ways of representing or describing one and the same material object. Thus spoke David Lewis:

> We have one thing. What we have two of, besides names for it, are ways of representing. There is some kind of equivocation built into representation *de re*, and the equivocation shows up when we get conflicting answers. … It reeks of double counting to say that here we have a dishpan, and we also have a dishpan-shaped bit of plastic that is just where the dishpan is, weighs just what the dishpan weighs (why don't the two together weigh twice as much?), and so on. This multiplication of entities is absurd on its face. (Lewis 1986: 252)

We resort to different descriptions, or ways of representing, to highlight different features or roles of the object. Of course, in a given context some ways of representing can be more appropriate than others. We can regard a given thing as a cat or as a mereological sum of such and such parts, and then some predicates will be more appropriate than others to describe that thing. Compare: it would have been linguistically inappropriate to refer to Kurt Gödel with the expression 'the man who proved the completeness of first-order logic' before 1929; but this does not mean that the proof of the completeness of first-order logic entailed the birth of a new man besides the old one, so that now 'Kurt Gödel' and 'the man who proved the completeness of first-order logic' refer to two different persons. For monists, it is a fallacy of descriptive ontology to infer from a difference in our language, or in our systems of representation of the world, to a worldly distinction.

An issue with this view, raised by Fine 2003, is where unification is to stop, and to what extent the counter-intuitiveness of the entailed prescriptive ontology counts against it. By parity of reasoning, the monist ontologist may have to identify material objects with events or processes. Take Alpha Centauri: a star born when some huge mass of hydrogen reached the critical pressure, and nuclear fusion of hydrogen into helium began. Call 'Alphusion' the prolonged event consisting of such a nuclear fusion. Alpha Centauri will end its career as a star when Alphusion ceases. So where Alpha Centauri is, there is Alphusion. When the one begins and ceases, the other begins and ceases. If they are co-located, nothing stops us from identifying the object and the event, just as we identify Tibbles with Tibs. This was indeed Quine's view, as well as Goodman's 1951. They recognized no real distinction between the categories of material object and event: what we refer to as material objects are nothing but 'monotonous events'.

Then why does the unifier not go around claiming 'That nuclear fusion is round'? At most, because it is inappropriate to refer to something of which we claim that it is round by means of event-kind words such as 'nuclear fusion'. If Alpha Centauri *is*

Alphusion, and Alpha Centauri is round, then by the Indiscernibility of Identicals, the process of a nuclear fusion is round.

In some strongly monistic ontologies of material objects, which have been grouped under the label of *stuff theory* (see Sidelle 1998; Heller 1990; Jubien 1993), objects are taken as mere spatiotemporal occupiers ('objects *in extenso*', to quote Fine 2003: 207). What actually is out there in the material world is just *stuff*. Our carving activities select some spatiotemporal portions of the world as salient, but this depends on our cognitive apparatus, more than on the world itself. We tend to carve, to qualify as 'objects' (and, say, to restrict our quantifiers to), those hunks of matter that display interesting or salient features; in the world out there, though, there are no intrinsic sorts or essences (some stuff theorist may claim that the only essential property in the material world is *being the occupier of some spatiotemporal region*; but from the point of view of mainstream sortalism this would be a trivial sortal property).

The monist ontologist may however refuse to distinguish even between material objects and the regions of space they occupy. We ascribe properties to material objects as spacetime occupiers, but those are actually properties of the regions of spacetime themselves. We commonly claim that Tibbles, at a given time, inhabits a place in the world, a certain region of space. Call such a region *s*. Suppose Tibbles now moves a bit. One could argue that Tibbles has just moved away from *s*, so by the Indiscernibility of Identicals, Tibbles is not *s*. What stops the unifier short of rejecting this argument, just as she rejected the difference between Tibbles and Tibs? It is not that Tibbles occupies this place, *s*: Tibbles just *is s*. Then despite intuitive appearances, either regions of space can move, or material objects cannot.

If Tibbles is *s*, 'This region of space has four legs and a tail' is just an inappropriate way of expressing oneself. Given our cognitive needs or semantic conventions, it is inappropriate to call this thing a region of space when we want to claim of it that it has legs and a tail. If we want to say that this thing has legs and a tail, we had better refer to this thing as a cat. But what we had better say does not sustain the ontologically demanding claim that we have a distinction between a material object and the place it occupies.

6 Diachronic identity

Besides occupying some place by way of their having spatial parts (unless they *are* the place they occupy, that is), material objects are also subject to the inexorable flow of time as they undergo change and becoming, generation and corruption. Parallel to ontological issues of synchronic identity, we have for them issues of *diachronic* identity. The problem here is to establish under which conditions object x, which exists at a given time t_1, is the same as object y, which exists at a different time t_2. On the one hand, we have the strong intuition that material objects can, in general and often, *persist* through change (see Hawley 2001): this armchair, which is red at t_1 (say, in the morning) can be painted in blue at t_2 (say, in the evening). We are inclined to think of it as being the same armchair throughout the day, despite its undergoing such a change. On the other hand, this seems to fly in the face of the Indiscernibility of Identicals again: how can the same armchair bear two incompatible properties like being red and being blue, thus, not being red?

The first obvious thought consists in considering disambiguations of the general form '*x* is *P* at time *t*', where *x* is the relevant material object, *P* the relevant property, and 'at time *t*' expresses a temporal qualification, or relativization to a time. The armchair is not both red and not red at the same time – this is what cannot be. It is red at one time – in the morning – and blue at another – in the evening. However, philosophers differ on how 'at time *t*' is to work, and on the temporal ontology underlying the divergence (the following exposition is greatly indebted to Varzi 2001: Ch. 5, and to fruitful discussions with Achille himself).

6.1 Three-dimensionalism

There are three main proposals on the market. The first view can be understood as attaching the qualification 'at time *t*' ('in the morning', 'in the evening') to the predicate: the armchair is red-in-the-morning, the armchair is blue-in-the-evening. What needs to be temporally qualified is the having of features by objects, not the objects themselves. Material objects are three-dimensional things: they extend along the three dimensions of space and have spatial parts; but they have nothing like *temporal* parts. The view is also called *endurantism*, after Lewis 1986: 202 (who claims to follow William Johnson on terminology). Material objects persist in time by enduring – by being wholly present at each time at which they exist.

Three-dimensionalism dates back to Aristotle's traditional account of change and becoming. According to Aristotelian metaphysics, that of which we claim that it changes, the *substratum* of change, is also that which persists through change. The starting point (*terminus a quo*) of becoming is the having of some property by the relevant thing (the armchair's being red), while the endpoint (*terminus ad quem*) is the having of a different property by the same thing (the armchair's being blue). Time flows from the *terminus a quo* to the *terminus ad quem*, and the changing *substratum* (the armchair) has to persist in existence throughout the process.

Three-dimensionalism has many subscribers – possibly the majority of modern analytic ontologists: Simons 1987, Lowe 1989, van Inwagen 1990 and Wiggins 2001. It is claimed to have the advantage of respecting common-sense intuitions about material objects; it is friendly to a generally descriptive approach to the methodology of ontology.

Three-dimensionalism is forced to attach some temporal qualification to any predicate standing for an intrinsic (not purely relational), but inessential or non-permanent feature of material objects. Each time we say that the armchair has a certain shape, or temperature or mass (supposing these are intrinsic features), these claims should be considered as implicitly indexed to times, for we want to claim that numerically one and the same armchair can change – from one temperature to another, etc.

Hence comes one objection to three-dimensionalism, raised by Lewis 1986 under the label of the *problem of temporary intrinsics*: intrinsic but temporary features of enduring, changing things. To claim that temporary intrinsic properties must be relativized to times is to misrepresent properties as relations to times. Redness should be a *property* of the armchair, not a *relation* between the armchair and some time. Similarly, having a bent shape should be one's property insofar as one is sitting, not a relation one bears to the time at which one is sitting. But then 'the solution to the problem of temporary intrinsics is that there aren't any temporary intrinsics'; and 'this is simply incredible, if we are speaking of the persistence of ordinary things. … If we know what a shape is, we know that it is a property, not a relation' (Lewis 1986: 204).

6.2 Four-dimensionalism

Four-dimensionalism can be understood as attaching the qualification 'at time *t*' to the subject of the relevant sentences: the armchair-in-the-morning is red, the armchair-in-the-evening is blue. What gets temporally qualified now are the objects themselves. This makes sense if material objects, besides extending across the three dimensions of space by having spatial parts, also extend across the dimension of time by having *temporal* parts. Four-dimensionalism is also called *perdurantism* (see again Lewis 1986: 202): material objects persist in time by 'perduring', that is by having different temporal parts, which are present at different times. That the armchair is red in the morning is to be understood as the claim that a certain temporal part or stage of the armchair is red. That the armchair is blue in the evening is to be understood as the claim that a different temporal part or stage of the armchair is blue.

Also four-dimensionalism has its subscribers: Quine, Goodman 1951, Lewis 1986, Heller 1990 and Jubien 1993. The view requires no relativization of the having of properties to times: it discharges the issue to the (temporal) mereological structure of objects. Different temporary features are ascribed to different temporal parts, while the temporal parts have their intrinsic properties absolutely: this temporal part of the armchair, its morning stage, is red – full stop.

As material objects have temporal as well as spatial parts, four-dimensionalism comes with a strong analogy between space and time (too strong for some, as we are about to see). Statements like ‘The armchair is red in the morning’, or ‘The armchair is blue in the evening’, are not that different from statements like ‘The armchair is red on its top’, or ‘The armchair is blue on its bottom’: we have pairs of compatible sentences, in which redness and blueness are not ascribed to the armchair as a (spatial, temporal) whole, but to different (spatial, temporal) parts of the chair.

Four-dimensionalism seems to be far less conservative than three-dimensionalism with respect to our commonsensical intuitions: try and think of ordinary material objects as ‘time worms’ with temporal slices, as the usual four-dimensionalist story goes. It thus looks like a prescriptive or a revisionary, rather than descriptive, approach to the ontology of material objects. Some have claimed it is ‘crazy metaphysics’ (Thomson 1983: 210). However, according to many of its supporters, four-dimensionalism can match with relativistic physics and the idea of a space-time continuum much better than three-dimensionalism. Also ordinary talk seems to show that, at least sometimes, we do treat material objects as having temporal parts: we claim that the *fin-de-siècle* Vienna was awesome, and that the later Wittgenstein hated formalisms (Varzi 2001: 120).

One common objection to four-dimensionalism (Mellor 1981) is this: to claim that change is just the having of different properties by different temporal parts, rather than an explanation of change, is a denial of the very phenomenon. The left third of the French flag is blue, the middle third is white and the right third is red: there is no event of anything changing in any sense, just diversity across space. But then, to claim that the morning-temporal-part of the armchair is red, or the evening-temporal-part of the armchair is blue, is just to point at diversity across time. We have missed the very idea that changes should be *events*, in which, as Aristotle remarked, one and the same *substratum* persists across different times while switching properties.

A staunch reply, to be found in Heller 1992, is that this is not a problem, but an advantage of the theory! It makes of change and becoming phenomena no more mysterious than the having of different properties by different spatial parts. That things change, for four-dimensionalists, means that different temporal slices of things have different properties. This is structurally just like different spatial slices of things’ having different properties: red here, white there and blue over there. One may object that we are mixing material objects, which change across time, with the events or processes their changing consists in. But as we already hinted above in this chapter, this may be a welcome result for some ontologists. Many four-dimensionalists, including Quine, believe that we are inclined to attach the qualification of ‘object’ to some ‘monotonous events’ because of their uniformity, but this marks no ontologically significant distinction. There is no difference, out there in the world, between Alpha Centauri, which fuses hydrogen into helium, and Alphusion, the fusion of Alpha Centauri’s hydrogen into helium.

6.3 Sequentialism

A third approach to the issue of diachronic identity is often called *sequentialism* (in fact, some doubt that this is really a third option, as we will soon see). The main idea is that material objects properly speaking are instantaneous things: they only exist for a single moment in time. In this view, which can be traced back to Chisholm 1976, and is supported by Varzi 2001, there just is no problem of diachronic identity: there is no such thing as identity across different times. Nothing survives change, for each real material object is locked in its own instant and does not survive any longer than that. Consider the structural analogy with Lewis' counterpart-theoretic view in modal ontology. There is no issue of trans-world identity, for there is no such thing: no object can be in different worlds, as objects are locked in their worlds. Similarly, there is no such thing as trans-temporal identity for sequentialists: no object can be in different times, as objects are locked in their instants.

How do we account for our intuition of persistence for material objects – that armchairs persevere through different times, at least when they undergo changes that are not too radical, like colour changes? According to sequentialists, ordinary material objects are but *entia successiva*. We identify lots of instantaneous armchairs as one single object that persists through time, but this is, in Chisholm's words, a 'loose and popular' (as opposed to the 'strict and philosophical') sense of identity: our red morning armchair actually is but a sequence of instantaneous red armchairs. They are similar enough to each other to have us count them, for practical purposes, as one thing. Our blue evening chair also is but a sequence of instantaneous blue armchairs. The blue armchairs are less similar to the red armchairs than the red armchairs are similar to each other; but still similar enough for us to want to loosely treat the things in the whole sequence as one. Such a treatment is largely conventional, though, as shown by the fuzziness of our intuitions in various cases of (non-)persistence: how many players can the coach change before we stop talking of the same playing team? (Compare counterpart theory again, where what is similar enough to object x, locked in world w, to count as a counterpart of x at worlds other than w, can be a matter of degree, so that it may be conventional where we draw the line).

Sequentialism seems deeply revisionary and counterintuitive. While revisionary ontologists may just bite the bullet, others may label it as 'crazy metaphysics' as much as four-dimensionalism. In fact, one objection to sequentialism, to be found in Sider 2001, is that it *is* just four-dimensionalism in disguise. To say that this armchair is but a temporal sequence of instantaneous objects is just to say, in a different tone of voice, that this armchair is but a four-dimensional worm ultimately made of instantaneous parts. A sequentialist may reply, though, that there is still a difference, which can be understood again in mereological terms. Just because she accepts the relevant instantaneous things, she is not committed to accepting in her ontology their temporal mereological sum, that is the time-worm itself. In the 'strict and philosophical' sense, there is no such thing as a temporally extended being, the armchair, whose temporal parts are the instantaneous armchairs.

We conclude the chapter with one methodological point. The debate on diachronic identity for material objects has been largely conducted within a Quinean metaontological framework, that is in terms of quantification and ontological commitments. This framework is bound to make such positions as sequentialism more revisionary and counterintuitive than they would look in a different metaontological approach. Just as for mereological nihilism or quasi-nihilism *à la* van Inwagen, which plays by the Quinean criterion of ontological commitment, there literally are no armchairs to be included in our ontological catalogue, only mereological simples spatially arranged armchair-wise; so for sequentialism (so understood) there literally are no armchairs, only instantaneous objects temporally arranged armchair-wise. But suppose we rephrase the point in terms, say, of grounding theories (as far as we know, no such rephrasing is found in the literature yet). Then we may understand sequentialism as the claim that the fundamental or grounding entities in the temporal world are instantaneous. We need not deny the existence of ordinary armchairs (of course there are such things!). What we deny is their ontological independence: they are grounded in the instantaneous entities that supposedly make for the basic temporal bricks of the material world.

Further Reading

Varzi 2009 is an excellent and not too technical introduction to mereology, while Casati and Varzi 1999 and Simons 1987 cover more advanced ground. van Inwagen 1990 is a must on the ontology of material objects. A general survey of the ontological issues concerning identity is Noonan and Curtis 2014. On sortalism and synchronic identity, see Lowe 1989 and Wiggins 2001. On diachronic identity, see Gallois 2011 and the beautiful collection of essays Haslanger and Kurtz 2006.

13

Fictional Objects

Chapter Outline

In this chapter we deal with things mentioned and described in works of fiction, such as Sherlock Holmes, Gandalf and the Fantastic Four. These objects raise a number of difficult puzzles for ontologists. Section 1 introduces the topic and a common distinction between two ways of speaking of fictional things, called *intra-fictional* and *extra-fictional* discourse. Section 2 describes *realist abstractionism*, the most popular account of such objects developed within the mainstream Quinean metaontology: fictional objects are real and to be included in our ontological catalogue. They are abstract artefacts, produced by the creative activities of authors. Sections 3 and 4 explore two alternative views: the former deals with the fictionalist strategy according to which there are no such things as fictional objects, and talk about them essentially involves make-believe; the latter introduces the Meinongian approach, which takes such objects as non-existent.

1 Fiction

Fantasy stories, narrations, plays, tales and other works of fiction, *prima facie* speak about – refer to, quantify over – a vast multiplicity of objects: Sherlock Holmes, Mr Pickwick, Anna Karenina, Batman and Robin, the Fantastic Four, Gregor Samsa,

Gandalf, Frodo and the dark army of Mordor's orcs. Call these (*purely*) *fictional objects*. At times the adverb 'purely' is needed, for fictional stories occasionally feature things that really exist, or have really existed. *War and Peace* speaks about Napoleon and Dante's *Comedy* speaks about Virgil, but both Napoleon and Virgil are, or at least have been, very real and existing persons (this view is, in fact, not uncontroversial: according to some, such works speak respectively about a fictional Napoleon and a fictional Virgil, different from the actually existed men; for criticisms of this view, see Berto 2012: Ch. 8). While non-purely-fictional objects also raise some interesting philosophical issues, our focus in this chapter will be on purely fictional things; we can thus omit the 'purely' from now on.

Some philosophers include in the category of fictional objects also mythical objects like Zeus, Thor, Atlantis and objects introduced by false scientific theories, like phlogiston, or the planet Vulcan, postulated by the astronomer Leverrier to account for the anomalies of Mercury's orbit. We will not deal specifically with such objects here. Unlike the objects of known fiction, these things are such that that the myths or theories introducing them were initially taken by and large seriously, that is as truthful representations: some scientists believed in the existence of phlogiston; the ancient Greeks generally believed in Zeus. Some philosophers want these objects be accounted for differently from fictional things, while others take this appeal to original intentions as too shaky to ground an ontological difference.

A characteristic feature of fiction is its being representational: we are inclined to qualify a work of art as fiction to the extent that it somehow represents something as being such-and-such and so-and-so. Fairy tales, stories and narrations of various kinds immediately come to mind, but also movies and plays qualify; sculptures and paintings may or may not fit the bill (think of the elusive shape of some abstract contemporary sculpture, as opposed to a statue of Napoleon: the latter certainly represents the historical man, while it is doubtful whether the former represents anything beyond itself). The interesting ontological issues arise when we have representation, for then our familiar twofold question is triggered, namely whether something is actually represented, and if so, what sort of thing it is.

Though somewhat marginal in our overall picture of the world, fictional objects make for a difficult test case for ontological theories, for the way we talk and think of them is puzzling. We say, on the one hand, that Sherlock Holmes doesn't exist, its purely fictional status involving precisely this. On the other hand, we also say that there is such a fictional character as Sherlock Holmes. We may take the claim that Holmes is a detective as somewhat true: it certainly fares better than the claim that Sherlock Holmes is a cobblestone. However, if asked why can't Holmes help the police to solve crimes, we are likely to reply that, well, he is just a fictional detective, not a detective for real: he cannot do such things. These contrasting intuitions make of fictional objects a difficult ontological subject.

Before we delve into specific accounts of fictional objects, we need to introduce a distinction between two kinds of fictional discourse, which will be of general utility.

Some features are ascribed to fictional objects *within* the fictional works in which they appear, by their authors or by those who report the works' contents: in the respective fictions, Holmes is a detective, Gandalf is a wizard, the Fantastic Four wear blue uniforms and Frodo arrogated to himself the Ring on Mount Doom. But we also ascribe to fictional objects features that are nowhere to be found within the fictions. Literary critics as well as laypersons can say that Gandalf is a literary character invented by Tolkien, that Holmes inspires the work of many existent detectives or that the Tin Man from *The Wizard of Oz* symbolizes the dehumanization of workers in industrial societies. As Kit Fine claimed, fictional objects appear to lead a double life: 'they have certain properties within the contexts in which they appear: they love and hate, thrive and fail'; but also, they 'relate to the real world: they are created by authors, read by readers, and compared, for better or worse, with one another and with what is real' (Fine 1982: 97). A distinction is thus widely acknowledged in the literature, as we will say, between *intra*-fictional and *extra*-fictional discourse.

With such a distinction under our belt, we will now explore three very different accounts of fictional objects. The first, *realist abstractionism*, is probably the most popular among the ontologists who follow a broadly Quinean metaontology. The second and third are applications of two alternative metaontological approaches, namely fictionalism and Meinongianism. The three views can be quickly classified according to how their proponents reply to the simple question: What in the world does 'Sherlock Holmes' refer to? According to realist abstractionists, it refers to an existent, abstract artefact. According to Meinongians, it refers to a non-existent object. According to fictionalists, it refers to nothing at all.

2 Realist abstractionism

Realist abstractionism comprises a group of theories at times quite different from each other, developed by such authors as Saul Kripke, Nicholas Wolterstorff, Amie Thomasson, Peter van Inwagen, Stephen Schiffer, Tatjana von Solodkoff and others. The view can be initially motivated by noticing that we quantify in complex ways over fictional characters in seriously asserted, and often true, sentences. Two examples due to van Inwagen 1977:

> There are characters in some nineteenth-century novels who are presented with a greater wealth of physical detail than is any character in any eighteenth-century novel.
>
> Some characters in novels are closely modelled on actual people, while others are wholly products of the literary imagination, and it is usually impossible to tell which characters fall into which of these categories by textual analysis alone.

Realist abstractionists stress that it is difficult to devise a systematic paraphrase strategy to free us from such complex quantificational constructions. If sentences such as these are true, and to be taken at face value, then since we quantify over fictional characters in them, and fictional characters are fictional objects, then by the Quinean criterion we are ontologically, that is existentially, committed to fictional objects.

Realist abstractionism gets its name because, in *nearly* all versions of the view, fictional objects are abstract productions. Just like chairs and tables, they are artefacts: brought into existence by the human activity. But unlike chairs and tables, they are abstract objects, things closer to concepts, functions and sets in this respect. Holmes' abstractness is to explains why we cannot stumble upon him in the real world, kick him or kiss him: abstract objects are devoid of such causal powers and of spatio-temporal location. But unlike functions or sets (at least, on a realist-platonist view of such objects), Holmes has been created by Doyle and essentially depends on him: fictional objects owe their being to the creative activities of the authors of fiction. Not all realist abstractionists are, in fact, so explicit on this artefactual nature of fictional objects. Wolterstorff seems to go for the view that Holmes is, rather, in some sense already there before Doyle thinks about him: Holmes is selected by Doyle, rather than produced by the novelist's creative activities. Thomasson goes for an explicitly artefactualist view, while van Inwagen is noncommittal.

Realist abstractionists usually maintain that the apparatus of predication and property-ascription for fictional objects is ambiguous. Extra-fictional ascriptions are taken literally: it is literally true that Holmes or Gandalf are fictional characters and that (let us suppose) some characters of nineteenth-century novels are presented with a greater wealth of physical detail than any character of any eighteenth-century novel.

Intra-fictional ascriptions, on the other hand, have a special status, which may be generically labelled as fictional. Different realist abstractionist theories differ on how to account for this status. It is generally agreed that the claim that Holmes is a detective is not to be taken at face value, but is to be understood as implicitly prefixed by a proviso:

(1) According to fiction F: Sherlock Holmes is a detective.

'According to fiction F' is (the schematic form of) a sentential operator of the kind we met in our chapter on fictionalism. In particular, it is not factive: one cannot move, in general, from asserting 'According to fiction F: *P*', to asserting *P*. 'F' stands in case (1) for the Doyle stories. While it is really the case that Holmes is a fictional character, only within the relevant fiction(s) is it the case that Holmes is a detective. As Holmes is a literary character, thus an abstract object, he cannot literally be a detective any more than a concept or a function can. Different theorists differ on the precise characterization of intra-fictional ascriptions.

In some lectures given at Princeton and at the University of California, and in the John Locke Lectures, Kripke defended a realist abstractionist view, roughly along the following lines (we refer to Salmon 1998, and to McGinn 2000, who attended some of those lectures; part of Kripke's work on fictional objects is, at the time of our writing these lines, about to be published in the collection of Kripke's writings, *Philosophical Troubles*.

An author, for instance, Doyle, pretends, with no intention to deceive, to refer to someone when he writes his novels, using the name 'Sherlock Holmes'. The name, as originally introduced and used by Doyle in many phrases of his stories, does not refer to anything. Claims like 'Sherlock Holmes is a detective', taken as part of the Doyle novels, work in such a way that 'Sherlock Holmes' has no denotation there. Thus, sentences like (1) in general do not entail such claims as 'Sherlock Holmes is such that *he* is a detective-according-to-fiction-F', involving full-fledged reference to Holmes, and confining the element of make-believe in the property ascription. However, an abstract object is meanwhile created by Doyle's storytelling activities. 'Sherlock Holmes' can then be used in extra-fictional contexts in order to refer to the literary character created by Doyle: 'language allows a grammatical transformation – so Kripke is claimed to have claimed – of a fictional name for a person into a name of a fictional person' (Salmon 1998: 294).

Van Inwagen 2003, too, may be interpreted as considering intra-fictional discourse as involving an aspect of sheer pretence. We can say that fictional characters *hold* the properties ascribed to them by internal fictional discourse; or that properties are intra-fictionally *ascribed to* fictional characters, ascription being a three-place relation: property *K* is ascribed to fictional character *x* somewhere in work of fiction F (there is, in fact, a different possible interpretation of van Inwagen's position, in which the *holding* and *being ascribed* relations constitute special kinds of predication, similar in some respects to the *encoding* of dual copula Meinongianism, which we met in the first part of the book).

A theoretical virtue often granted to realist abstractionism is that it can take many ordinary claims, those belonging to external discourse, at face value: the view can afford the ontological commitment entailed by those sentences. Fictional objects are admitted in the ontological catalogue, and the peculiarity of their metaphysical status, for instance, their being nowhere to be found in the physical world, is accounted for in terms of their abstractness.

However, the view faces various problems. One is connected to the view that fictional objects are created (Yagisawa 2002). We understand fairly well what creation is for concrete things – what it means for a craftsman to create a chair, or for a mother to create her baby. But it is a bit mysterious what kind of creation is involved when it's about bringing into existence an abstract thing. What rough materials did Doyle resort to, in order to produce Holmes? If creation is a causal process, how can one create abstract objects devoid of causal features?

Besides, even if we could link creativity in fiction to the mental activities of thinking beings, the relevant process may look fuzzy: the conditions under which a fictional object comes into being are unclear. Exactly when did Holmes start to exist? When did Doyle first set out to write a novel involving a detective? When did he write down the first sentence including the name 'Sherlock Holmes'? Or perhaps the first novel, or the first two? Or does the reality of Holmes require some kind of collective intentionality (how many readers must have read the Doyle novels, then? Ten or ten thousands?)

Another problem has to do with negative existentials: sentences in which we deny the existence of something. Sensible adults deny in all seriousness that things like Superman, Holmes or the Fantastic Four exist. A father who reveals to his son that Superman doesn't exist aims to speak the strict and literal truth. Negative existentials typically count as extra-fictional discourse, not as intra-fictional ascriptions: in Doyle's stories, Holmes is very much existent. 'Holmes does not exist' seems to call for a treatment along the same lines as 'Holmes is a fictional character'. Realist abstractionists are compelled to break this intuitive uniformity. One solution considered by Thomasson 1999 consists in claiming that negative existentials on fictional characters must be literally false. In *Creatures of Fiction*, van Inwagen says that, given his theory, what to do with 'Mr. Pickwick does not exist' is 'a very complicated question' (van Inwagen 1977: 308).

Sometimes realist abstractionists suggest that true denials of existence for fictional objects should be interpreted as implicitly restricted quantifications. We are not really claiming that there is no such thing as Mr Pickwick at all. Rather, we are claiming that Mr Pickwick is not to be found in the domain of concrete objects, for it's an abstract thing (another option explored in Thomasson 1999). However, as Walton 2003 has stressed, negative existentials in ordinary English are naturally interpreted as *un*qualified denials. When we use 'there is' and 'there is not', we often have implicitly restricted quantification in play. If at the zoo of Berlin one says 'There are no dolphins', she probably means: there are no dolphins in this zoo. That is: quantifying only over things in the zoo, none of them is a dolphin. One doesn't mean that no dolphin exists (anymore), that dolphins are extinct. But if one says 'Dolphins do not exist', one would normally mean exactly (and, luckily, falsely) that dolphins are indeed extinct, that they do not exist *simpliciter*, not that they are not to be found in a domain of things of a specific kind, or located in some specific place. Existential sentences often just cannot cope with domain restrictions: we cannot sensibly say things like 'Obama does not exist in Texas'; or 'A man existed at the door this morning, looking for you.' Those who deny the existence of Santa or the Big Bad Wolf seem not to have such restrictions in mind.

A related point is made by Sainsbury 2010. According to Sainsbury, Thomasson's account of denials of existence for fictional characters in terms of denial of concreteness 'represents a mistake about ontological category as a mistake about whether something exists' (109). If a person mistakes a material being X, to which that person refers via the name 'X', for an immaterial thing, we wouldn't correct him or her by saying anything like 'Look, X does not exist', but rather by telling that person that X is not immaterial.

3 Talk of fictional objects as fictional talk

Contrary to realist abstractionism, the aim of fictionalism on fictional objects is to free us from ontological commitment to such things. We already know from Chapter 6 of our book that fictionalism is a general strategy to deal with ontological issues. Fictionalism about some kind of discourse we care about generally takes claims in the area as valuable but not literally true. Talk of fictional objects seems to make for the ideal and pristine field of application. Both Gregory Currie and Kendall Walton originally developed their views having fiction in their sights. For Currie 1990, authors of literary works operate with the intention, shared by their readers or intended audiences, to make-believe the propositions expressed by the relevant sentences. In Walton's 1990 general theory of representation and fiction, people play collective games of make-believe. The rules of the games specify that so-and-so must be represented or imagined or simulated. What is represented is not true in reality, but only in the appropriate make-believe game. However, things 'true inside the game', or 'true in a certain story', are in general not true in the real world.

Applying the view to fictional objects like Holmes, we have: that it holds in the relevant fiction that Holmes lives in Baker Street means that it is fictional (it is a component of the game of make-believe, and is to be imagined within the game) that Holmes lives in Baker Street. This can be motivated intuitively by stressing that, when Doyle wrote that Holmes lived in Baker Street, he didn't actually assert the sentence expressing this proposition. Doyle just pretended, in a non-deceptive way, to perform this linguistic act, so he was not committed to the content of his claim's being actually the case.

Roughly, one should be able to extend to discourses apparently on fictional things the strategy of the 'according to the fiction' operator that we saw above. Some objections against fictionalist accounts of fictional objects are then just objections against fictionalism in general, as a strategy in metaontology. Having explored such general objections in our chapter on fictionalism, we can be brief here. A point often raised against fictionalism on fictional objects (van Inwagen 2003) is that the strategy of prefixing non-factive fictional operators does not seem to work in general. Take the extra-fictional claims that Holmes is a fictional character of Doyle's stories, and that he is played by Robert Downey Jr in some recent Hollywood movies. If we put an 'according to the fiction' proviso in front of the relevant ascriptions, we get:

(2) According to fiction F: Holmes is a fictional character.
(3) According to fiction F: Holmes is played by Robert Downey Jr.

These seem to be false (contrast sentence (1) above) if F = Doyle's stories (and it's not clear what else F could sensibly be). In Doyle's stories, Holmes is not a fictional character but a very real and concrete person, and nobody else plays him. True extra-fictional ascriptions to fictional characters usually do not ascribe them properties those characters have within the respective stories, such as the property of being a detective.

In general, sentences involving fictional characters like 'If no character appears in every novel, then some character is modelled on another character' (van Inwagen 2003: 137) appear to be seriously asserted, without any explicit or implicit pretence. Nobody would criticize Doyle for having written the literal falsity that Holmes lived in 221b Baker Street. That's true in the story, not in the real world. But someone engaged in literary criticism may be rightly criticized (or approved) for having written that Holmes is an epitome of the values of the Victorian age. People making such claims appear to aim at saying literal truths about the actual world. They seem to make genuine assertions, and to commit themselves, with no make-believe involved. It would be difficult to convince ordinary speakers that they are pretending, not only when they claim that Holmes lives in Baker Street, but also when they say that Holmes is Doyle's main literary character.

However, one may say the same of other areas of discourse targeted by fictionalist metaontologists. If fictionalism does work for them nonetheless, then one or another of the strategies explored in Chapter 6 may apply to extra-fictional discourse about fictional objects too. Also mathematicians appear to assert their theorems with no element of pretence involved. Perhaps the sentences of literary criticism, or extra-fictional claims like the aforementioned ones, make for a *different* fiction from the one the Holmes narratives consist in. They are external to Doyle's fiction, but still, they are fiction: if mathematics is 'good without being true', the same may be said of literary criticism.

4 Fictional objects as non-existents

Meinongianism on fictional objects simply considers these things as a kind of non-existents. Fictional objects are often taken as providing a case, if there is any, for believing that some things are non-existent. Meinongianism comes as a form of realism on fictional objects: there really are such things, we can quantify over them and say true things of them. On the other hand, as we know, for Meinongians quantification is not perforce existentially committing: these things can be really there although they fail to exist.

Meinongians often treat fictional objects on a par with any other non-existent, so most of what they claim on such objects is but a specification of what we saw in Chapter 7 on Meinongianism in general, in the first part of the book. On the other hand, fictional objects can differ in various respects from other candidate non-existents (e.g. past and future existents, *possibilia*) – and can create problems of a peculiar kind, as we are about to see.

One pro of the Meinongian view is that negative existentials like 'Gandalf does not exist' or 'The Fantastic Four do not exist' obtain the proper truth-values and a straightforward treatment. These are literal truths, seriously asserted by competent speakers: no paraphrase or convoluted story about them is required. Fictional objects can bear properties and make the corresponding statements true. Meinongianism in principle easily accommodates extra-fictional ascriptions, like 'Gandalf is a purely fictional character', which can be true *simpliciter* – true in the real world.

On the other hand, some Meinongian theories, those of the nuclear kind, for example, tend to have what has been called by Fine 1982 a *literalist* approach to intra-fictional claims. Not only is Holmes literally a non-existent object, but also, he is literally a detective, living in Baker Street, etc. After all, these are typical nuclear properties, and ones that characterize the object called 'Sherlock Holmes' by the Nuclear Comprehension Principle of the theory. So 'Holmes is a detective' and 'Holmes lives in Baker Street' should be taken at face value and with no implicit, non-factive operator prefixed to them.

This, however, may look strange: if Holmes really is a detective, why can't we in principle shake hands with him? If he really lives in Baker Street, why can't we just go there to meet him and shake hands? The nuclear Meinongian's typical reply is that Holmes is a detective, but a non-existent one, and that he lives in a non-existent street. But this may sound unconvincing: such a complete independence of *Sosein* from *Sein* forces us to sever the intuitive link between some (nuclear) properties and existence. The intuition that the view fails to accommodate is that if something literally and really is a detective, and really lives in some real street (as Baker Street in London happens to be, unless one assumes that, in the Holmes case, we are dealing with a doppelganger of the real street), then it is a concrete object with a spatio-temporal address and causal powers – thus, it exists.

It is fair to say that other Meinongian theories, such as the dual copula view, may fare better in this respect. In this version of Meinongianism, recall, things like Holmes are abstract non-existent objects that don't really have, that is they don't exemplify such features as being a detective or living at some address: they only encode such properties. While encoding them is taken as determining such objects in some way, to the extent that encoding is distinct from exemplification, it seems to be a representational, nonliteral way of having such features. Holmes only encodes, but does not exemplify, the property of being a detective. Thus, we should not expect him to be able to chase real criminals, as things exemplifying the property of being a detective are supposed to do.

The main problem Meinongianism has with fictional objects, though, is different. It's an issue specific to non-existent objects of fiction, while it may be less pressing for other kinds of non-existents. Typically, as already claimed, Meinongians have a realist attitude to fictional objects. This does not mean, in the context, that such objects *exist* independently from us (from our beliefs, mental constructions and artistic activities) – for they just do not exist. But it means that non-existent objects do not depend on us, in that they are what they are, and in general have the properties they have, autonomously from us. When Doyle thinks of a non-existent object who is to be the main character of his stories, and pins a name on it – 'Sherlock Holmes' – this looks more like picking out the object from a pre-determined realm, than like producing it.

But how can this be? We cannot have causal interactions with non-existents. Being devoid of physical location, they are nowhere to be found in the material world. If they are already there and endowed with their properties, we are expected to be able to select them somehow. To give a name to a non-existent, characterize it and make true claims on it, one needs to single *it* out in the domain of the totality of objects. How? This has been called by Sainsbury (2010: Ch. 3), the Selection Problem.

Notice that this is not a problem of identity criteria, or identity conditions, in the sense explained in Chapter 3 on the Standard View, and picked up in Chapter 7 on Meinongianism, in the first part of our book. Meinongian theories provide, as we saw there, various identity criteria for their objects (these may or may not work, but that's not at issue here). Rather, we now have a problem of individuation: when Doyle starts to write his first novel on Holmes, how can he single *him* out among all the things that, existing or not, are out there, and talk about *Holmes* throughout the various stories?

One reply may be that, although we cannot single out a non-existent and pin a name on it by physically pointing at it, we may be able to single it out via a definite description. But it is doubtful that we can do this, in general, for fictional objects. If a Comprehension Principle of some kind or other delivers things like the non-existent Holmes by characterization, it is likely to deliver things extremely similar to Holmes, too. Aren't there too many things quite like Holmes out there to allow for a specific one to be picked out by Doyle? Descriptions like 'the detective living in 221b Baker Street' (or, 'the super-hero wearing a red and blue costume with a big "S" on the chest', 'the herb-pipe smoking wizard from Middle Earth who was a great friend of hobbits', etc.), taken by the Meinongians as characterizing fictional non-existents, by their own ontological view, apply to just too many things. There may be lots of numerically distinct fictional characters satisfying the whole characterization of Holmes embedded in the Doyle stories, but differing in other features (one is an inch taller than the other, both are a few grams heavier than a third one and so on). Which one is the Holmes Doyle meant to refer to?

A reply may be available to a Meinongian who admits radically incomplete objects: the relevant non-existent *only* has the properties it is explicitly characterized as having in the fiction. This does not seem to work intuitively well with many fictional things, though. Doyle does not tell us whether Holmes is left- or right- handed (or ambidextrous). It seems implausible, though, that within the Doyle stories Holmes is then to be neither left- nor right-handed (nor ambidextrous). Doyle also doesn't tell us (say) Holmes' exact height, but it seems strange to think of Holmes as a vague object in the stories – one with no precise height, or with fuzzy borders. Intuitively, fictional objects should have additional properties with respect to the ones they are explicitly characterized as having in the relevant fictions.

The problem is specifically pressing for fictional objects as non-existents. As we saw in the first part of our book, some Meinongians take past existents as (currently) non-existent objects, and there is no general selection problem for them. Even if Thomas Jefferson is currently a non-existent object, we managed to single him out in the past, and (presumably, via his parents) pinned his name on him, when he was existent and causally active. We nowadays refer back to him, just via our intention to retain the referent of the name 'Thomas Jefferson' as it has been passed on to us.

Even mere *possibilia*, things which exist at some other possible world but not at the actual one, can in some cases be singled out and referred to (we need not be able to single out *all* of them, of course, but still we can quantify over them, if quantification, as many assume, does not presuppose the possibility of singular reference to the objects in the range of the quantifiers). Divers 2002 and others use to this effect procedures which allow to build definite descriptions that intuitively refer to exactly one *possibile* by relying on recombinations of descriptive accounts of actuality.

None of these moves seems to be easily extended to fictional objects, however. One staunch reply to the selection problem for them, advanced in Priest 2005, consists in claiming that we can select non-existents via some purely mental, nonphysical act of pointing. But how can a mental act pick out, all by itself, an extra-mental, mind-independent object? Invocation of a mental faculty ('noetic rays', David Lewis once jokingly claimed) capable of singling out objects we have no causal acquaintance with, is likely to leave critics unmoved.

Another reply available to the Meinongian, sketched by Fine 1982 and developed by Berto (2012: Ch. 9), consists in dismissing the realist (in the aforementioned sense) assumption. At least some non-existents – the fictional ones – are not independent from us. Rather, they supervene on the mental activities of authors. Holmes was not already there to be picked out by Doyle: he is available to be referred to, and as an object in the domain of quantification of our actual reality, as a result of Doyle's narrative and inventive activities.

This view successfully addresses the Selection Problem: Doyle didn't have to select Holmes from a pre-established domain. Doyle somehow produced Holmes and made him accessible for us. But the view looks quite similar to realist abstractionism on fictional objects, in that such objects seem to be, again, somehow created by authors. Thus, it faces the problems of such creationism, hinted at above: the exportation of the notion of creation from the familiar realm of concrete chairs and humans to exotic things like abstract or non-existent objects is not harmless.

The creationist Meinongian view also faces an additional, semantic objection. 'To create' is ordinarily taken as meaning 'to bring into existence'. This is fine for realist abstractionists, as for them Holmes does exist (and is brought to existence by Doyle). But for the Meinongians following this anti-realist line Holmes does not exist despite supervening on Doyle's mental activities. If one is now claiming that we can 'create non-existents', one seems to be challenging the ordinary meaning of words.

Further Reading

Kroon and Voltolini 2011 is a general introduction to the ontology and metaphysics of fiction, while Voltolini 2006 presents both an overview and an original syncretistic theory. Sainsbury 2010 presents and critically discusses the main realist theories of fictional objects in its first part, and defends an anti-realist view in its second part. Brock and Everett's 2014 collection is bound to become a classic on fictional names.

14

Beyond Particulars: Properties and Events

Chapter Outline

On a simple picture, the world is made of *individual objects:* this table, this chair, that person and so on. Different individuals, however, can apparently share the same properties. This table and this chair, for instance, are both solid. Is this not a good reason to think that there is something beyond individual objects, that is, the properties they share?

Section 1 is about the existence of properties. This relates with the traditional debate about so-called *universals.* On one possible account of properties, the distinction between objects and properties just is the distinction between particulars of individuals and universals. This may however be misleading. Some philosophers identify properties with universals, but some do not. The theory of universals is just one possible account of what properties are. Once a terminological distinction between 'properties' and 'universals' is made, one can see that the choice is not just between holding that there are universals (Section 1.1) and thinking there are no such things as properties (Section 1.2). One could also maintain that properties exist, but they are not universals (Section 1.3). We review the pros and cons of each of these alternatives. Finally, in Section 1.4 we mention a very important topic in the metaphysics of properties, namely the idea that different theories of properties can account for different roles properties are claimed to play.

Other entities which seem to be different from (individual) objects are events, that is things that happen, like a party, a soccer game or a show. In Section 2 we briefly review the main reasons to accept the existence of events and some accounts of their nature.

1 Introducing properties and universals

Consider a world – we may call it 'the lonely world' – made only of a red pullover, a red rose and a red house. If someone asked you how many things there are in that world, what would you answer? A natural answer would be 'Three': didn't we tell you that the lonely world is populated just by a pullover, a rose and a house?

Natural as it may sound, this answer is not obviously the correct one. Forgetting for the moment about the possibility of countenancing the mereological sum or fusion of the three objects just mentioned, there is another problem with the natural answer. It is true that, in describing the lonely world, the only objects we mentioned were the pullover, the rose and the house. But we also told you that they are all red. Is not this enough to conclude that *there is something* that these three objects share, that is the property of redness?

This is a simple version of what is called the 'one over many' argument for properties (see for instance Armstrong 1989: Ch. 1). Different things can be considered of the same kind. The aforementioned inhabitants of the lonely world are three, but they are also of just one colour. How do we account for their similarity? One way is to hold that there is something, that is the colour red, or the property of redness, that the three objects share. Moreover, admitting the existence of properties allows us to give a simple analysis of the meaning of sentences like:

(1) Humility is a virtue. (Lewis 1983b)
(2) Spiders and insects share many anatomical properties. (van Inwagen 2004)

Terms like 'humility' figuring in (1) seem to be singular terms aiming to refer to some object. If this is correct, and if, as it seems to be the case, (1) is true, then 'humility' does refer to something. Friends of properties can simply say that it refers to the property of humility. Apparent quantification over properties, displayed in sentences like (2), is another phenomenon that needs to be accounted for. If quantification over properties cannot be eliminated or paraphrased away from our best theories of the world, this gives to those who stick with Quine's metaontology a reason for accepting the existence of properties.

If one accepts at least one of such arguments, one believes there are properties. It remains to be settled what properties are. On a popular account, properties are *universals*. We will discuss the theory of universals and its problems in Section 1. But it is possible to reject universals without rejecting properties. This brings us to a terminological point we already hinted at. In Chapter 9 we have labelled as 'nominalists' those philosophers who reject abstract objects. This is the modern sense associated to the term. In another, more traditional sense, nominalism is taken to be the rejection of universals. In this chapter we are going to use the term 'nominalism' to refer to the doctrine that there are no universals. This leaves open the possibility of being a nominalist while accepting the existence of properties. This may sound strange, if one's reason to reject universals is that one thinks – as some medieval philosophers did – that there are only particular or individual objects.

Of course, one way to reject universals is just to reject properties. But as we will see, a *class nominalist*, a nominalist (in the sense of this chapter) who however accepts such abstract objects as classes, can reject universals but accept properties, taking them to be some kind of classes, that is, collections of things. A class nominalist like Lewis 1983b, or a nominalist who accepts abstract mathematical objects like the mature Quine, are examples of philosophers who are nominalists in the sense of the present chapter, but platonists in the sense of Chapter 9. On the other hand, David Armstrong, arguably the most prominent advocate of universals in the contemporary scene, is a nominalist in the sense of Chapter 9, given that he takes universals to be *concrete* entities and rejects abstract objects (see, for instance, Armstrong 1997: 41).

Now that we got clear about this admittedly tangled terminology, let us focus on the view that accepts properties and takes them to be universals.

1.1 There are properties, and they are universals

According to the proponents of a theory of universals, different things can be similar to each other in virtue of their being all particular examples or instances of the same universal property. The use of the phrase 'in virtue of' should remind us of the grounding relations discussed in Chapter 8. The fact that all red things resemble each other, on this account, can be seen as grounded in (due to, holding in virtue of) the fact that they all share the same property (this does not mean that friends of universals automatically are grounding theorists: people such as Armstrong wrote many of their works on the topic before grounding theories flourished). Universals are introduced here to explain similarities and thus solve the 'one over many' issue hinted at in Section 1.

One theory of universals usually attributed to Plato and Russell (Edwards 2014: §2.2) considers universals as abstract entities, devoid of causal features and spatiotemporal location, distinct and separated from individual things. One speaks in this case of *transcendent* or *ante rem* universals. The property of beauty, on this picture, is separate from all beautiful things and is located nowhere.

This poses some problems. If universals are separate abstract objects, lacking spatiotemporal location, causal powers, etc., they are of a very different kind from concrete, particular things. But then it is just difficult to see how particular and universals can be *related*. Plato is well known to have faced this issue concerning the relations between his world of pure forms or ideas and the material world.

Moreover, it is usually assumed that the causal powers of individual things are grounded in their properties. A stone can break a glass window due to its solidity; one's red pullover would make a bull angry due to its colour; etc. But if properties are universals and universals are abstract entities, this would be problematic. How could abstract entities, devoid of any causal power, confer such powers upon individual things?

For this reason, the most discussed theory of universals nowadays is that of Armstrong, which takes universals to be concrete entities, endowed with causal powers and located wherever there is an object instantiating them. In this case, one speaks of *immanent* or *in re* universals. The universal of redness, for instance, is located *in its entirety* wherever there is a red region of space (Sider 1995 proposes this interpretation). This means that, according to Armstrong, the property of redness is not exactly a sparse object in the sense of one located partly here and partly there, like the mereological fusion of all red objects (see Section 1.3 of this chapter). The whole of redness is everywhere there is a red region. So the universal of redness occupies more than one place at the same time. This may sound weird, but the weirdness of this aspect of Armstrong's theory is mitigated by noticing that the intuition that an object can occupy only one place at a time may arise from our habit of considering only particular, individual, objects and not universals (see Lewis 1983b). One may say that this just *is* the salient feature of universals, distinguishing them from particulars: each particular has a unique location in spacetime, while universals can be multiply located.

There is, in any case, a problem for all theories of universals in accounting for the relation between universal properties and the particular objects that instantiate them. The problem has to do with the fact that relations are themselves universals. So far we have been concerned only with universals like the property of redness, which are called *monadic* properties, given that they are instantiated by just one object at a time. But we should also take into account relational properties, like love, that can be instantiated by more than one pair of objects. Romeo and Juliet love each other and so do Bonnie and Clyde. This means, according to the supporter of universals, that the ordered pair <Romeo, Juliet> and <Bonnie, Clyde> are both instances of the relation of being in love.

A word on the symbolism and terminology being used here: the notation '<*a, b*>' indicates in this chapter an ordered pair, and such an ordered pair is just a pair of which *a* is the first member and *b* the second. This means that <*a, b*> is different from <*b, a*>. The difference may matter: if <*a, b*> is an instance of the relation of love, but <*b, a*> is not, this means that *a* loves *b*, but *b* does not love *a*. Note that talk of ordered pairs here works just as a convenient way of speaking. Instead of saying that the pair <*a, b*> instantiates the relation *R* we could have said that the relation *R* holds between *a* and *b*.

If one accepts the existence of universals and thinks that they serve as the denotations of (both monadic and relational) predicates, then it is tempting to account for the truth of claims of the form '*Fa*' ('*a* is *F*') as due to the fact that object *a* instantiates property *F*, for the truth of claims of the form '*R*(*a, b*)' ('*a* is *R*-related to *b*') as due to the pair <*a, b*>'s instantiating relation *R*, and so on.

Were this account of the semantics of predicates correct, though, we would run into a famous *regress*. The truth of a claim like:

(U1) My pullover is red.

Would entail that of:

(U2) My pullover instantiates the property of being red.

If *instantiation* is itself a relation, one should analyse (U2) by saying that the pair <my pullover, being red> is an instance of the relation of instantiation. This means that there is a relation of instantiation that is instantiated by the triple <my pullover, being red, instantiation>. It would be better to call this latter relation, the one that holds between my pullover, the property of being red and the relation of instantiation, *instantiation*$_2$, to distinguish it from *instantiation*$_1$, the relation instantiated by the couple <my pullover, the property of being red>. There are logical reasons, related to Russell's paradox (see below), to make such a distinction between relations of instantiation. Moreover, positing just one relation of instantiation would lead us to say that *a* instantiates the property of *F*-ness because *a* and the property of *F*-ness instantiate the property of instantiation, which looks circular. The thought is that it is circular to explain facts about the relation of instantiation in terms of facts about the very same relation of instantiation.

So we have that:

(U3) My pullover and being red instantatiate$_2$ the relation of instantiation$_1$.

If we want to account for the truth of (U3) in the same way as we did for other relational claims, we should now say that the quadruple <my pullover, being red, instantiation$_1$, instantiation$_2$> is an instance of the relation of instantion$_3$:

(U4) My pullover, being red and instantiation$_1$ instantatiate$_3$ the relation of instantiation$_2$.

This is another relational claim, which calls for explanation. If we want to follow the same analysis we applied to the previous cases, we end up introducing another relation of instantiation, instantiation$_4$, and a new relational claim to be accounted for. And we are off and running. The analysis of claims of the form '$R(a, b)$' in terms of the sequence of objects $<a, b>$ being an instance of relation R generates an infinite sequence of relational claims and an infinite series of relations of instantiation. This has been seen by many philosophers as a case of *vicious* regress: the analysis of a claim of the form '$R(a, b)$' is never completed (this is known as Bradley's regress: see Bradley 1893).

Now for a related problem. The regress just considered is generated by the assumption that every predicate (be it monadic or relational) denotes a property. Intuitive as this assumption might look, there is an argument based on purely logical considerations against the idea that every predicate denotes a property. Russell's Paradox, which we encountered in Chapter 9, admits of a variant in terms of properties, rather than classes. The property of being a lion is not itself a lion. On the other hand the property of being a property is itself a property. Echoing the distinction between normal and non-normal classes we saw when dealing with Russell's paradox, we can thus distinguish between properties that cannot be self-instantiated, like the property of being a lion, and properties that can be self-instantiated, like the property of being a property.

Let us use the predicate 'is Russellian' to mean that something either is not a property or is a property that cannot be instantiated by itself. According to this definition, the following Russellian schema holds:

(RS) The property of being … is Russellian if and only if the property of being … is not … .

Now suppose that 'Russellian' denotes a property. Then by filling the dots we get a version of Russell's paradox for properties:

(RP) The property of being Russellian is Russellian if and only if the property of being Russellian is not Russellian.

But this, being of the form 'P if and only if $\sim P$', gives a contradiction in classical logic. This seems to show that there are general logical reasons to reject the idea that every predicate expresses a property.

There is also another, more metaphysical reason to reject a naïve correlation between predicates and properties. On the one hand, properties should explain genuine similarities between things. Predicates, on the other hand, can be true of things that are not similar in any interesting respect. Take the predicate 'is blue or green'. This is true of all blue things and of all green things. But green things *qua* green do not resemble blue ones *qua* blue. So if properties track genuine similarities among things, then there should not be anything like the property of being blue-or-green, corresponding to the predicate 'is blue or green'. According to many philosophers, the same holds for negative predicates like 'not red', for it seems very hard to find some unique, determinate respect of similarity in the vast variety of things that fail to be red.

Armstrong accepts this conclusion. He rejects an *abundant* conception of properties, the view that there is a property corresponding to every predicate. Properties are *sparse*, on Armstrong's view, and their identification is the target of *a posteriori*, empirical procedures. This fits well with the idea that properties are to mark genuine worldly similarities among concrete entities: they are then independent from the way human beings classify the world, which on the other hand is reflected by the kinds of predicates present in our natural language.

This feature of Armstrong's view fits well with his solution to the regress problem. According to Armstrong, there just is no relational property of instantiation. Particulars and universals are united – this pullover is united with redness, for instance –, and their union is said to be a *state of affairs*, like the state of affairs consisting of this pullover's being red. But this should not be accounted for by appealing to a universal relation of instantiation. Facts about the union of universals and particulars are what we are going to call, in the following section, *primitive facts*: facts that are not to be explained in terms of other facts. There seems to be nothing especially problematic with this move. Arguably, no theory can explain everything (one cannot even define each given concept in terms of other concepts, or we would end up in a – possibly quite large – *circulus in definiendo*). Taking something as primitive is a legitimate move. Still, as we are going to see in the next session, it is as legitimate for the nominalist on universals as it is for Armstrong.

1.2 There are no properties

The most radical alternative to the account of properties as universals is the view that there are no such things as properties in the first place. To say that the pullover, the house and the rose of our lonely world above are all red is just to take note of a fact about these three objects. But there is no need to appeal to a common or shared property to account for it. One prominent advocate of this position was Quine himself:

> One may admit that there are red houses, roses, and sunsets, but deny, except as a popular and misleading manner of speaking, that they have anything in common. The words 'houses', 'roses', and 'sunsets' are true of sundry individual entities which are houses and roses and sunsets, and the word 'red' or 'red object' is true of each of sundry individual entities which are red houses, red roses, red sunsets; but there is not, in addition, any entity whatever, individual or otherwise, which is named by the word 'redness', nor, for that matter, by the word 'househood', 'rosehood', 'sunsethood'. That the houses and roses and sunsets are all of them red may be taken as ultimate and irreducible, and it may be held that McX is no better off, in point of real explanatory power, for all the occult entities which he posits under such names as 'redness'. (Quine 1948: 10)

The first thing to note is that Quine's criterion of ontological commitment is implicitly in play here. Quine maintains that it is admissible to say that:

(ON1) There are red pullovers, red houses and red roses but there is no such thing as the property of redness.

('ON' stands for 'ostrich nominalism': see below). The reason is that one natural way to translate (ON1) in the canonical notation yields a consistent sentence:

(ON1b) $\exists x$(x is a pullover and x is red), $\exists y$(y is a rose and y is red), and $\exists z$(z is a house and z is red), but it is not the case that $\exists w$(w = the property of redness).

In Chapter 2 we explained the strategy of ontological commitment detection in terms of inconsistency of certain sets of claims. We said that sentence *P* (once rendered in canonical notation) is committed to entities of kind *F* just in case '*P*, but there are no *F*s' is inconsistent. Another way to make the same point is to say that *P* is committed to the existence of *F*s if *P* entails that there are *F*s. This seems to yield the same result as before. Consider the following:

(ON2) There is an x such that x is a pullover and x is red.

Pending subtleties (see Chapter 3), it seems natural to say that (ON2) entails that there are red pullovers, pullovers and red things – these are its interesting ontological commitments. This means that (ON2) is not ontologically committed to properties. Of course advocates of properties may question Quine's criterion of ontological commitment. This can be done in a variety of ways, as we have seen in the chapters on non-standard approaches to ontology; but it won't work with nominalists like Quine, who typically adopt, well, Quine's methodology for ontological disputes.

A less question-begging attempt is to argue that the picture of the world sketched by Quine, in which there are red things but no properties of redness, leaves something *unexplained*. The advocate of universals typically claims that the similarities we experience among things just call for an explanation. The Quinean nominalist *refuses* to give an explanation. As we have just seen, that all the inhabitants of the lonely world are red is, according to Quine, an 'ultimate and irreducible' fact. A nominalist of this kind has thus been accused of behaving like an ostrich, so to speak putting its head in the sand to avoid meeting a reasonable request (Armstrong 1978: 12–16).

But to call nominalists like those we are considering 'ostrich' may be a bit unfair. Nominalists like Quine maintain that there is no explanation of the similarities we experience among things. This is not like pretending that a question about what grounds similarities between things cannot be asked. It is just about acknowledging that ostrich nominalists have no answer to give to such a question. This, by itself, is not a fatal problem. As first rate philosophers like Aristotle, Wittgenstein and Lewis have argued, we cannot explain everything (Wittgenstein 1953: §1; Lewis 1986: 154). As explanations must stop somewhere, every theory will leave *some* facts unaccounted for. These facts will be brute, or primitive. Similarly, we cannot explain every notion we use, on pain of an infinite regress or of the aforementioned *circulus*, which means that some notions will be taken as primitive, that is as irreducible to any other notion.

One could wonder whether a realist about universals like Armstrong is really better off than the ostrich nominalist in this respect. We have seen that Armstrong too takes something as primitive, that is the union of universals and particulars in states of affairs. In Quinean talk of 'ontology' and 'ideology': by admitting universals, a realist pays an ontological price that an ostrich nominalist does not pay. Both pay an ideological price in term of primitives: the ostrich nominalist's brute similarity facts vs. the realist's union of universals and particulars into states of affairs. Unless the realist shows that the latter is in some sense a better primitive, she may be worse off on overall theoretical balance.

Sometimes discontents of ostrich nominalism claim that the view does not provide a *truthmaker* for statements like 'The rose is red' (Armstrong 1989: 89). Truthmaker theory is very difficult to state precisely (MacBride 2014), but one idea behind it is that the truth of a statement depends on the way the world is (remember again the grounding relations discussed in Chapter 8). In particular, if a statement is true, then there must be something in the world responsible for that; something that makes it true: a truth-maker.

This by itself does not seem to rule out nominalism, however. Asked to point out what in the world makes true the sentence 'The rose is red', the nominalist has a natural candidate: the (red) rose itself! Friends of universals can of course rejoinder that the rose is inadequate as a truthmaker, because it could have been of other colours besides red, but it is doubtful that this helps. As Parsons 1999 pointed out, the nominalist is going to maintain that what makes true 'The rose is red' is the rose *as* it is, namely red. It is not clear how this line of objection against the ostrich nominalism can be developed in a promising way.

Ostrich nominalism and paraphrases

We are now in the position to appreciate that the ostrich nominalist has no particular problems in accounting for the truth of a claim like:

(ON3) *a* and *b* are both red.

Ostrich nominalists could just say that this is true in virtue of the fact that *a* is red and *b* is red (see Devitt 1980). And we have seen that, as we confine ourselves to first order logic, it is logically consistent to say that something is red but there is nothing like redness, so that the claims that *a* is red and that *b* is red are nominalistically acceptable.

Apparently more complicated is the case where one says that two things share a property without telling what property it is (see Lewis 1983b):

(ON4) *a* and *b* share some property.

If one allows oneself the account of quantification developed by Hofweber, and reviewed in Chapter 5, there is a way out of this problem. (ON4) is taken as just a way to track the fact that the following proto-sentence can be turned into a true sentence by replacing the dots with some predicate:

(ON4*) *a* is … and *b* is … , too.

Alternatively, one could see (ON4) as an infinite disjunction (see Section 6 of Chapter 9) like:

(ON4**) Either *a* is tall and *b* is tall, or *a* is short and *b* is short, or *a* is slim and *b* is slim, or… .

In order for this theory to be adequate, every putative property must be expressible in the language employed by the nominalist – presumably a natural language like English. Is this assumption plausible? If we shift our attention to other languages from our own, there seem to be putative properties that could not be expressed in such languages. There seems to be no predicate of ancient Greek expressing the properties of *being a quark* and the relation of *tasting better than Coke*. Hofweber is aware of the difficulty. He presents and discusses these and other examples in Hofweber 2006, offering interesting replies (recall how in Section 2.3 of Chapter 10 we discussed an analogous problem having to do with the issue of inexpressible *propositions*). In any case, some ontologists who stick with a standard metaontological perspective, like van Inwagen, despite some sympathy for nominalism reject such an account of quantification (see van Inwagen 2004: 124). For them, if quantification over properties cannot be paraphrased away, then asserting claims like (ON4) does signal commitment to the existence of properties.

1.3 There are properties, but no universals

If one thinks that the task of paraphrasing away talk about properties is not feasible and is not willing to adopt a view of quantification like that of Hofweber, then one must probably admit properties in one's ontology, at least on a standard metaontological view. Even in this case, though, there is room for rejecting universals. One could do this by making the more metaphysical move of identifying properties with some kind of object already present in various ontological frameworks, like classes, mereological fusions or predicates. These accounts of properties are considered nominalistically kosher, thus one finds them labelled as predicate, class or mereological *nominalism* respectively.

Predicate nominalism

Nominalism, as the name suggests, can and has been considered the doctrine that universals are not things, but just *nomina*, that is words. One way to understand this view is to identify properties with predicates and to understand the claim that *a* is *F* as equivalent to the claim that *a* falls under the predicate '*F*'.

The problem is that predicates are words, and in many contexts – for instance, often in linguistics – words are naturally conceived as types (recall Section 1 of Chapter 10 on the type-token distinction). Consider the sentences in the following two lines:

(R1) This rose is red.
(R2) This pullover is red.

If we count tokens, there are two predicates in (R1) and (R2), so it would not be true that the rose and the pullover fall under the *same* predicate. This suggests that predicate nominalists had better conceive of predicates as types. But the nominalist wants to replace universals with predicates. If predicates are types, they are universals; this means that this account of properties identifies them with universals. It is not easy to evaluate how serious this difficulty is. There are ingenious attempts, like that of Sellars 1962, to paraphrase away talk of types in terms of talk of tokens, but they have been challenged by some serious objections (see Wetzel 2011). As usual, there is always the available move of paying an ideological coin by taking the relation *falling under the predicate 'F'* as primitive, not trying to account for it in any way.

Another way to understand predicate nominalism is to think of properties as *shadows of predicates* (Schiffer 2003). This kind of neo-Carnapian view (see Chapter 5) concedes that properties exist, but treats them as second rate or pleonastic entities. According to this approach, for my pullover to possess the property of redness just is for my pullover to be red (Rayo 2013). The existence of properties like redness is a trivial consequence of uncontroversial facts, like my pullover's being red, plus the principles that define the concept of property. It is worth reminding that Hofweber's interpretation of quantification over properties is also compatible with this approach. The account of properties in terms of predicates is in any case an abundant one. It thus seems ill suited to make properties what grounds genuine similarities among things, for the reasons reviewed in Section 1.1 above.

Properties as classes (natural or not)

Another possibility is to identify properties with classes, that is collections of things. A class of things is said to have members, which belong to the class in question. The relation of membership holding between the elements of a class and the class they belong to is the subject matter of set theory, and should not be confused with the relation of parthood studied by mereology. The mereological sum of all and only the red things is itself red, and has red objects as parts; but the class of red things in no sense has red objects as parts, and it is itself not a red object.

A good thing about construing properties as classes is that this construction yields precise identity criteria for properties. As we have seen in Section 2.2 of Chapter 3, one of the chief complaints Quine made against the introduction of properties into one's ontology is that it is hard to tell in general when the property of *F*-ness is identical to the property of *G*-ness. According to his 'No entity without identity' view, this was a good reason to reject properties. But if properties are classes, then the challenge to find precise identity criteria for them can be met. As we have seen in Chapter 3 on standard metaontology, classes do have identity criteria: class x is identical with class y if and only if they have exactly the same members, that is if and only if everything that is a member of x is a member of y and vice versa.

The bad thing about construing properties as classes is that they seem to provide the *wrong* identity criteria for properties. Back to the Fregean example again: *being renate* seems to be a different property from *being cordate*, even though, as a matter of fact, everything that has a heart has kidneys too, and vice versa. So it seems wrong to identify different properties, such as being renate and being cordate, with the same class (that of cordate/renate things).

One way to address this difficulty has already been discussed in Chapter 11 on possible worlds. The idea is to construe properties as classes of *possible objects*, as in David Lewis' account (see Lewis 1983b, 1986). A world containing creatures with a heart but devoid of kidneys seems a possible one, and if one accepts *possibilia* into one's ontology, then the class of all possible renate beings will be different from that of all possible cordate beings. Of course, this does not help with properties which are intuitively distinct but hold of the same entities as a matter of necessity. All triangles are trilateral objects, and vice versa, in all possible worlds. This means that the class of all possible triangular things is identical with the class of all possible trilateral things even in Lewis' framework, even though 'being triangular' is not synonymous with 'being trilateral'.

The view of properties just sketched is clearly an abundant one. For every predicate (or, for every predicate free from the risk of delivering logical paradoxes: see Section 1.1 of the current chapter), there is a corresponding class. Moreover, there are collections of things that are not picked out by any predicate. So this view seems even more abundant than predicate nominalism. Even on such an abundant picture of properties, it is still possible to mark some kinds of classes as privileged. As we noted in Section 1.1 of Chapter 4, the property of being red is more natural than that of being red or blue, in the sense that red things *qua* red are more similar to each other than red-or-blue ones *qua* red-or-blue. The idea of Lewis 1983b, 1986 is to construe properties as classes and distinguish between more and less natural classes in terms of the degree to which members of these classes resemble each other:

> In fact, the properties are as abundant as the sets themselves, because for any set whatever, there is the property of belonging to that set. It is these abundant properties, of course, that I have identified with the sets. The sparse properties are another story. Sharing of them makes for qualitative similarity, they carve at the joints, they are intrinsic, they are highly specific, the sets of their instances are ipso facto not entirely miscellaneous, there are only just enough of them to characterise things completely and without redundancy. … Probably it would be best to say that the distinction between natural properties and others admits of degree. Some few properties are perfectly natural. Others, even though they may be somewhat disjunctive or extrinsic, are at least somewhat natural in a derivative way, to the extent that they can be reached by not-too-complicated chains of definability from the perfectly natural properties. The colours, as we now know, are inferior in naturalness to such perfectly natural properties as mass or charge; grue and bleen are inferior to the colours; yet even grue does not plumb the real depths of gruesomeness. If it did, we would not have been able to name it. (Lewis 1986: 60–1)

Two things resemble each other to a lower or higher degree depending on the degree of naturalness of the classes to which both they belong. *Resemblance nominalism* (Rodriguez-Pereyra 2002) reverses this order of explanation. According to this view, the claim (ON4) above, that *a* and *b* share some property, should be paraphrased as:

(ON4***) *a* resembles *b*.

By parity of reasoning, one would expect the division between natural and non-natural classes to depend, for a resemblance nominalist, on the degree to which its members resemble each other. It is objected to this view that *resemblance* is itself a relation, thus a universal (this goes back to Russell 1967: 48). If this is meant to indicate that a predicate like 'resembles' or 'is similar' must denote something, we should be familiar from the section on ostrich nominalism with the reply a Quinean is likely to give:

> Why should 'fish', or 'aquatic' or 'similar' be put on a par with names such as 'Chicago', and 'Truman' and 'Parthenon'? Many words are admissible in significant sentences without claiming to name; witness 'the' and 'of' and 'sake' and 'kilter'. Why not 'fish' and 'aquatic' and 'similar'? (Quine 1966: 204)

Of course, if one tried to account for the fact that *a* resembles *b* in terms of the pair <*a*, *b*> resembling the relation of resemblance, this would lead to vicious regress again. The resemblance nominalist may take the relation of resemblance as a primitive – a legitimate move, as we know from Section 1.2.

The fusion of all red things, we said, is different from the class of red things. But one could try to identify the property of being red with the former. On this account, the property of redness is but the scattered red object located everywhere there is something red, and only there. This account, known as *mereological nominalism*, is not very popular (see Quine 1950; Amstrong 1978: 35; see Edwards 2014: Section 5.4, for critical discussion), but it deserves some consideration. If any predicate is to denote a property, the account requires accepting *mereological universalism* (see Section 4 of Chapter 12), but mereological universalism may be independently defended and motivated.

Mereological nominalism also seems to reverse the traditional direction of explanation: something is red in virtue of its being part of the fusion of all red things, whereas we would expect something to be part of the fusion of all red things in virtue of its being red. Also the view that the whole is explanatorily prior to its parts can be defended (see Schaffer 2010). If set theory is really indispensable (see section 5.1 of Chapter 9), and we have to admit classes in our ontology, then it is worth using classes to do the work of properties. Then, conversely, mereological nominalism may be of interest to those who take seriously attempts to reduce set theory to mereology, such as Lewis 1993.

Properties as tropes

Sometimes properties are mentioned in causal accounts, accounts of why some things happen. Francesco is good at giving advice due to *his* wisdom, this glass broke when I threw it against the wall due to *its* fragility, an electron attracts a proton due to *its* charge, etc. But what kind of properties are we mentioning in these claims? It may be that, in general, the property of wisdom helps in giving good advice. But it doesn't seem that wisdom in general made Francesco give Matteo that precise piece of good advice that he gave. Analogously, the breaking of a certain window at a given time seems to be a particular episode. It is something that happened just one time and will never happen again. And particular events seem to call for particular causes: it was the solidity of that particular stone that caused that particular window to break.

This suggests the possibility of viewing *particular properties* as the real bearers of causal powers. Particular properties are taken here as things like the wisdom of Francesco – that particular wisdom which is only Francesco's – or the solidity of this stone, etc. Particular properties are often called *tropes* in contemporary literature. Tropes may be seen, in a sense, as halfway between individual objects and universals (see Williams 1953; See also Campbell 1990; Mertz 1996, and Maurin 2013b for an overview). They can be taken as conceptually close to properties in that they are features of things; but unlike traditional universals, they are strictly tied to individuality: even considering two apples that have exactly the same shade of red, the redness of *this* apple is different from the redness of *that* other apple.

According to some, tropes or particular properties can be taken as the building blocks of the world: what Williams called the 'elements of being'. Universal properties can be reconstructed as bunches of tropes, that is scattered groups of exactly similar tropes. The general property of wisdom is constituted by the wisdom of Socrates, the wisdom of Plato, etc. This may offer a solution to the problem of coextensive properties which are intuitively different. Your being renate is a qualitatively different trope from your being cordate (they even occupy different spacetime regions), so the set of renate-tropes is different from the set of cordate-tropes.

Objects can be similarly reconstructed as bundles of co-localized tropes of different kinds. My pullover is constituted by its being red, its mass, its shape, etc. It is natural to think that similarities among things are grounded in the kind of particular properties that they possess. My pullover resembles the rose because the redness of the pullover resembles the redness of the rose. This of course raises the issue of how similarities between tropes are to be understood. There is the possibility of a regress, if one thinks that the resemblance between tropes themselves is to be explained by tropes having second-level tropes that resemble each other. But it seems natural to think that the resemblance between tropes is due to the nature of the tropes themselves, whereas with objects things are not so. Its being red is not an essential feature of one's pullover (one could paint it in blue). Therefore, one's pullover could fail to resemble the rose. The same is not true of tropes, though: the redness of one's pullover could not fail to be similar to the redness of the rose (see on this Campbell 1990 and Maurin 2002).

Another possible source of regress has to do with the account of *compresence* of tropes in the same bundle (see Daly 1994). Should we account for compresence in terms of compresence tropes? This is likely to trigger the usual regress: if t_1 and t_2 are comprensent tropes, this entails the existence of a comprensence trope c_1, which in turn is compresent with t_1 and t_2, which in turn entails the existence of a compresence trope c_2, etc. (see Ehring 2011).

There seem to be various options for trope-theorists to tame this problem. One is to simply count the relation of compresence as a primitive. More elaborated ones are developed by Simons 1994, Maurin 2002, 2010, 2013b and Ehring 2011. Some attempts to solve the puzzle recognize the regress here, but argue that it is not vicious: see Molnar 2003.

1.4 Too much of a burden

Being the referents of predicates. Explaining similarities between things. Grounding their causal powers. This is what we ask from properties. As authors like Lewis 1983b and Edwards 2014 suggest, maybe this is too much a burden for a single account of properties. Why should we think that all these tasks may or should be carried out by just one kind of entity? Natural properties are better suited to account for the similarities among things than abundant properties, which in turn may be the best candidates to play the role of the meanings of predicates. Pluralism about properties (see again Edwards 2014) holds that is possible to consider different accounts of properties as individuating suitable candidates for different roles property are to play. For instance, one could combine universals, invoked to account for sparse-natural properties, with classes, invoked to account for the abundant ones.

The issue is important from a metaphysical point of view, that is in order to understand what properties are. It is also important from an ontological point of view, that is to understand the reasons we have to admit properties in our ontology. The 'one over many' argument, for instance, is a metaphysical argument which should have nothing to do with the kinds of predicates we use. The argument based on apparent quantification over and reference to properties, on the other hand, is a more semantic one. It is important not to confuse them, as may be done, for instance, by asking nominalists to account for the fact that we apply the same predicate (e.g. 'red') to many things. If this is supposed to be an argument for universals, it is not a good one, given that Armstrong himself accepts that there are predicates that do not pick out a property. On the other hand, if the problem of finding referents for all our predicates is a real one, then it should be noted that this is as much a problem for Armstrong as for the nominalist. Turning to tropes, it is worth noting that they help to paraphrase apparent quantification over properties only if classes are also admitted into one's ontology. To be fair to the ostrich nominalists, advocates of properties should get clear on which argument they are pressing.

2 Events

Many ontologists add to their list of the furniture of the world another category of things which seem *prima facie* quite different from (individual) objects: the category of *events*, that is of things that happen. Examples include exams, parties, flights, discussions, car accidents and naps. Events seem to behave differently from objects with respect to the category of time: events occur, whereas objects exist or fail to exist at a given time. Related to this, it is easier to speak of the temporal borders of an event than of those of an object. It also sounds more natural to attribute the property of being dynamic or static to events rather than to objects.

Talk of events is ubiquitous in ordinary language. Not only terms like 'Matteo's birthday' or 'Federer's last match' seem to refer to events, but we also count events ('Federer played 100 matches last year') and we appear to quantify over them ('There was a meeting at 4p.m.'). Events may also be taken as the content of our perceptions, as when we say that we saw (or heard) our friend crying (Higginbotham 1983). Moreover, events seem to be the proper terms of causal relations (as alluded to in Section 1 of Chapter 9): it is this stone's hitting the window that caused that window to break (a particularly interesting kind of events in this ballpark are actions, whose properties are relevant for important subjects like the one of moral responsibility).

Also in this case there have been attempts to paraphrase away reference to and quantification over events. It is easy enough to rephrase sentences like 'John took a walk' with 'John walked'. One could also try to express the content of 'There were two explosions last night' by saying: 'Two things exploded last night'. But starting from Davidson 1967, it has been pointed out that quantification over events provides a smooth account of apparently sound inferences. And this has been seen as a case for the admission of events (we saw in Section 2.1 of Chapter 10 a parallel situation in the case of propositions). For instance: from John's having walked slowly, John's having walked seems to follow by sheer logic. This can be accounted for if we render 'John walked slowly' and 'John walked' respectively as:

(E1) There is an *x* such that *x* is a walk and John took *x* and *x* was slow.

And:

(E2) There is an *x* such that *x* is a walk and John took *x*.

The inference from (E1) to (E2) is clearly valid, whereas it turns out not be easily proved valid if we take 'walk' and 'walk slowly' just as two different predicates. Like numbers, propositions and properties, events have been considered in some neo-Carnapian approaches as entities whose existence is guaranteed by the adoption of the event-framework, plus some uncontroversial facts. Again, Rayo 2013 submits that the only condition to be met in order for the event of John's death to occur is that John dies.

Turning to the metaphysics of events and the debate on their nature, it is natural to wonder whether events are better conceived as particulars or as universals (see Casati and Varzi 2010, and references therein). One reason to think that events are universals is that when we say that Francesco takes the same walk every Sunday we seem to be referring to a *type* of walk, which can recur many times, rather than to a particular walk that occurs only one time. This may not be such a strong argument, though. One can also say that Francesco eats the same cake every Sunday, but this is naturally interpreted as indicating that Francesco eats the same kind of cake every Sunday – which is of course compatible with cakes being particular objects. Moreover, as we have already hinted, according to some, tropes may be better suited than universals to account for causation. If we accept this, and want events to be the *relata* of causal relations, it is natural to simply *identify* events with tropes (see Section 1.3): Juliette's smiling, on this account, is the particular property of being a smile of Juliette's. And it is this event, this trope, that caused another trope/event – say, Romeo's smiling or the smile of Romeo's.

Another hotly debated issue in this area is that of identity criteria for events. There have been several proposals. Davidson 1967 suggested that event *x* and event *y* are identical if they have the same causes and the same effects. But the view looks circular: in order to establish whether *x* and *y* are the same event we should have a criterion to tell, for example, whether event *z*, caused by *x*, is the same event as event *w*, caused by *y*.

A more promising and often discussed proposal is that event *x* is the same as event *y* if *x* and *y* occurred at the same time and place. Monists, like Quine 1960, accept this criterion, whereas pluralists, like Kim 1966, do not. The debate parallels that about the identity criteria for material objects reviewed in Section 6.2 of Chapter 12. Pluralists on co-located material objects claim that we should distinguish Tibbles from the mereological sum of its parts: Tibbles could survive the destruction of its tail whereas the sum of its parts, by definition, could not. Similarly, pluralists about events distinguish the killing of Caesar from the stabbing of Caesar, given that Caesar could survive the latter but not the former, by definition.

The reply by the monist on events may then be similar to the one of the monist on co-located material objects: 'stabbing' and 'killing' are not synonymous, but this does not mean that they cannot be used to refer to the same event, just like 'Brutus' and 'the killer of Caesar' are not synonyms, but they denote the same person nonetheless. Once again, the point would be that we should not be easily led from multiple ways of referring to ontological multiplications. It seems fair to say that the issue of finding adequate identity criteria is just as problematic in the case of events as in that of material objects. Given that usually it is not taken to be insurmountable in the case of material objects, this gives to advocates of events reasons not to lose hope.

Further Reading

Chapter 8 of Conee and Sider 2005 is a highly readable introduction to the metaphysics of properties. For an extensive and illuminating discussion of the topic we recommend Edwards 2014, which inspired the structure of this chapter and which also contains useful suggestions for further readings. Mellor and Oliver 1997 is an important collection of papers on universals and the issues they raise. For a survey of work on the ontology of events, Casati and Varzi 2010 is the place to start. Casati and Varzi 1997 is an annotated bibliography of work on events from 1947 to 1997.

References

Adams, R. (1974), 'Theories of Actuality'. *Noûs* 8: 211–31.
—(1981), 'Actualism and Thisness'. *Synthèse* 49: 3–41.
Alexander, D. (1920), *Space, Time and Deity*. London: Macmillan.
Armstrong, D. M. (1978), *Universals and Scientific Realism*, Vols. I and II. Cambridge: Cambridge U.P.
—(1989), *Universals: An Opinionated Introduction*. New York: Westview.
—(1997), *A World of States of Affairs*. Cambridge: Cambridge U.P.
Azzouni, J. (2004), *Deflating Existential Consequence: A Case for Nominalism*. New York: Oxford U.P.
Baker, L. R. (1997), 'Why Constitution Is Not Identity'. *Journal of Philosophy* 94: 599–621.
Balaguer, M. (1998), *Platonism and Anti-Platonism in Mathematics*. Oxford: Oxford U.P.
—(2011), 'Fictionalism in the Philosophy of Mathematics', in Zalta (ed.) *The Stanford Encyclopedia of Philosophy*, http://plato.stanford.edu/entries/fictionalism-mathematics/.
Benacerraf, P. (1965), 'What numbers could not be'. *Philosophical Review* 74: 47–73.
—(1973), 'Mathematical Truth'. *Journal of Philosophy* 70: 661–79.
Bergmann, G. (1967), *Realism*. Madison: University of Wisconsin Press.
Berto, F. (2011), 'Modal Meinongianism and Fiction: The Best of Three Worlds'. *Philosophical Studies* 153: 313–34.
—(2012), *Existence as a Real Property*. Dordrecht: Synthèse Library, Springer.
Berto, F. and Tagliabue, J. (2012), 'Cellular Automata', in Zalta (ed.) *The Stanford Encyclopedia of Philosophy*, http://plato.stanford.edu/entries/cellular-automata/.
Boolos, G. (1971), 'The Iterative Conception of Set'. *Journal of Philosophy* 68: 215–31.
—(1984), 'To Be Is to Be a Value of a Variable (Or to Be some Values of Some Variables)'. *Journal of Philosophy* 81: 430–49.
—(1985), 'Nominalist Platonism'. *Philosophical Review* 94: 327–44.
Borges, J. L. (1962), 'Tlön, Uqbar, Orbius Tertious', translated by the Spanish by Alastair Reid, in Kerrison (ed.), *Ficciones*. New York: Grove Press.
Bradley, F. H. (1893), *Appearance and Reality*. Oxford: Clarendon Press.
Brock, S. (1993), 'Modal Fictionalism: A Response to Rosen'. *Mind* 102: 147–55.
Brock, S. and Everett, A. (eds) (2014), *Fictional Names*. Oxford: Oxford U.P. (forthcoming).
Bueno, O. (2014), 'Nominalism in the Philosophy of Mathematics', in Zalta (ed.), *The Stanford Encyclopedia of Philosophy*, http://plato.stanford.edu/entries/nominalism-mathematics/.

Burgess, J. P. (1983), 'Why I Am Not a Nominalist'. *Notre Dame Journal of Formal Logic* 24: 93–105, repr. in Burgess (2008a): 31–45.
—(2002), 'Mathematics and Bleak House'. *Philosophia Mathematica* 12: 18–36, repr. in Burgess (2008a): 46–65.
—(2005), 'Being Explained Away'. *The Harvard Review of Philosophy* 13: 41–56, repr. in Burgess (2008a): 85–103.
—(2008a), *Mathematics, Models, and Modality: Selected Philosophical Essays*. Cambridge: Cambridge U.P.
—(2008b), 'Cats, Dogs, and so on', in Zimmerman (ed.), *Oxford Studies in Metaphysics*. Oxford: Oxford U.P., pp. 4–56.
Burgess, J. P. and Rosen, G. (1997), *A Subject With No Object*. Oxford: Oxford U.P.
—(2005), 'Nominalism Reconsidered', in Shapiro (ed.), *The Oxford Handbook of Philosophy of Mathematics and Logic*. Oxford: Oxford U.P., pp. 515–35.
Cameron, R. P. (2008), 'Truthmakers and Ontological Commitment: or How to Deal with Complex Objects and Mathematical Ontology without Getting into Trouble'. *Philosophical Studies* 140: 1–18.
Campbell, K. (1990), *Abstract Particulars*. Oxford: Blackwell.
Carnap, R. (1932), 'Überwindung der Metaphysik durch logische Analyse der Sprache'. *Erkenntnis* 2: 219–41.
—(1950), 'Empiricism, Semantics and Ontology'. *Revue Internationale de Philosophie* 4: 20–40, repr. with minor changes in Carnap (1956): 205–21.
—(1956), *Meaning and Necessity: A Study in Semantics and Modal Logic*, Enlarged edition. Chicago: University of Chicago Press.
Carrara, M. and Varzi, A. C. (1997), 'Ontological Commitment and Reconstructivism'. *Erkenntnis* 55: 33–50.
Carroll, L. (1871), *Through the Looking-Glass and What Alice Found There*, page references are to the reprint in *The Annotated Alice: The Definitive Edition*, ed. Gardner. Harmondsworth: Penguin 2000.
Casati, R. and Varzi, A. C. (1994), *Holes and Other Superficialities*. Cambridge, MA: MIT Press.
—(1997), *Fifty Years of Events. An Annotated Bibliography 1947 to 1997*. Bowling Green (OH), Philosophy Documentation Center.
—(1999), *Parts and Places: The Structures of Spatial Representation*. Cambridge, MA: MIT Press.
—(2010), 'Events', in Zalta (ed.), *The Stanford Encyclopedia of Philosophy*, http://plato.stanford.edu/entries/events/.
—(2014) 'Holes', *The Stanford Encyclopedia of Philosophy* (Spring 2014 Edition), http://plato.stanford.edu/entries/holes.
Chakravartty, A. (2013), 'Scientific Realism', in Zalta (ed.), *The Stanford Encyclopedia of Philosophy*, http://plato.stanford.edu/entries/scientific-realism/.
Chalmers, D., Manley, D., Wasserman, R. (eds) (2009), *Metametaphysics. New Essays on the Foundations of Ontology*. Oxford: Clarendon Press.
Chateaubriand, O. (1971), *Ontic Commitment, Ontological Reduction, and Ontology*. Berkeley: University of California Press.

Chihara, C. (1968), 'Our Ontological Commitment to Universals'. *Noûs* 2: 25–46.
—(2005), 'Nominalism', in Shapiro (ed.), *The Oxford Handbook of Philosophy of Mathematics and Logic*. Oxford: Oxford U.P., pp. 483–514.
Chisholm, R. M. (1976), *Person and Object*. La Salle, IL: Open Court.
Clark, M. J. and Liggins, D. (2012), 'Recent Work on Grounding'. *Analysis* 72: 812–23.
Cohen, M. (2012), 'Aristotle's Metaphysics', in Zalta (ed.), *The Stanford Encyclopedia of Philosophy*, http://plato.stanford.edu/entries/aristotle-metaphysics/.
Colyvan, M. (2001), *The Indispensability of Mathematics*. New York: Oxford U.P.
—(2010), 'There Is No Easy Road to Nominalism'. *Mind* 119: 285–306.
—(2011), 'Indispensability Arguments in the Philosophy of Mathematics', in Zalta (ed.), *The Stanford Encyclopedia of Philosophy*, http://plato.stanford.edu/entries/mathphil-indis/.
—(2012), *An Introduction to the Philosophy of Mathematics*. Cambridge: Cambridge U.P.
Conee, E. and Sider, T. (2005), *Riddles of Existence: A Guided Tour of Metaphysics*. Oxford: Oxford U.P.
Correia, F. and Schnieder, B. (eds) (2012), *Metaphysical Grounding. Understanding the Structure of Reality*. Cambridge: Cambridge U.P.
Crane, T. (2013), *The Objects of Thought*. Oxford: Oxford U.P.
Crane, T. and Farkas, C. (eds) (2004), *Metaphysics. A Guide and Anthology*. Oxford: Oxford U.P.
Cresswell, M. (1972), 'The World Is Everything That Is the Case'. *Australasian Journal of Philosophy* 50: 1–13.
Currie, G. (1990), *The Nature of Fiction*. Cambridge: Cambridge U.P.
Daly, C. (1994), 'Tropes'. *Proceedings of the Aristotelian Society* 94: 253–61, repr. in Mellor and Oliver (eds) (1997): 140–59.
—(2012), 'Scepticism about Grounding', in Fabrice Correia and Benjamin Schnieder (eds), *Metaphysical Grounding: Understanding the Structure of Reality*. Cambridge: Cambridge U.P., p. 81.
Daly, C. and Liggins, D. (2010), 'In Defence of Error Theory'. *Philosophical Studies* 149: 209–30.
—(2011), 'Deferentialism'. *Philosophical Studies* 156: 321–37.
Davidson, D. (1967), 'The logical form of action sentences', in Rescher (ed.), *The Logic of Decision and Action*. Philadelphia: University of Pittsburgh Press, pp. 81–95, repr. in Davidson D. (1980), *Essays on Actions and Events*. Oxford: Clarendon Press, pp. 105–22.
—(1977), 'The Method of Truth in Metaphysics'. *Midwest Studies in Philosophy* 2: 244–54, repr. in Id. (1984), *Inquires Into Truth and Interpretation*. Oxford: Oxford U.P., pp. 199–213.
—(1991), 'What is Present to the Mind?'. *Philosophical Issues* 1: 197–213.
Devitt, M. (1980), '"Ostrich Nominalism" or "Mirage Realism"?'. *Pacific Philosophical Quarterly* 61: 433–9, repr. in Mellor and Oliver (eds) (1997), pp. 93–100.
Divers, J. (2002), *Possible Worlds*. London-New York: Routledge.
Divers, J. and Hagen, J. (2006), 'The Modal Fictionalist Predicament', in MacBride (ed.), *Identity and Modality*. Oxford: Oxford U.P.

Dorr, C. (2005) 'What We Disagree About When We Disagree About Ontology', in Kalderon (ed.), *Fictionalism in Metaphysics*. Oxford: Oxford U.P., pp. 234–86.
Dummett, M. A. (1991), *Frege: Philosophy of Mathematics*. Cambridge, MA: Harvard U.P.
Edwards, D. (2014), *Properties*. Cambridge: Polity Press.
Ehring, D. (2011), *Tropes: Properties, Objects, and Mental Causation*. Oxford: Oxford U.P.
Eklund, M. (2006a), 'Metaontology'. *Philosophy Compass* 1: 317–34.
—(2006b), 'Neo-Fregean ontology'. *Philosophical Perspectives* 20(1): 95–121.
—(2007), 'The Picture of Reality as an Amorphous Lump', in Sider, Hawthorne and Zimmerman (eds), *Contemporary Debates in Metaphysics*. Oxford: Blackwell.
—(2011a), 'Fictionalism', in Zalta (ed.), *The Stanford Encyclopedia of Philosophy*, http://plato.stanford.edu/entries/fictionalism/.
—(2011b), 'Book Review. *Quantifier Variance and Realism: Essays in Metaontology*. Eli Hirsch', *Notre Dame Philosophical Review*, http://ndpr.nd.edu/news/24764-quantifier-variance-and-realism-essays-in-metaontology/.
—(2013), 'Carnap's Metaontology'. *Noûs* 47: 229–49.
Enoch, D. (2010), 'The Epistemological Challenge to Metanormative Realism'. *Philosophical Studies* 148: 413–38.
Field, H. (1980), *Science without Numbers: A Defence of Nominalism*. Oxford: Blackwell.
—(1984), 'Review of Gottlieb, *Ontological Economy*'. *Noûs* 18: 160–5.
—(1988), 'Realism, mathematics and modality'. *Philosophical Topics* 19: 57–107, repr. in Id. (1989): 227–81.
—(1989), *Realism, Mathematics and Modality*. Oxford: Blackwell.
—(2008), *Saving Truth from Paradox*. Oxford: Oxford U.P.
Fine, K. (1982), 'The Problem of Non-Existents, I: Internalism'. *Topoi* 1: 97–140.
—(2000), 'A Counter-Example to Locke's Thesis'. *The Monist* 83: 357–61.
—(2001), 'The Question of Realism'. *Philosophers' Imprint* 1: 1–30.
—(2003), 'The Non-Identity of a Material Thing and Its Matter'. *Mind* 112: 195–234.
—(2009), 'The Question of Ontology', in Chalmers, Manley and Wasserman (eds), *Metametaphysics. New Essays on the Foundations of Ontology*. Oxford: Clarendon Press, pp. 157–77.
Fitting, M. and Mendelsohn, M. (1998), *First-Order Modal Logic*. Dordrecht: Synthèse Library, Springer.
Frege, G. (1884), *Die Grundlagen der Arithmetik. Eine logisch-mathematische Untersuchung über den Begriff der Zahl*. Hamburg: Felix Meiner Verlag, 1986; repr. with English translation by J. Austin as *The Foundation of Arithmetic*. Oxford: Blackwell, 1950.
Gallois, A. (2011), 'Identity over Time', in Zalta (ed.), *The Stanford Encyclopedia of Philosophy*, http://plato.stanford.edu/entries/identity-time/.
Garrett, B. (2006), *What Is This Thing Called Metaphysics?*. London & New York: Routledge.
Geach, P. (1968), 'What Actually Exists'. *Proceedings of the Aristotelian Society* 42: 7–30.
Goodman, N. (1951), *The Structure of Appearance*. Cambridge, MA: Harvard U.P.
Goodman, N. and Quine W. V. O. (1947), 'Steps Toward a Constructive Nominalism'. *Journal of Symbolic Logic* 12: 105–22.

Grossmann, R. (1974), *Meinong. The Arguments of Philosophers*. London: Routledge.
—(1992), *The Existence of the World*. London: Routledge.
Haack, S. (1977), 'Lewis' Ontological Slum'. *Review of Metaphysics* 33: 415–29.
Hahn, L. E. and Schlipp, P. A. (eds) (1986), *The Philosophy of W.V.O. Quine*. La Salle: Open Court.
Hale, B. and Wright, C. (2001), *The Reason's Proper Study. Essays Towards a Neo-Fregean Philosophy of Mathematics*. Oxford: Oxford U.P.
—(2005), 'Logicism in the Twenty-first Century', in Shapiro (ed.), *The Oxford Handbook of Philosophy of Mathematics and Logic*. Oxford: Oxford U.P., pp. 166–202.
—(2009), *The Metaontology of Abstraction*, in Chalmers, Manley and Wasserman (eds), *Metametaphysics. New Essays on the Foundations of Ontology*. Oxford: Clarendon Press, pp. 178–212.
Hart, W. D. (ed.) (1996), *The Philosophy of Mathematics*. Oxford: Oxford U.P.
Haslanger, S. and Kurtz, R. M. (eds) (2006), *Persistence: Contemporary Readings*. Cambridge, MA: MIT Press.
Hawley, K. (2001), *How Things Persist*. Oxford: Clarendon Press.
Hawthorne, J. (2009), 'Superficialism in Ontology', in Chalmers, Manley and Wasserman (eds), *Metametaphysics. New Essays on the Foundations of Ontology*. Oxford: Clarendon Press, pp. 213–30.
Heller, M. (1990), *The Ontology of Physical Objects*. Cambridge: Cambridge U.P.
—(1992), 'Things Change'. *Philosophy and Phenomenological Research* 52: 695–704.
Hellman, G. (1989), *Mathematics without Numbers*. Oxford: Clarendon Press.
—(2005), 'Structuralism', in Shapiro (ed.), *The Oxford Handbook of Philosophy of Mathematics and Logic*. Oxford: Oxford U.P., pp. 536–62.
Hempel, C. G. (1945), 'On the Nature of Mathematical Truth'. *American Mathematical Monthly* 52: 543–56, repr. in Benacerraf and Putnam (eds) (1983), *Philosophy of Mathematics: Selected Readings*. Cambridge: Cambridge U.P., pp. 377–93.
Higginbotham, J. (1983), 'The Logic of Perceptual Reports: An Extensional Alternative to Situation Semantics'. *Journal of Philosophy* 80: 100–27.
Hilbert, D. (1971), *Foundations of Geometry*. La Salle III: Open Court.
Hirsch, E. (2009), 'Ontology and Alternative Languages', in Chalmers, Manley and Wasserman (eds), *Metametaphysics. New Essays on the Foundations of Ontology*. Oxford: Clarendon Press, pp. 231–59.
—(2011), *Quantifier Variance and Realism: Essays in Metaontology*. Oxford: Oxford U.P.
Hofstadter, D. (1979), *Gödel, Escher, Bach: An Eternal Golden Braid*. New York: Basic Books.
Hofweber, T. (2005a), 'Number Determiners, Numbers, and Arithmetic'. *Philosophical Review* 114: 179–225.
—(2005b), 'A puzzle about Ontology'. *Noûs* 39: 256–83.
—(2006), 'Inexpressible Properties and Propositions', in Zimmerman (ed.), *Oxford Studies in Metaphysics*, Vol. 2. Oxford: Oxford U.P., pp. 155–206.
—(2007), 'Review of *Deflating Existential Consequence: A Case for Nominalism* by Jody Azzouni'. *Philosophical Review* 116: 465–7.

—(2009), 'Ambitious, yet Modest, Metaphysics', in Chalmers, Manley and Wasserman (eds), *Metametaphysics. New Essays on the Foundations of Ontology*. Oxford: Clarendon Press, pp. 260–89.

Iacona, A. (2002), *Propositions*. Genoa, Italy: Name.

—(2003), 'Are There Propositions?'. *Erkenntnis* 58: 325–51.

Jacquette, D. (1996), *Meinongian Logic. The Semantics of Existence and Nonexistence*. Berlin-New York: De Gruyter.

Jeffrey, R. (1965), *The Logic of Decision*. Chicago: McGraw-Hill.

Joyce, R. (2001), *The Myth of Morality*. Cambridge: Cambridge U.P.

—(2009), 'Moral Anti-Realism', in E. Zalta (ed.), *The Stanford Encyclopedia of Philosophy*, http://plato.stanford.edu/entries/moral-anti-realism/.

Jubien, M. (1993), *Ontology, Modality and the Fallacy of Reference*. Cambridge: Cambridge U.P.

Kaplan, D. (1973), 'Bob and Carol and Ted and Alice', in J. Hintikka, Patrick Suppes and Julius Moravcsik (eds), *Approaches to Natural Language*. Dordrecht: Reidel, pp. 490–518.

Kim, J. (1966), 'On the Psycho-Physical Identity Theory'. *American Philosophical Quarterly* 3: 277–85.

Kripke, S. (1972), *Naming and Necessity*, rev. ed. Oxford: Blackwell 1980.

—(2011), *Philosophical Troubles*. New York: Oxford U.P.

Kroon, F. and Voltolini, A. (2011), 'Fiction', in Zalta (ed.), *The Stanford Encyclopedia of Philosophy*, http://plato.stanford.edu/entries/fiction/.

Ladyman, J. and Ross, D. (2007), *Every Thing Must Go*. Oxford: Oxford U.P.

Lambert, K. (1983), *Meinong and the Principle of Independence*. Cambridge: Cambridge U.P.

Lewis, D. K. (1980) 'Index, Context and Content', in Id. (1998): 21–44.

—(1983a), *Philosophical Papers*, Vol. 1. Oxford: Oxford U.P.

—(1983b), 'New Work for a Theory of Universals'. *Australasian Journal of Philosophy* 61: 343–77, repr. in Mellor and Oliver (eds) (1997): 118–227.

—(1986), *On the Plurality of Worlds*. Oxford: Blackwell.

—(1990), 'Noneism or Allism?'. *Mind* 99: 23–31.

—(1991), *Parts of Classes*. Oxford: Blackwell.

—(1993), 'Mathematics is Megethology'. *Philosophia Mathematica* 3: 3–23.

—(1998), *Papers in Philosophical Logic*. Cambridge: Cambridge U.P.

Lewis, D. and Lewis, S. (1970), 'Holes'. *Australasian Journal of Philosophy* 48: 206–12.

Liggins, D. (2006), 'Is There a Good Epistemological Argument Against Platonism?'. *Analysis* 66: 135–41.

—(2007), 'Anti-Nominalism Reconsidered'. *The Philosophical Quarterly* 57: 104–11.

—(2008a), 'Quine, Putnam, and the "Quine-Putnam" Indispensability Argument'. *Erkenntnis* 68: 113–27.

—(2008b), 'Modal Fictionalism and Possible-Worlds Discourse'. *Philosophical Studies* 138: 151–60.

—(2010a), 'Epistemological Objections to Platonism'. *Philosophy Compass* 5: 67–77.

—(2010b), 'The Autism Objection to Pretence Theories'. *The Philosophical Quarterly* 60: 764–82.

—(2012), 'Fictionalism'. *Oxford Bibliographies Online Philosophy*, doi: 10.1093/obo/9780195396577-0034.

Linnebo, Ø. (2012a), 'Reference by Abstraction'. *Proceedings of the Aristotelian Society* 112(1pt1): 45–71.

—(2012b), 'Metaontological Minimalism'. *Philosophy Compass* 7(2): 139–51.

—(2013), 'Platonism in the Philosophy of Mathematics', in Zalta (ed.), *The Stanford Encyclopedia of Philosophy*, http://plato.stanford.edu/entries/platonism-mathematics/.

Lowe, E. J. (1989), *Kinds of Being. A Study of Individuation, Identity and the Logic of Sortal Terms*. Oxford: Blackwell.

Lyon, A. (2012), 'Mathematical Explanations of Empirical Facts and Mathematical Realism'. *Australasian Journal of Philosophy* 90: 559–78.

Loux, M. J. (ed.) (1979), *The Possible and the Actual. Readings in the Metaphysics of Modality*. Ithaca, NY: Cornell U.P.

Ludlow, P. (2013), 'Descriptions', in Zalta (ed.), *The Stanford Encyclopedia of Philosophy*, http://plato.stanford.edu/entries/descriptions/.

MacBride, F. (1999), 'Listening to fictions: A study of fieldian nominalism'. *British Journal for the Philosophy of Science* 50(3): 431–55.

—(2003), 'Speaking with Shadows: A Study of Neo-Logicism'. *British Journal for the Philosophy of Science* 54: 103–63.

—(2014), 'Truthmakers', in Zalta (ed.), *The Stanford Encyclopedia of Philosophy* http://plato.stanford.edu/entries/truthmakers/.

Mackie, J. L. (1977), *Ethics: Inventing Right and Wrong*. London: Harmondsworth Press.

Mackie, P. and Jago, M. (2013), 'Transworld Identity', in Zalta (ed.), *The Stanford Encyclopedia of Philosophy*, http://plato.stanford.edu/entries/identity-transworld/.

Maddy, P. (1990), *Realism in Mathematics*. Oxford: Oxford U.P.

—(1997), *Naturalism in Mathematics*. Oxford: Oxford U.P.

Majors, B. (2007), 'Moral Explanation'. *Philosophy Compass* 2: 1–15.

Malament, D. (1982), 'Review of Field's *Science Without Numbers*'. *Journal of Philosophy* 79: 523–34.

Manley, D. (2009), 'Introduction: A Guided Tour of Metametaphysics' in Chalmers, Manley and Wasserman (eds), *Metametaphysics. New Essays on the Foundations of Ontology*. Oxford: Clarendon Press, pp. 1–37.

Markosian, N. (1998), 'Simples'. *Australasian Journal of Philosophy* 76: 213–28.

—(2008), 'Time', in Zalta (ed.), *The Stanford Encyclopedia of Philosophy*, http://plato.stanford.edu/entries/time/.

Maurin, A. S. (2002), *If Tropes*. Dordrecht: Kluwer Academic Publishers.

—(2010), 'Trope Theory and the Bradley Regress'. *Synthèse* 175: 311–26.

—(2013a), 'Metametaphysics'. *Oxford Bibliographies Online: Philosophy*, doi: 10.1093/obo/9780195396577-0217

—(2013b), 'Tropes', in Zalta (ed.), *The Stanford Encyclopedia of Philosophy*, http://plato.stanford.edu/entries/tropes/.

McDaniel, K. (2009), 'Ways of Being', in Chalmers, Manley and Wasserman (eds), *Metametaphysics. New Essays on the Foundations of Ontology*. Oxford: Clarendon Press, pp. 290–319.

McGinn, C. (2000), *Logical Properties. Identity, Existence, Predication, Necessity, Truth*. Oxford: Oxford U.P.

McGrath, M. (2012), 'Propositions', in Zalta (ed.), *The Stanford Encyclopedia of Philosophy*, http://plato.stanford.edu/entries/propositions/.

Meinong, A. (1904), 'Über Gegenstandstheorie', in Id. (1904) (ed.), *Untersuchungen zur Gegenstandstheorie und Psychologie*. Leipzig: J. A. Barth, pp. 1–51.

Melia, J. (1998), 'Field's programme: Some Interference'. *Analysis* 58: 63–71.

—(2000), 'Weaseling Away the Indispensability Argument'. *Mind* 109: 455–79.

Mellor, D. H. and Oliver, A. (eds) (1997), *Properties*. Oxford: Oxford U.P.

—(1981), *Real Time*. Cambridge: Cambridge U.P.

Menzel, C. (1990), 'Actualism, Ontological Commitment, and Possible Worlds Semantics'. *Synthèse* 85: 355–89.

—(2008), 'Actualism', in Zalta (ed.), *The Stanford Encyclopedia of Philosophy*, http://plato.stanford.edu/entries/actualism/.

—(2013), 'Possible Worlds', in Zalta (ed.), *The Stanford Encyclopedia of Philosophy*, http://plato.stanford.edu/entries/possible-worlds/.

Mertz, D. W. (1996), *Moderate Realism and Its Logic*. New Haven and London: Yale U.P.

Molnar, G. (2003), *Powers: A Study in Metaphysics*, ed. S. Mumford. Oxford: Oxford U.P.

Moltmann, F. (2003) 'Propositional Attitudes without Propositions'. *Synthèse* 135: 77–118.

Moore, J. (1999), 'Propositions, Numbers, and the Problem of Arbitrary Identifications'. *Synthèse* 120: 229–63.

Neale, S. (1990), *Descriptions*. Cambridge: MIT Press.

Nolan, D. (2011), 'Modal Fictionalism', in Zalta (ed.), *The Stanford Encyclopedia of Philosophy*, http://plato.stanford.edu/entries/fictionalism-modal/.

Noonan, H. (1988), 'Reply to Lowe on Ships and Structures'. *Analysis* 48: 221–3.

Noonan, H. and Curtis, B. (2014), 'Identity', in E. Zalta (ed.), *The Stanford Encyclopedia of Philosophy*, http://plato.stanford.edu/entries/identity/.

Panza, M. and Sereni, A. (2013), *Plato's Problem*. London and New York: Palgrave Macmillian.

Papineau, D. (2009), 'Naturalism', in Zalta (ed.), *The Stanford Encyclopedia of Philosophy*, http://plato.stanford.edu/entries/naturalism/.

Parsons, C. (1979), 'Mathematical Intuition'. *Proceedings of the Aristotelian Society* 80: 145–68.

Parsons, J. (1999), 'There Is No 'Truthmaker' Argument Against Nominalism'. *Australasian Journal of Philosophy* 77: 325–34.

Parsons, T. (1980), *Nonexistent Objects*. New Haven, CN: Yale U.P.

Plantinga, A. (1974), *The Nature of Necessity*. Oxford: Clarendon Press.

Plato, *Sophist*, in *Platonis Opera*, 5 vol., ed. Burnet, Oxonii, 1900–07, trans. in *The Sophist & The Statesman*, ed. Taylor. London: Nelson & Sons, 1961.

Priest, G. (2000), *Logic: A Very Short Introduction*. Oxford: Oxford U.P.

—(2002), *Beyond the Limits of Thought*, 2nd edition. Oxford: Oxford U.P.
—(2005), *Towards Non-Being. The Logic and Metaphysics of Intentionality*. Oxford: Oxford U.P.
—(2008), *An Introduction to Non-Classical Logic. From If to is*. Cambridge: Cambridge U.P.
Putnam, H. (1971), *Philosophy of Logic*. New York: Harper Torchbooks.
—(1975), *Mathematics, Matter and Method*. Cambridge: Cambridge U.P.
—(1987), *The Many Faces of Realism*. La Salle: Open Court.
—(1994), 'The Question of Realism', in Id. (1994), *Words and Life*. Cambridge, MA: Harvard U.P., pp. 295–312.
—(2004), *Ethics Without Ontology*. Cambridge, MA: Harvard U.P.
Quine, W. V. O. (1948), 'On What There Is'. *Review of Metaphysics* 2: 21–38, repr. in Id. (1953).
—(1950) 'Identity, Ostension, and Hypostasis'. *Journal of Philosophy* 47: 621–33, repr. in Id. (1953).
—(1951a), 'Two Dogmas of Empiricism'. *Philosophical Review* 60: 20–43, repr. in Id. (1953).
—(1951b), 'Ontology and Ideology'. *Philosophical Studies* 2(1): 11–15.
—(1953), *From a Logical Point of View*. Cambridge, MA: Harvard U.P.
—(1960), *Word and Object*. Cambridge, MA: MIT Press.
—(1966), *The Ways of Paradox and Other Essays*. New York: Random House.
—(1969), *Ontological Relativity and Other Essays*. New York: Columbia U.P.
—(1969a), 'Propositional Objects', in Id. (1969): 139–60.
—(1969b), 'Existence and quantification', in Id. (1969): 91–113.
—(1975), 'On the Individuation of Attributes', in Anderson, Barcan and Martin (eds), *The Logical Enterprise*. New Haven, CN: Yale U.P.
—(1981), *Theories and Things*. Cambridge, MA: Belknap Press.
—(1986a), 'Reply to Alston', in Hahn and Schlipp (eds), *The Philosophy of W.V.O. Quine*. La Salle: Open Court, pp. 73–5.
—(1986b), 'Reply to Charles Parsons', in Hahn and Schlipp (eds), *The Philosophy of W.V.O. Quine*. La Salle: Open Court.
Rayo, A. (2013), *The Construction of Logical Space*. Oxford: Oxford U.P.
Rayo, A. and Yablo, S. (2001), 'Nominalism Through De-Nominalization'. *Noûs* 35: 74–92.
Reicher, M. (2010), 'Nonexistent Objects', in Zalta (ed.), *The Stanford Encyclopedia of Philosophy*, http://plato.stanford.edu/entries/nonexistent-objects/.
Rodriguez-Pereyra, G. (2002), *Resemblance Nominalism: A Solution to the Problem of Universals*. Oxford: Oxford U.P.
Rosen, G. (1990), 'Modal Fictionalism'. *Mind* 99: 327–54.
—(1993) 'A Problem for Fictionalism About Possible Worlds'. *Analysis* 53: 71–81.
—(2006), 'Jody Azzouni: Deflating Existential Consequence. A Case for Nominalism'. *Journal of Philosophy* 103(6): 312–18.
—(2010), 'Metaphysical Dependence: Grounding and Reduction', in Hale and Hoffmann (eds), *Modality: Metaphysics, Logic, and Epistemology*. Oxford: Oxford U.P., pp. 109–35.

—(2012), 'Abstract Objects', in Zalta (ed.), *The Stanford Encyclopedia of Philosophy*, http://plato.stanford.edu/entries/abstract-objects/.

Rosen, G. and Dorr, C. (2002), 'Composition as a Fiction', in Gale (ed.), *The Blackwell Guide to Metaphysics*. Oxford: Blackwell, pp. 151–74.

Routley, R. (1980), *Exploring Meinong's Jungle and Beyond*. Canberra: Australian National University, RSSS.

Russell, B. (1903), *The Principles of Mathematics*. Cambridge: Cambridge U.P.

—(1905), 'On Denoting'. *Mind* 14: 479–93.

—(1919), *Introduction to Mathematical Philosophy*. London: Allen & Unwin.

—(1967), *The World of Universals*, in Id., *The Problems of Philosophy*. Oxford: Oxford U.P., pp. 52–7, repr. in Mellor and Oliver (eds) (1997): 45–56.

Ryle, G. (1932), 'Systematically Misleading Expressions'. *Proceedings of the Aristotelian Society* 32: 139–70.

Sainsbury, M. (2010), *Fiction and Fictionalism*. London & New York: Routledge.

Salmon, N. (1998), 'Nonexistence'. *Noûs* 32: 277–319.

Schaffer, J. (2003), 'Is There a Fundamental Level?'. *Noûs* 37: 498–517.

—(2009), 'On What Grounds What', in Chalmers, Manley and Wasserman (eds), *Metametaphysics. New Essays on the Foundations of Ontology*. Oxford: Clarendon Press, pp. 347–83.

—(2010), 'Monism: The Priority of the Whole'. *Philosophical Review* 119: 31–76.

Schiffer, S. (1996), 'Language Created, Language Independent Entities'. *Philosophical Topics* 24: 149–67.

—(2003), *The Things We Mean*. Oxford: Clarendon Press.

Sellars, W. (1962), 'Naming and Saying'. *Philosophy of Science* 29: 7–26.

Shapiro, S. (2000), *Thinking about Mathematics*. Oxford: Oxford U.P.

Sidelle, A. (1989), *Necessity, Essence, and Individuation*. Ithaca, NY: Cornell U.P.

Sider, T. (1995), 'Sparseness, Immanence, and Naturalness'. *Noûs* 29: 360–77.

—(1999), 'Global Supervenience and Identity Across Times and Worlds'. *Philosophy and Phenomenological Research* 59: 913–37.

—(2001), *Four-Dimensionalism. An Ontology of Persistence and Time*. New York: Oxford U.P.

—(2011), *Writing the Book of the World*. Oxford: Oxford U.P.

Sider, T., Hawthorne, J., Zimmerman, D. W. (eds) (2007), *Contemporary Debates in Metaphysics*. Oxford: Blackwell.

Simons, P. M. (1987), *Parts. A Study in Ontology*. Oxford: Clarendon Press.

—(1994), 'Particulars in Particular Clothing: Three Trope Theories of Substance'. *Philosophy and Phenomenological Research* 54: 553–75.

Skyrms, B. (1976), 'Possible Worlds, Physics and Metaphysics'. *Philosophical Studies* 30: 323–32.

Sober, E. (1993), 'Mathematics and Indispensability'. *Philosophical Review* 102: 35–57.

Spolaore, G. (2012), 'Not Just a Coincidence. Conditional Counter-examples to Locke's Thesis'. Thought 1(2): 108–15.

Stalnaker, R. (1976), 'Possible Worlds'. *Noûs* 10: 65–75.

Stanley, J. (2001), 'Hermeneutic fictionalism'. *Midwest Studies in Philosophy* 25: 36–71.

Strawson, P. F. (1959), *Individuals. An Essay in Descriptive Metaphysics*. London: Methuen.
Thomasson, A. (1999), *Fiction and Metaphysics*. Cambridge: Cambridge U.P.
—(2009), 'The Easy Approach to Ontology'. *Axiomathes* 19: 1–15.
—(2013), 'Fictionalism vs. Deflationism'. *Mind* 122(488): 1023–51.
Thomson, J. J. (1983), 'Parthood and Identity Across Time'. *Journal of Philosophy* 80: 201–20.
—(1998), 'The Statue and the Clay'. *Noûs* 32: 149–73.
Turner, J. (2010), 'Ontological Pluralism'. *Journal of Philosophy* 107: 5–34.
—(2011), 'Ontological Nihilism', in Bennett and Zimmerman (eds), *Oxford Studies in Metaphysics*. Oxford: Oxford U.P., pp. 3–54.
Urquhart, A. (1990), 'The Logic of Physical Theory', in Irvine (ed.), *Physicalism in Mathematics*. Dordrecht: Kluwer, pp. 145–54.
van Inwagen, P. (1977), 'Creatures of Fiction. *American Philosophical Quarterly* 14: 299–308.
—(1981), 'The Doctrine of Arbitrary Undetached Parts'. *Pacific Philosophical Quarterly* 62: 123–37.
—(1986), 'Two Concepts of Possible Worlds'. *Midwest Studies in Philosophy* 11: 185–213.
—(1990), *Material Beings*. Ithaca, NY: Cornell U.P.
—(1998), 'Meta-Ontology'. *Erkenntnis* 48: 233–50, repr. in Id. (2001): 13–31.
—(2001), *Ontology, Identity and Modality. Essays in Metaphysics*. Cambridge: Cambridge U.P.
—(2002), 'The Number of Things'. *Philosophical Issues* 12: 176–96.
—(2003), 'Existence, Ontological Commitment, and Fictional Entities', in Loux and Zimmermann (eds), *Metaphysics*. Oxford: Oxford U.P., pp. 131–57.
—(2004), 'A Theory of Properties', in Zimmerman (ed.), *Oxford Studies in Metaphysics*, Vol. 1. Oxford: Oxford U.P., pp. 107–38.
—(2006), 'McGinn on Existence'. *The Philosophical Quarterly* 58: 36–58.
Varzi, A. C. (2000), 'Mereological Commitments'. *Dialectica* 54: 283–305.
—(2001), *Parole, oggetti, eventi e altri argomenti di metafisica*. Rome: Carocci.
—(2009), 'Mereology', in Zalta (ed.), *The Stanford Encyclopedia of Philosophy*, http://plato.stanford.edu/entries/mereology/.
Voltolini, A. (2006), *How Ficta Follow Fiction. A Syncretistic Account of Fictional Entities*. Dordrecht: Springer.
Walton, K. (1990), *Mimesis as Make-Believe: on the Foundations of the Representational Arts*. Cambridge, MA: Harvard U.P.
—(1993), 'Metaphor and Prop Oriented Make-Believe'. *European Journal of Philosophy* 1: 39–57.
—(2003), 'Restricted Quantification, Negative Existentials, and Fiction'. *Dialectica* 57: 239–42.
Wetzel, L. (2011), 'Types and Tokens', in Zalta (ed.), *The Stanford Encyclopedia of Philosophy*, http://plato.stanford.edu/entries/types-tokens/.
Wiggins, D. (2001), *Sameness and Substance Renewed*. Cambridge: Cambridge U.P.

Williams, D. C. (1953), 'On the Elements of Being II'. *Review of Metaphysics* 7: 171–92.
Williamson, T. (2007), *The Philosophy of Philosophy*. Oxford: Blackwell.
—(1987), 'Equivocation And Existence'. *Proceedings of the Aristotelian Society* 88: 109–27.
—(2011a), 'What is naturalism?', *New York Times* (online), 4 September 2011, http://opinionator.blogs.nytimes.com/category/the-stone/ .
—(2011b), 'On ducking challenges to naturalism', *New York Times* (online), 28 September 2011, http://opinionator.blogs.nytimes.com/category/the-stone/ .
Wilson, J. M. (2014), 'No Work for a Theory of Grounding'. *Inquiry: An Interdisciplinary'. Journal of Philosophy* (forthcoming).
Wittgenstein, L. (1953), *Philosophical Investigations*. New York: Macmillan.
Wolstertorff, N. (1961), 'Referring and Existing'. *The Philosophical Quarterly* 11: 335–49.
Woodward, R. (2008), 'Why Modal Fictionalism is Not Self-Defeating'. *Philosophical Studies* 139: 273–88.
—(2012), 'A Yablovian Dilemma'. *Thought* 1: 200–9.
Wright, C. (1983), *Frege's Conception of Numbers as Objects*. Aberdeen: Aberdeen U.P.
Yablo, S. (1998), 'Does Ontology Rest on a Mistake?'. *Proceedings of the Aristotelian Society* Suppl. Vol. 72: 229–61, repr. in Yablo (2010): 117–44.
—(2000), 'A Paradox of Existence', in Hofweber and Everett (eds), *Empty Names, Fiction, and the Puzzles of Non-Existence*. Stanford: CSLI Publications, pp. 275–312.
—(2001), 'Go Figure: A Path Trough Fictionalism'. *Midwest Studies in Philosophy* 25: 72–102, repr. in Yablo (2010): 177–99.
—(2002), 'Abstract Objects: a Case Study'. *Philosophical Issues* 12: 220–40, repr. in Yablo (2010): 200–20.
—(2005), 'The Myth of the Seven', in Kalderon (ed.), *Fictionalism in Metaphysics*. Oxford: Clarendon Press, pp. 88–115, repr. in Yablo (2010): 221–45.
—(2006), 'Non-Catastrophic Presupposition Failure', in Thomson and Byrne (eds), *Content and Modality: Themes from the Philosophy of Robert Stalnaker*. Oxford: Oxford U.P., repr. in Yablo (2010): 269–95.
—(2009), 'Must Existence-Questions Have Answers?', in Chalmers, Manley, and Wasserman (eds) *Metametaphysics. New Essays on the Foundations of Ontology*. Oxford: Clarendon Press, pp. 507–25, repr. in Yablo (2010): 296–14.
—(2010), *Things: Papers on Objects, Events, and Properties* (Philosophical Papers, vol. II). Oxford: Oxford U.P.
—(2012), 'Explanation, Extrapolation, and Existence'. *Mind* 121: 1007–29.
—(2014), *Aboutness*. Princeton: Princeton U.P.
Yagisawa, T. (2002), 'Against Creationism in Fiction'. *Noûs* 35: 153–72.
Zalta, E. (1983), *Abstract Objects: an Introduction to Axiomatic Metaphysics*. Dordrecht: Reidel.
—(1988), *Intensional Logic and the Metaphysics of Intentionality*. Cambridge, MA: MIT Press.

Author Index

Subject Index